TAB Guide 2013 to
Money, Pensions and Tax
Jill Kerby, Sandra Gannon, Neil Brooks

7 Lower Fitzwilliam Street, Dublin 2.

Telephone: (01) 6768633   Fax: (01) 6766576

email: info@tab.ie

www.tab.ie

This book has been prepared as a general guide for use in the Republic of Ireland and is based on our understanding of present law and practice. While every effort has been made to ensure accuracy, neither the publisher nor editor are liable for any errors or omissions.

Published by

TAB TAXATION SERVICES LTD.

7 Lower Fitzwilliam Street, Dublin 2.

Telephone: (01) 6768633

E-mail: catherine@tab.ie

Web Site: www.tab.ie

ISSN No: 0790 9632

ISBN No: 978-0-9558110-5-0

Jill Kerby   - Sunday Times Personal
Finance Journalist

Co Author of TAB Guide
to Money, Pensions & Tax.

Sandra Gannon - TAB Taxation
Services Ltd.

Co Author of TAB Guide
to Money, Pensions & Tax.

Neil Brooks - TAB Financial Services Ltd

Co Author of TAB Guide
to Money, Pensions & Tax

Table of Contents

1	Risk and rewards	Page	9
2	Making the most of your savings	Page	15
3	Investing wisely	Page	33
4	Borrowing and managing debt	Page	63
5	Buying a home	Page	77
6	Insurance	Page	93
7	Income tax	Page	107
8	PAYE	Page	133
9	Self employment	Page	167
10	Working abroad/Foreign income	Page	181
11	Capital gains tax	Page	199
12	Social welfare benefits	Page	207
13	Redundancy	Page	247

"A pension that's ahead of the curve. That's it. I'm moving to Zurich."

When it comes to pensions, Zurich Life has the best managed fund returns in Ireland over the last twenty years.* And, you can have peace of mind knowing that we are part of the Zurich Insurance Group which has an internationally recognised financial strength rating of AA-.† Little wonder then that Zurich Life remains the best choice for your retirement savings.

Find out why more and more people are moving to Zurich.

Talk to your broker.
Call Zurich on 1850 202 102.
Click on zurichlife.ie

* Annualised returns, 20 years to 30th September 2012; independent survey, source: Rubicon Investment Consulting Limited.
† Financial strength rating is for the Zurich Insurance Group, source: Standard & Poor's 19th October 2012.
Zurich Life Assurance plc is regulated by the Central Bank of Ireland.

14   Pensions - financial planning for
      retirement   Page   257

15   Marriage   Page   301

16   Separation & divorce   Page   309

17   Death and taxes   Page   329

      Index   Page   345

1 Risk and rewards

Your personal finances involve more than putting a little money aside every week, or buying a life insurance policy to ensure a decent burial. Irish people have never been so aware of not just how their money is earned and spent, but how and where it is taxed, saved and invested. These past few years have been a huge wake up call that not all the purchases and investments we made - in property, pensions, stocks and shares, and consumer goods were necessarily very wise. Hundreds of millions have been wiped off the wealth side of our personal balance sheets, not to mention the nations'. The very income that allowed so many of us to buy homes, grow businesses and experience material comforts that our grandparents could only dream of, has also been decimated by what is now being referred to as Ireland's 'Great Recession'.

Never before has there been a greater need or urgency for personal financial planning. During the boom years, most people spent more time planning a two week summer holiday than planning for their 20 year retirement. Undoubtedly many regret the hours spent choosing a new car, which may have been better spent choosing the best way to educate their children through to third level.

Proper financial planning doesn't take place in a vacuum: a young person starting their first job may not be ready to think about a pension plan, but may still need to find the best finance package for a first car or to move into a home of their own. Does it make sense to keep renting or to buy in this depressed property market, they should be asking. And what is the most tax-efficient way to be paid now that tax rates have soared? How can you protect your savings from higher taxation and the potential threat of price inflation?

Life doesn't come to a halt because the economy is faltering. Young couples are always looking to the future.   They may be planning a family, moving house, taking on all kinds of responsibilities. They need to make their Wills, get the best finance deal for their new home, make sure they have insured each other's lives (especially when a baby arrives) and they need to set up a viable family budget.

Children bring enormous joy - and bills! If a parent does not stay at home with the baby, someone else may have to be hired to provide childcare. Either way a significant cost is going to be incurred.

Since your child is going to have to be fed, dressed, educated and amused for the next two decades, the sooner you start planning for all these costs the better - difficult as it may be, it is always advisable to start putting aside even a modest amount of money each week or month. Beginning to save or invest regularly two or three years before secondary or third level school fees fall due is really about 10 years too late.

"Children bring enormous joy - and bills."

If you don't have an occupational pension scheme at your workplace to join, you should also be considering ways to invest for your retirement, perhaps in a PRSA or AVC (Additional Voluntary Contribution) if you are unlikely to have full-service years as a member of an occupational scheme. You also need to review your life and health insurance policies. Debt management should also be a high priority this year.

The financial needs of someone middle aged are very different from those of a single person or a young parent. Though your monthly outlay may be high, there is light at the end of the child-rearing tunnel; ideally you are earning more and will have built up some equity in your home and in some kind of savings or investment funds. You may still have 15 or 20 years before retirement, but do you have a pension plan? How has it fared during the economic downturn? Is your occupational scheme meeting its legal funding standard requirements?

For the over 60's, retirement can be a blessing or a burden. Without an adequate pension or other assets, day to day spending may have to be curtailed and outstanding debts may provoke a serious financial crisis. For the financially secure, retirement can provide exciting new opportunities to enjoy life at your own pace. Whether you work for someone else or have your own business, you certainly need to take stock of your financial position, including your assets and debts, plus your short and long term health care provisions.

Aside from matters like budgeting, home ownership, saving and investing, and social welfare entitlements, this book also takes you through a number of financial issues that must be dealt with when somebody dies:

Wills, Inheritance Tax, Probate, Intestacy and the tax adjustments that come with widowhood.

Financial planning is best done with a trusted advisor and independent, objective advice is by far the best option; the fee you pay such a person may well be one of the best investments you will ever make.

Risk and rewards

Everyone takes chances at some time in their lives. One of the ingredients of success, aside from talent and luck, is the ability to take a few risks to achieve a difficult task or goal.

"The challenge is to take educated risks."

Unfortunately, reckless lending and borrowing in recent years, by institutions and individuals, resulted in reckless investing and the global financial crisis that began in late 2007 has taken its toll not just on the wealth of the profligate, but the prudent as well. The appetite of many for risk-taking has undoubtedly been tempered by the big losses many people have suffered on property, their pensions and the stock market. Nevertheless, it is still higher risk investment strategies that produce potentially higher rewards. The challenge is to take educated risks.

There are financial institutions - and yes, some of them are even banks and building societies - that recognise this reluctance on the part of many people to take chances with their income or savings and offer both deposit accounts and a range of capital guaranteed savings certificate and bond products with little or no risk and thus low long term rewards.

Low growth/low risk

Deposit-based bank, building society and post office accounts that operate in this State have come under the Government deposit guarantee schemes, including the 100% deposit guarantee for Irish institutions, see page 15 for more details. Interest rates have ebbed and waned since the financial crisis began in 2007 but deposit rates in Irish owned banks in particular are very generous, though mortgage lending rates are higher than they were a year or two ago. The European Central Bank rate was reduced to 0.75% in 2012 as the great eurozone debt crisis began threatening the very existence of the euro. By the end of 2012 signs of a double dip recession in many European countries had strengthened and there are now increased worries of both deflation and inflation risks if the ECB continues its issuing of Eurobonds and its new support mechanisms (like the ESM) in attempts to recapitalise struggling banks and peripheral

EU governments.

Difficult as it may be to believe, given how volatile asset markets have been since 2007, a higher reward is usually the prize taken away by genuine, calculated, risk takers. If you still want a higher reward than is paid by a deposit account, you first need to look at your ability to deal with risk taking into account your age, your general financial circumstances and your ability to absorb any losses.

For example, an elderly widow relying on a State pension for her income is not a suitable candidate to invest her savings in the stock market no matter how buoyant the performance of shares. A younger person with a steady rising income, or a professional with existing assets and excellent earning potential, on the other hand, is a good candidate to take some short or long term risks, even after our recent market experience.

Living with risk

To establish your own level of risk, you need to ask yourself the following questions:

- Can I afford to lose my money? Will I be able to meet all my regular, day-to-day obligations if it disappears?

- Am I prepared for the fact that investment markets are cyclical and values are likely to go down as well as up?

- Can I wait for investment markets to recover, if they go down?

If you answer no to any of these questions, then you probably have a relatively low risk threshold. Investing directly in the stock market, or even in unitised funds or property - which all require relatively long term investment periods - may not be for you.

Risk also needs to be related to age. A young person taking out a pension plan which will mature in 40 years should take some risk with the underlying investments in the fund in the early years while someone in their 50's investing in a pension needs to be more cautious, especially if retirement is coming up in just five or ten years time. Parents of young children who want to save for their education, need to take fewer risks than a long term pension investor since time may not be on their side.

Matching the risk

Tax-free State Savings Certificates, Bonds and Instalment Savings Plans have always been considered good options for low risk savers (like pensioners) or people with short term funding needs. Aside from the credit and solvency risk that the banking system has produced since September 2008, the biggest danger associated with deposit type products historically has been that they are not always inflation proof and your capital is eroded by the rise in the price of everyday goods (and higher tax). Today, unfortunately, savers must also consider sovereign default risk and possibly even devaluation losses.

Unitised investment products, especially those that are well diversified, either geographically or by industrial sector but more often by asset classes that include the likes of property, bonds, cash and commodities as well as equities (stocks and shares), have been designed for people with low to medium risk personal profiles who could save on a regular or lump sum basis for up to 10 years or more.

"An independent financial advisor could be of great assistance ....."

For people who were willing to take more investment risk, there are opportunities to move into more specialised equity asset funds spread between investment sectors, such as all financial, industrial or retail shares; companies in 'developed' geographic locations like Europe, America or Japan, and increasingly into 'emerging markets' like Brazil, Russia, India and China (the BRIC nations). Commodities like steel, coal, oil, precious metals and grains can also be purchased as pooled 'funds', either purchased through an investment firm or increasingly as a direct investment in the form of low cost Exchange Traded Funds that trade on stock markets in the form of a single share. Bought in this form, you need to be willing to do your own research and of course, to take full personal responsibility for all your buying decisions.

Independent financial advice

Volatility has never been greater as the world comes to terms with the fallout from the financial and banking crisis and the huge sums that governments and central banks have pumped into the system to keep it afloat.

Unless you are a financial expert yourself, the huge variety and types of savings and investment products on the market make it very difficult for you to know which one is suitable for your particular needs and circumstances. An independent financial advisor could be of great assistance in helping you choose which deposit account to open and which savings policy, pension or stocks and shares to buy.

Independent financial advice is not available from the Post Office, banks or building societies, stockbrokers or life assurance companies since they all want you to buy their individual products. A bank official is not going to recommend that you take out a State Savings Instalment Plan, even if it happens to pay more interest than the bank's equivalent scheme. The credit union will not recommend that you borrow from the building society, even if the society's interest rate is lower. A life assurance company wants you to buy into their managed equity fund, not go directly to the stock market.

Commissions are still paid by financial institutions as a sales reward to the broker or sales agent when you opt to buy one of their products. The size of the commission will vary in size from institution to institution and also depends on whether you are contributing a lump sum or are making regular monthly or even weekly payments.

Many people advertise themselves as 'independent' financial advisers on mortgages, general and life assurance policies, pensions, deposit accounts and investment funds. Yet nearly all of them accept commission payments from the institution. Those institutions which do not pay broker commissions - the Post Office, some banks and building societies (depending on the product), are unlikely to be recommended by a broker or salesperson who relies solely on commission for their own income.

Avoid misselling

The best way to reduce the danger of being missold an expensive financial service or product is to seek advice from a genuinely independent financial advisor, who charges a fee. Knowing that their time and expertise is being rewarded, regardless of whether you buy a product, your wider financial situation will more likely be taken into account and the risk of you being sold an unsuitable product should be lessened.

Such advisors may be specialist life and pensions brokers, mortgage brokers and/or investment brokers, accountants and management consultants who deal with the personal finances of their private clients.

If you prefer to deal with a commission-based advisor rather than pay a fee, make sure they explain why they are recommending one product or policy over another, and satisfy yourself that they are not being influenced by the size of the commission they are being paid.

2 Make the most of your savings

At the height of the global banking and stock market crisis, the Irish Government moved to guarantee bank deposits.

All banks and credit unions operating in Ireland, are covered either by the €100,000 deposit guarantee, the 100% deposit guarantee that has now been extended for fixed rate deposits in excess of €100,000 in participating ELG scheme (Eligible Liability Guarantee) banks and/or the deposit guarantee scheme of their own country, if they are a non-Irish institution. State savings schemes (available in the post office) continue to be 100% State guaranteed.

The ELG scheme has now been extended to the end of June 2013.

With State Savings™ (available in the post office) your money is with the Irish Government and there is no upper limit on the amount the Government protects and the Government's obligation to repay you does not have an expiry date.

The worst of the uncertainty about the Irish banking sector has been eased by the capitalisation of the five main Irish banks, but you still should not do business with any financial institution until you ask yourself the following questions:

- Why you are saving?

- How accessible do you want your money to be?

- What is the interest rate on offer?

  and

- How secure is this institution? Will I get a return on my money, but more importantly will I get my money returned?

- Can this institution accommodate a foreign currency account and what costs and charges are involved? Will it pay interest or not?

If your business has no borders, why should your bank?

In today's global economy there are no traditional borders. All that matters is the ability to reach out and grasp opportunities wherever they exist. That's why we're introducing new standards for how we support and service our customers who operate both locally and internationally. It's why we are establishing an even more customer-oriented organisation that operates under one name: Danske Bank. Our new structure means we can be more agile and react faster to international market demands. A new structure that will be of huge benefit to our customers. To learn more please visit newstandards.ie

Danske Bank

New Standards

Deposit guarantee and compensation schemes

Deposit Guarantee Scheme

The Deposit Guarantee Scheme provide compensation to depositors if a regulated firm covered by the scheme goes out of business. The maximum each individual can claim for under the scheme is €100,000 for each bank, building society or credit union regulated by the Financial Regulator. This means that even if you have an amount greater than €100,000 in deposits with an institution, you will only be entitled to a maximum of €100,000. The Deposit Guarantee scheme does not have an end date. The following institutions are covered by the deposit guarantee scheme.

Name of Institution
ACC Bank
Allied Irish Bank plc (AIB)
Irish Bank Resolution Corporation Ltd t/a IBRC (formerly Anglo Irish Bank Corporation)
Bank of Ireland
Bank of Scotland (Ireland) t/a Halifax
Credit unions
EBS Building Society
ICS Building Society (also trades as The Mortgage Store)
Permanent tsb
KBC Bank Ireland Plc
Danske Bank Note 1
Northern Rock Note 2
Pfizer International
Ulster Bank

Note 1   Also covered by the Danish guarantee fund for depositors and investors.

Note 2   Also covered by the UK scheme

Sterling savings accounts now available

Life is all about choices.
Now we're giving you even more of them.

- A range of Sterling account types

- Fixed or variable rates

- Manage Euro and Sterling accounts easily in one place
  - Online
  - Post
  - Phone
  - In branch

- Foreign Exchange service for Euro/Sterling conversions

VISIT **nationwideuk.ie** | CALL **1800 800 280**
ASK **3 Spencer Dock, Dublin 1 or 13 Merrion Row, Dublin 2**

A safe haven for your savings

Eligible liabilities guarantee scheme (ELG)

In December 2009 the Government introduced the Eligible Liabilities Guarantee Scheme (ELG) for term deposit accounts exceeding €100,000. The scheme covers term deposits until they mature (up to a maximum of five years), provided the bank was covered by the scheme when the deposit was placed. This scheme has been extended to 30 June 2013 with EU State Aid approval.

The following institutions are covered by the ELG scheme.

Name of Institution
Allied Irish Bank
Irish Bank Resolution Corporation Ltd t/a IRBC (formerly Anglo Irish Bank Corporation)
Bank of Ireland
EBS Building Society
ICS Building Society
Irish Life & Permanent (permanent tsb)
Irish Nationwide

"Savings Certificates are another very tax-efficient way to save money."

Some banks that operate in Ireland are regulated in their home country and operate here under the EU rules. The Deposit Guarantee Scheme guarantees all deposits up to €100,000 for the following financial institutions within Ireland:

Name of Institution	
Danske Bank t/a NIB	Covered up to €100,000 through combined protection under the national deposit protection schemes in Denmark and Ireland.
Investec Bank Plc	Financial Services Compensation Services (www.fscs.org.uk) 100% of the first £100,000 per person
Leeds Building Society	Financial Services Compensation Services (www.fscs.org.uk) 100% of the first £100,000 per person
Nationwide Building Society/ Nationwide UK (Ireland)	Financial Services Compensation Services (www.fscs.org.uk) 100% of the first £100,000 per person
Northern Rock	Accounts opened before 24th May 2010 are guaranteed by the Bank of England and HM Treasury. For accounts opened after this date they are covered by Financial Services Compensation Services (www.fscs.org.uk) 100% of the first £100,000 per person
RaboDirect	100% of the first €100,000 per person.

Type of deposit accounts

Fixed term accounts

These accounts require you to leave your money with the deposit institution for an agreed period of time - usually from one to 12 months. Normally, the interest paid on these type of accounts is higher than on normal demand deposit accounts. The downside of these accounts is that you cannot access your funds until the maturity date. If you do you will be liable to an interest penalty.

Regular savings accounts

These accounts reward the regular saver with a slightly higher interest rate than is paid by a demand deposit account. For this, you must save an agreed amount over a set period of months. The account may include a number of withdrawal terms and penalties for not adhering to conditions regarding the size of your deposit.

Regular income accounts

These are ideal for someone who needs a regular income, though they usually require a minimum initial deposit. Interest rates can be quite low, however some banks/building societies offer a high rate if you agree to certain restrictions on the amounts you can withdraw at any one time. The income may vary if interest rates go up or down.

Fixed interest accounts

A sort of savings bond, these accounts are extremely popular and involve the bank or building society guaranteeing to pay a fixed amount of interest for a minimum sum over a specific period.

State Savings™ (sold through An Post and the Prize Bond company

State Savings™ is the brand name used by the National Treasury Management Agency (NTMA) to describe the range of savings products offered by the State to personal savers. State Savings™ are sold through the NTMA's agents An Post and the Prize Bond Company. When you place your money in State Savings™ you are placing your money directly with the Irish Government, there is no upper limit on the amount of your money that the Government protects and the Government's obligation to repay you does not have any expiry date.

Savings Bonds are a three year investment and require a minimum investment of €100. At the end of the three years, you will currently earn 10% tax-free or an annual compound rate of 3.23%. Since the interest is cumulative, and increases towards the latter part of the savings period, you should avoid encashing savings bonds early. Withdrawals are subject to seven days notice.

Savings Certificates are another tax-efficient way to save your money, at no risk. With a minimum purchase of €50, savings certificates pay 21% interest guaranteed and tax-free over a five year and six month period. This is the equivalent of an average annual compound interest rate of 3.53% per annum.

National Instalment Savings

To join State Savings'™ Instalment Savings Scheme, the saver - who must be at least age seven - must make regular monthly payments for a minimum of one year, of between €25 and €500. Left for another five years, your accumulated savings will then earn 20% tax free. Or a typical compound rate of 3.37%, including the first 12 month contribution period, when no interest is paid.

Instalment Savings are a popular - and tax free way - to watch savings grow over the medium to longer term. They are a good way to save for a child's education and other domestic goals. Many parents take advantage of the automatic facility on offer which deposits the monthly child benefit allowance (worth €130 a month per child for the first three children, €140 for the fourth and subsequent children (from 1 Jan 2013), directly into the Instalment Savings Scheme as well as into Savings Certificates and other An Post accounts.

Deposit accounts

State Savings™ offer a number of deposit accounts comparable to bank and building society demand accounts.

Prize bonds

Prize Bonds are another product in the State Savings™ suite of products. They pay no interest and are therefore vulnerable to the ravages of inflation if you hold them for a long time, but each eligible Prize Bond is entered into the top monthly prize draw of €1,000,000. A top prize of €20,000 is awarded each week, other than when the monthly €1,000,000 prize is awarded. Over 8,500 €75 prizes are also awarded each week. Prize Bonds are sold in units of €6.25, (there is a minimum purchase of €25 for 4 units). They can be cashed in at any time after an initial period of three months.

National solidarity bond

The National Solidarity Bond is a savings product which gives a gross return of 50% over 10 years. This is paid in 10 annual payments of 1% which are subject to DIRT at 30% and 40% as a tax free lump sum, paid at the end of the 10 years. The minimum contribution is €500 but you can save to reach this amount through regular lodgements of €25 or more. The maximum contribution is €250,000 or €500,000 from two joint applicants or €750,000 from three joint applicants.

The four year National Solidarity Bond pays a gross return of 15% over four years. This is paid in four annual interest payments of 1% subject to DIRT at 30% plus a tax free bonus of 11% after four years.

Budget 2013

The rate of DIRT will increase to 33% with effect from 1 January 2013.

Credit union

The credit union movement has 3 million members in the 32 counties and total assets of approximately €14 billion. Credit unions are essentially financial co-ops in the community or at the saver's place of work. Members come together to save on a regular basis and to provide loans to each other from the collective savings fund.

Members can save in two ways in a credit union:

- Shares which pay a dividend which is determined at the end of the credit union financial year

- Deposits which pay interest which may be determined in advance. Not all credit unions operate deposit accounts.

Loan protection insurance

Many people choose to take out insurance to cover outstanding loans in case of death. In a credit union the loan balances of all insurable members are automatically covered (up to certain limits) at no direct cost to the member. This means that insurable members can borrow in the confidence that their dependents will not be obliged to repay the outstanding loan balance in the event of their death. Should a member with an outstanding loan balance die, the balance is repaid in full, subject to certain cover limits and conditions which apply.

Life cover

Credit unions can insure their members' savings up to a limit of €7,700, €10,200, €12,700 or €20,000. The board of each credit union decide the limit that will apply to their credit union's members. Any savings made after the member's 70th birthday are not insured. On the death of a member, subject to the relevant limit, the amount of life cover paid is calculated on the balances in your account as follows, in accordance with the terms and conditions of the insurance policy.

Example

An individual has the following insurable savings in their account

Share balance and your age	%
Share balance at age 55 (or lowest balance thereafter)	100%
Share balance at age 60 minus share balance at age 55 (or lowest balance thereafter)	75%
Share balance at age 65 minus share balance at age 60 (or lowest balance thereafter)	50%
Share balance at age 70 minus share balance at age 65 (or lowest balance thereafter)	25%

At age	€
55	€2,000
60	€5,000
65	€7,000
70	€9,000

The individual died aged 71 - their credit union has an insurable saving limit of €12,700.

The total amount due on the individual's death is €14,750 i.e. €9,000 savings + €5,750 life cover calculated as follows:

	Balance	Savings	Savings Insured	% Insured	Amount Insured
A	At age 55	€2,000	€2,000	100%	€2,000
B	At age 60	€5,000	€3,000 (B - A)	75%	€2,250
C	At age 65	€7,000	€2,000 (C - B)	50%	€1,000
D	At age 70	€9,000	€2,000 (D - C)	25%	€500
Total insurance cover					**€5,750**

Tax

As a credit union member, the tax treatment of your dividend or interest depends on whether you have a Regular Share, Special Share or Deposit account. Alternatively you can avail of significant tax-free allowances with medium term or long term savings accounts, subject to certain terms and conditions.

Regular share accounts

If you have a Regular Share Account, you are required to declare your dividend in your annual tax return and are liable to pay tax on it at your marginal income tax rate. You may also be liable for levies on this income.

Special share accounts

If you opt to have a Special Share account, your credit union will automatically deduct DIRT at 30% (33% from 1 January 2013) from any dividend you receive on your shares. You have no further liability to tax on these dividends and you are not required to make any declaration to the Revenue Commissioners. This option should suit savers who pay income tax. If you or your spouse are aged over 65 or permanently incapacitated, and your total income is below the relevant Revenue limit, you may be exempt from DIRT. (See page 27 for DIRT exempt accounts).

Deposit accounts

Some credit unions also offer deposit accounts. DIRT at the prevailing rate (33% from 1 January 2013) is deducted automatically from interest earned on these accounts.

Medium term share accounts

If money invested in a Medium Term Share account remains in the account for three years, you can earn an annual dividend on that money up to €480 without having to pay any tax. Any dividend you earn above €480 will be taxed at 33% for 2013.

Long term share accounts

If money invested in a Long Term Share account remains in the account for five years, you can earn an annual dividend on that money up to €635 without having to pay any tax. Any dividend you earn above €635 will be taxed at 33% in 2013.

Each member can only have one Medium or Long Term Share account and penalties apply if you withdraw your savings early.

Summing up

Deposit accounts will never be a way to get rich quick. However, cash deposits do offer safety and ready access to your money. So it makes sense to use them:

- To provide cash reserves for emergencies.

- When you know you will need money for a particular purpose soon (a new car, wedding etc.).

- When you think other types of investments are particularly risky and you want to play safe.

"A healthy respect and under-standing of money is an invaluable gift you can pass onto your children."

Tax

Irish Interest

DIRT at 33% in 2013 is deducted at source from interest earned on deposit accounts. While no further tax is payable, interest earned should be included on your tax return as it may be liable to PRSI. Deposit interest is not liable to the universal social charge (USC).

From 1 January 2013 a DIRT rate of 36% is payable on interest earned on a deposit where the interest payments are made less frequently than annually.

UK interest

Where the UK tax has been deducted at source, the tax will be repaid in full from the UK tax authorities on completion of the appropriate form IRL/Individual/Int. You can obtain this form from the UK Inland Revenue website at www.hmrc.co.uk If you are resident in Ireland you will only be liable to tax in Ireland on deposit interest earned in the UK. The gross interest is taxed in Ireland under Case III Schedule D.

Other interest

Other interest arising abroad for Irish residents will be taxed whether or not it is remitted to this country. Any tax paid abroad will generally be available as a credit against tax payable here.

DIRT free deposit accounts for those aged 65 and over

These accounts allow you to receive any interest earned on money on deposit, paid to you without deduction of DIRT, where you satisfy certain conditions (outlined below).

If you meet these conditions, you can apply directly to your financial institution to have the interest paid without deduction of DIRT.

In order to claim exemption from DIRT you must complete a declaration form stating that you or your spouse/partner (if you are married or in a civil partnership) meet the following conditions:

- Are aged 65 or over when making the declaration.

- If married or in a civil partnership the total annual income for you and your spouse/partner will be below the relevant annual exemption limit. The current annual exemption limits are listed on page 111.

Saving for your children

Sometimes it seems as if there is no end to the financial sacrifices that parents will make for their children. For many young parents it begins with the high cost of pre-school childcare, which can be the equivalent of a second mortgage. On top of all the other family expenses will come the price of schoolbooks and uniforms, music and drama lessons, sports club membership, etc.

Tax relief, allowances and social welfare benefits make a very small contribution to the total cost of raising a child in Ireland today, estimated by some financial institutions to be as much as €100,000 from cradle to college.

Spread over 20 years or so, this annual outgoing will be diluted, but prudent parents will make provision for this huge outlay by undertaking to reassess their own spending habits, their earning capacity and their ability to save and invest on a regular basis.

A good place to start is with the monthly child benefit payment from the Department of Social Protection, which is €130 a month for the first second and third child, and €140 for the fourth and subsequent children.

Many new parents take advantage of the opportunity given to them at the maternity hospital to choose a deposit account from a list of financial institutions (including the tax free State Savings™) to which their monthly child benefit payment can be automatically transferred.

Over the course of 18 years, a monthly payment of €130 can grow to an amount of €28,080 (Deposit accounts attract 33% DIRT tax from 1 January 2013, and are also vulnerable to inflation.)

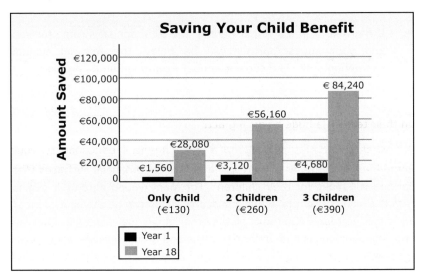

Investing your child benefit for such a long period should, based on historic past performance of stock and shares, produce even higher returns that will ideally offset both taxation and inflation. Given the huge volatility in stock markets however, you need to choose the fund or asset even more carefully for its growth potential, relative to the level of risk you are prepared to take.

Traditional unitised managed funds widely sold by life assurance companies, into which you invest on a monthly basis, are a popular but expensive choice because of high set-up and on-going charges and commissions unless you arrange the investment with a fee-based advisor who strips out the commission.

Lower cost indexed and sectoral funds, include those offered by popular on-line providers like RaboDirect. The lowest cost of all are ETFs (Exchange Traded Funds) which trade on stock markets like a single share and can be purchased directly through a stockbroker, who will charge a commission, or directly via your own on-line share-dealing account, where commission costs are lower. Online trading accounts are execution only, that is, without any advice from the stockbroker.

The attraction of buying investment funds on a regular, monthly basis is that you buy both on dips and rises and do not expose a lump sum from the start to sudden downward movements in asset markets.

Money knowledge doesn't grow on trees

Most parents try to do their best for their children, providing more than just a roof over their heads, food on the table and an education. Finding the money these days - what with incomes under pressure, higher taxation and unemployment - for holidays, entertainment and even braces on their teeth is a huge balancing act.

But what about also passing on a good financial education to your children, something they are unlikely to find on their everyday school curriculum? You might want to start by creating a proper family budget and getting your own personal finances in order. (see page 69).

First, open a joint savings account for each child in the Post Office, the credit union or bank; do it on-line if this is more convenient. Then come up with a consistent pocket-money plan that is both practical and flexible.

For example, it's not a very good idea to give your young children a few cent or euro every week if you think all they are going to spend it on are sweets and you are dead set against them rotting their teeth. Together you might want to set some junk food parameters.

Next, decide whether pocket money is awarded automatically, or on receipt of chores. Some parents prefer the compromise that promises a weekly sum that is then supplemented by the offer of extra pay for more time-consuming or 'difficult' jobs outside the usual household chores.

How much do you give? This too depends on the size of the family budget, number of children, their ages and the amount of peer pressure you get sucked into. It also depends on how much you spend on ice-creams, DVD rentals or a movie, the odd book or comic and clothes: kids don't 'need' to buy themselves anything when they have such willing parents.

A healthy respect and understanding of money is an invaluable gift you can pass on to them, especially in these difficult economic times.

It's never easy to know how much young children understand about money, but using your own judgement, the following are issues that you and your children should talk about on an on-going basis:

1   "Debt is the pits" or, "totally uncool".

Explain how not paying your bills on time is like not doing your homework - it can get you into a lot of trouble. Explain how banks and credit card companies are in business to make money from personal loans and credit cards.

2   Teach them about the importance of having savings.

Explain how savings leave them free to make choices about what to spend their money on. Debt, on the other hand is a form of slavery that gives that control to other people. (Any child "in debt" to an older sibling knows what that means).

3   Explain to them how money can make money.

The credit union, State Savings ™ (in the post office) or bank that accepts minimum €1 deposits - as opposed to their piggy bank - offers the best interest rate for small sums and reinforces the importance of a regular savings routine.

4   A little self-denial goes a long way.

Children like the idea of watching their savings grow (they always prefer to spend your money than their own). But you need to convince them that this will only happen if they forego that extra toy, the really expensive item of clothing or disco night (for older kids) in favour of putting that regular tenner into a savings fund which over a long time could actually make them rich. Just €10 a week into an indexed fund growing at 5% over 10 years will be worth over €6,700 gross over 10 years and nearly €18,000 gross over 20 years.

5   Take any opportunity to talk about the cost of running the family - but not in a hectoring way.

Older children should be told - approximately - how much income the family earns, and how much is spent on overheads: mortgage, food, utilities, holidays, etc.

6   Encourage children to create their own budget - to decide how much they want to save and how much to spend, and on what.

It will show them that splurging on a large, single item means going without something else. Older children who earn from babysitting, stacking shelves or other part-time work should be compelled to save a portion of their money for school expenses and to make an appropriate contribution to mam and dad for their personal upkeep.

7   Tell them not to fully trust anyone with their money except themselves.

As we have all found out to our peril, the world is full of people with get-rich schemes to share, or who want you to buy something from them (or for them). They need to learn to take responsibility for their own money and how it is spent, saved or wasted.

8   Encourage any entrepreneurial shoots you may see.

Explain how some of the best business people started selling surplus comic books (or computer games) to their friends.

10   Money doesn't buy happiness.

Having money does make it easier, however, to cope with some of life's hardships, such as poor health, especially in old age. It can also bring the greatest joy - when it's shared with others less fortunate.

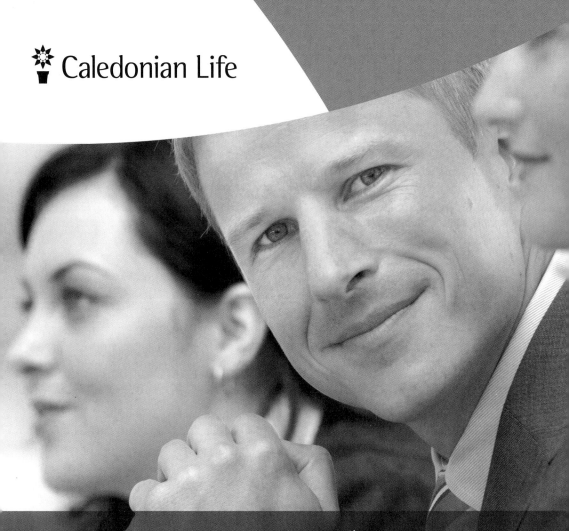

Protecting you and your world

For over 180 years in serving the needs of Irish people, **Caledonian Life** in one guise or another, has offered personalised client-focused service and some of the market's most competitive and comprehensive Life assurance products.

To find out more about how Caledonian Life can help you in 2013 and beyond, contact your local Financial Broker. They'll be delighted to hear from you!

3 Investing wisely

The Irish Government's 100% guarantee of all the deposits and liabilities of the Irish banks in September 2008 may have succeeded in preventing a melt-down of the Irish banking sector when it was first introduced, convincing most depositors that their funds were safe, but in the end, when the size of the Irish bank liabilities became clear, it proved to be a huge mistake. The Irish banking sector was effectively nationalised even as the capitalisation process continued, this time through the auspices of a seven year loan facility from the European Union/European Central Bank's European Financial Stability Fund and the International Monetary Fund in November 2010.

Our appetite for risk has certainly changed since the arrival of 'the Troika' in November 2010 and the heightening of the eurozone debt crisis. An increasing number of people are seeking safe havens for their savings and existing investment funds, including pensions. The most cautious are more concerned about the return of their money rather than a return *on* their money.

Cash is king for most of these people and they are seeking any instrument which will ensure that it is preserved – deposit funds here and abroad; in euro and non-euro currency; strong sovereign and inflation linked bonds and increasingly, precious metals.

Risk opportunities

Experienced investors who have a sharp understanding of risk –including sovereign risk – nevertheless see opportunities even in today's volatile markets. They subscribe to the contrarian investment view that fortunes can always be made when the fear factor is greatest.

Knowledgable, long term investors also see opportunities to buy assets at great value prices in these uncertain and difficult market conditions. There has been increasing interest in blue chip, or 'global dominator' type stocks that pay steady dividends and hold commanding positions in their industry.

These sharp investors, who truly understand how to accurately price a share, and understand stock market risks, might be sitting on a windfall, whether from an inheritance, a retirement or redundancy lump sum, and possibly even a gain from an asset that they have successfully sold. This person, like the experienced investor wants more than the guaranteed, but modest return on offer from their bank or credit union. They are determined to invest.

Investment options for individual investors mainly come in three basic forms:

- Bonds

- Stocks & Shares

- Property

Historically, high quality shares – those that represent successful companies with solid capital bases, low amounts of debt, strong management and recession-proof products or services, have, on average tended to give greater long term returns than any other class of investment, beating property, bonds and deposits.

Bonds

Beyond the security of the bank and building society deposits lie a whole family of fixed-income assets, which are dependent on fluctuations in the national and world economies for their day-to-day values.

When you understand how they work, bonds can be a very useful instrument for investment purposes, especially during time of extreme economic and financial volatility.

Bonds are long-term fixed-interest debt issued by companies and governments - particularly by governments. The 'safer' the government (or sovereign), as determined by the international debt ratings agencies, usually the more costly the bond and the lower the annual yield and capital. (You are paying for the security of knowing that the yield will be paid.) When you buy a bond, the government or corporation takes your money now, and promises to repay you your money at an agreed date in the future. As we have seen in the past year, there are no guarantees that government bonds will always be repaid or that you might not suffer significant losses if you trade or sell them inside your fixed maturity date.

Nominal value

This is the value guaranteed to be repaid to you by a government or company at maturity. The price of a particular bond is normally quoted in terms of €100 nominal value of the stock. For example, a price of €103.06 for the 4% Treasury Bond 2015, means that €100 of the nominal value of the stock could be bought today for €103.06.

Maturity date

Most bonds have a maturity date, i.e. the date at which the nominal value of the stock is guaranteed to be repaid to you by a government or company. Remember that the guaranteed payment at maturity is not the original sum you invested, but the nominal value of the stock you hold.

There is a wide choice of bonds available - with maturity dates that may only be a few months away or as much as 20 or more years away.

Gilts

Because they have always been regarded as being extremely safe, government bonds are often called 'gilt-edged' securities, or simply 'gilts'.

However, it is important to note that unlike bank or building society deposits, bonds are only completely safe if you are willing to hold them until they mature and the country that issues them is credit worthy. If you need to get at your money earlier you can sell your holding in the 'gilts market'. Gilts are traded in much the same way as shares and, as in the case with shares, prices fluctuate daily.

Coupon

The "coupon" is the term used to describe the rate of interest payable on a gilt. It is expressed as a percentage of the nominal value of stock. In the case of the 4% Treasury Bond 2015, the coupon is 4%. So, if you buy €100 nominal value of this stock, the annual payment guaranteed by the government is €4.

Stock types

Gilts are generally categorised by reference to their maturity dates:

Short term gilts: The maturity date of the stock is within the next five years

Medium term gilts: The maturity date of the stock is more than five and less than 15 years away

"In general, interest payments are made on gilts at six monthly intervals"

Long term gilts:	The maturity date of the stock is more than 15 years away.

Ex div/cum div

In general, interest payments are made on gilts at six monthly intervals. To facilitate these payments, the Register of Gilt Owners is closed 31 days before a dividend is due to be paid and each registered owner on this closing date is paid the upcoming dividend.

If you buy stock before this closing date you are said to buy it "cum div" and you will be entitled to receive all of the next dividend payment when it becomes due. If you buy a stock after this closing date, you are said to buy it "ex div" and you will not receive the upcoming dividend.

Tax

If you sell a gilt "cum div", the price you receive will reflect an interest element which the purchaser will receive. This interest element is liable to income tax at your marginal rate of tax.

Example

You invested €20,000 in 4% Guaranteed Stocks on 7 July 2012 and resold the stock on 28 November 2012 for €21,000. The details are as follows;

Last dividend date	01/07/12
Ex dividend date	02/12/12
Next dividend date	01/01/13

You held the stock for 145 days and received no interest payment. However the following interest will be deemed to have accrued and may be taxable,

$$€20,000 \times 4\% \times \frac{145}{365} = €317.80$$

No tax may be payable on this amount if:

● The stock transfer was between you and your spouse.

   or

● The stock has been held by you for a continuous period of two or more years.

If you are deemed to be trading in "gilts", the full gain will be taxed as income.

Other interest received from gilts will be taxed in the normal way under Schedule D Case III. If you made a capital gain on a gilt, no tax is payable unless you are deemed to be trading in gilts.

UK gilts

Where the UK tax has been deducted at source, the tax will be repaid in full from the UK tax authorities on completion of the appropriate form IRL/Individual/Int which is available for the UK Inland Revenue at www.hmrc.co.uk. The gross interest is taxed in Ireland.

Stocks and shares

In the past few years, Irish and global investors suffered some of the worst losses on the stock market in nearly 40 years as a result of the collapse of the banking and financial sector and subsequent unwinding of the huge market in sub-prime mortgage positions, collateralised debt obligations and other complicated derivative investments that have been under investment for mainly the past decade.

Most commentators now accept that the liberalising of banking and stock market regulations, poor supervision by financial regulators and the historically huge injection of low cost credit from 2001 in particular, created the huge credit fuelled asset bubbles (first the dot.com shares in the late 1990s and later, in property) that have now collapsed.

The consequence of this failure to regulate and set appropriate restrictions on the creation of credit is still unravelling, but the spectacular drop in stock market values from 2007 to the Spring of 2009 and again this past year undoubtedly produced some buying opportunities for knowledgeable investors who were able to identify high quality, underpriced, shares.

It is impossible to predict how these volatile markets will keep evolving, but it is worth revisiting the historic potential of stock market returns. For example, suppose that at the end of 1919, one of your relatives had invested €1,000 on the London Stock Exchange and reinvested the annual dividends, this portfolio would have been worth nearly €6.7 million in early 2007, before markets nose-dived.

Of course, €1,000, even in the heady early days of 2007, didn't buy what it used to in 1919 - in real terms the purchasing power of the €1,000 then would have turned into something like €222,003 in 2007 due to the ravages of inflation. Nevertheless, it represented a more than 30-fold increase in the wealth of the lucky shareholder by 2007. Hopefully, he or she was also lucky enough to sell out before their shareholding dropped by the average 30% that most stockholders around the world suffered by early 2009. Since then, much of these losses have been recovered, though not of course in Irish bank shares.

Dividend payments

When you buy stocks and shares, you become a part owner of the company and are usually entitled to a percentage of its profits by way of a dividend. Dividends are normally paid twice a year. Unlike the income from a bank or building society, share dividends are not directly related to the money you invest but, instead, are linked to the growth in the company's profits and its dividend policy. When you invest money in shares, you may be more interested in capital growth or the increase in the relevant stock market valuation.

However, if you are going to need your money next month or next year, shares are not for you - whether you are buying in a 'bear' or 'bull' market - you would be better off putting your money in a more secure place. On the other hand, if you can wait for five, ten or even twenty years for your investment to "mature" and can cope with periodic 'crashes' along the way, then well chosen shares still have the best potential to give you a very good return.

Buying shares is, as we all know now, a risky business and there is always the possibility of a bad investment and of losing some, if not all, of your money. This risk of loss usually diminishes over time, provided you spread your risk by choosing a widely diversified pool of assets.

If you decide to invest in shares, you may want to keep an eye on their performance by reading the financial pages of your daily newspaper (or by subscribing to a recommended financial newsletter or web-site). Take a good investing course (see www.investRcentre.com) that can help teach you about the markets and how they work. It's certainly useful to know how to read the markets columns on the financial pages of your newspaper, which looks like this.

High	Low	Company	Share Price	+ -	Div. yld	P/E	Times cover
14.05	8.70	ABC Ltd.	10.73	-0.47	3.10	10.60	2.80
20.40	11.22	XYZ Ltd.	14.70xd	0.00	1.91	9.70	5.14
11.15	6.26	Z Ltd.	7.23	+0.05	2.20	9.40	3.22

High and low

The first column usually gives the highest price paid for that individual share in the current year and the second column gives the lowest price. The idea is to buy as close as possible to the lowest price and sell as close as possible to the highest price.

Company

The next section gives the relevant company or stock name.

Share price

The share price in column four is usually the previous day's closing price.

Ex-dividend

As we said earlier, companies usually pay dividends twice a year. About six to eight weeks before a dividend is paid, the company announce what the next dividend will be. A week or two after this announcement, the company's share register is temporarily closed. Upcoming dividends will be paid to the registered shareholders on this date. The company's shares will then go ex-dividend and are marked "xd" in the paper. So, if you buy shares marked xd you will not get the upcoming dividend.

Rise or fall

Column five gives the difference between the opening and closing prices of each share in the previous day's trading.

Dividend yield

The dividend yield is the ratio of a share's annual dividend to the share price. Column six gives the gross dividend yield i.e. the dividend yield before tax.

Price earnings ratio (p/e)

Traditionally, many people related a share price to a company's net asset value. Another way of valuing a share is to relate the share price to the company's flow of profits. The price earnings ratio in column seven is calculated by dividing the company's share price by the after-tax earnings due to each share over the company's most recent financial year. This ratio can also be calculated using expected rather than historical earnings. A high P/E ratio shows that investors have a lot of confidence in that company's future prosperity. A low P/E ratio can mean an investor is getting earnings "cheap" or can imply a lack of confidence in that company's future prosperity.

Times cover

The times cover is the ratio of last year's profits to the dividends paid. In the case of XYZ Ltd., it is 5.14. In other words, if XYZ Ltd. had paid out all of its profits to shareholders, the dividend would have been 5.14 times higher.

Tax

Buying and selling shares can give rise to two taxes:

- Income tax on dividends you receive.
- Capital Gains Tax (CGT) on investment gains.

Dividend income

Dividend income is liable to income tax under Schedule F.

When you receive a dividend from an Irish resident company, withholding tax at the 20% standard rate tax is deducted by the company. If the amount of tax withheld exceeds your total tax liability you can claim a refund. However, if you are a higher rate taxpayer you will have to pay the difference between the standard rate and the higher rate.

Example

You receive a dividend of €1,000 in November 2012. Dividend withholding tax of €200 (20%) is withheld by the company. Assuming you have already used up your standard rate cut off point (see page 110) your tax liability will work out as follows:

		2012 €
	Irish dividend gross	€1,000
	Tax @ 41%	€410
Less:	Withholding tax	€200
	Additional tax payable	€210

PRSI and the universal social charge (USC) may also apply.

UK dividends

When you obtain a dividend from a UK company it will normally show:

(a)   The net dividend; and

(b)   A tax credit which is equivalent to 1/9th of the net dividend.

Only the net dividend is taxable in Ireland, i.e. the cash amount received exclusive of any tax credit.

Example

You get a net dividend from UK Ltd. of €1,800, your dividend voucher will also show a tax credit of €200 (1/9th). You pay Irish income tax as follows, assuming that your top rate of tax is 41% in 2012 (ignoring rates of exchange).

The UK tax credit of £200 is non-refundable even if you are a non-taxpayer.

	2012 €
UK dividend (€1,800 net)	€1,800
Tax @ 41%	€738

Capital gains tax

All realised gains in excess of your annual exemption limit (€1,270) will be liable to Capital Gains Tax at 30% (33% from 1 January 2013).

Exchange Traded Funds (ETFs)

Exchange Traded Funds (EFT's) are a low cost alternative to buying stocks and shares or indexed funds directly. An ETF represents a company whose only asset is a collection of shares (or even commodities).

The early ETF market was dominated by index-based ones that represented all or a selection of shares on a well-known stock market, such as the FTSE-100, the Dow Jones index, or even our own ISEQ 20, Ireland's top 20 capitalised private companies, which was launched in 2005. This single share trades just like any other share on the Irish exchange.

The attraction of ETF's are manifold: your risk is diversified between a number of companies, yet you only pay the transaction costs associated with a single share. The transaction and management costs are very low compared to actively managed funds. Typically, there are no entry charges other than a stock broking commission and annual management charges will often be 0.5% or less.

An ETF, like a stock market indexed fund, is considered a good long-term option for investors who prefer to hold their shares rather than actively trade them, on the grounds that 90% of fund managers never consistently beat the performance of a stock market.

Priced daily, you also always know the value of your ETF and can buy into and exit your position at the daily price quickly, something that is not possible with a unitised investment fund.

There are thousands of ETF's available, ranging from large stock market indices, geographical funds (such as a country ETF), to obscure industrial sectors. There are commodity ETF's that track the daily price of gold or silver, for example, or commodity-based ones that bundle together companies in local or global mining industries.

The energy sector is well represented with companies that explore for oil or water, as well as the firms that supply the rigs, pipes, drilling equipment, etc. and ETF investors can also buy 'soft' agri-commodities - wheat, corn, sugar, coffee, cotton, etc which are in increasing demand in developing economies.

The value risks associated with ETF's are no different than any other fund, and global ETF's have taken the same beating from stock market volatility that shares and funds have experienced in the past few years. You need to research your ETF and its underlying companies and assets carefully. Commodities are particularly volatile: a bad harvest can push up the price of wheat or corn, but a bumper harvest can push it down just as easily, which can not only affect the actual price of your ETF commodity, but also impact all they way up the line from the farmer to the combine harvesting company to the trucking and shipping lines that transport the wheat or corn halfway around the world.

Tax

There is no Stamp Duty on the purchase of ETF's in Ireland or the UK.

The ISEQ 20 ETF is regulated under the European UCITS framework and is subject to an exit tax of 33% (36% from 1 January 2013). You cannot offset losses from ETF's against other gains or claim your annual CGT tax-free allowance.

Non-European ETFs may be subject to withholding tax in the country of origin, and also a tax on income and/or capital gains tax when the ETF is sold.

"Typically, there are no entry charges other than stock-brokering commissions."

Property

The collapse of property prices here, and in other countries that experienced massive property inflation, especially from 2001, has devastated both net personal wealth and that of many State treasuries. As a result, property values have fallen dramatically, none more so than here in Ireland, where the biggest property boom of all was fuelled by a dangerous combination of cheap credit, substantial tax breaks for builders, investors and owner occupier's and our historic mania for property that was fed by a combination of the State, the property industry and the media.

It will take many years - decades perhaps - for the fallout of the bust to settle and for house prices to begin to rise again, but that doesn't mean that there isn't a genuine desire for home-ownership. Families will always want a home of their own in which to raise their children and to see out their retirement. It just won't be the kind of market that saw private homes turn into a quick source of wealth...at highly inflated prices.

The reason why, historically, property that is not necessarily your principal private residence can be a sound investment is because it does have long term investment opportunities, both as a generator of income, and for capital growth.

Professional landlords have understood these attractions, and many have become wealthy from a portfolio of well-priced properties. Leveraging the purchase price with some of the lowest interest rates available for any form of borrowing has always been one of the huge attractions of property as an investment asset. But no amount of cheap finance is worth the risk if the landlord cannot earn a profit from his rental yield after all taxes and expenses are paid: it was the idea that property values would only go up that was the cause of the collapse in the property market and the main contributor to the bursting of the global finance bubble.

The collapse of the Irish banks in 2008 and the setting up of NAMA (the National Assets Management Agency) which has purchased the biggest of the toxic property loans held by the banks means that the banks are under huge pressure to capitalise their balance sheets. With the banks restricting the number of loans and reverting to more prudent lending criteria, it has become more difficult and more expensive for recent home buyers to service their mortgages - at least half are in negative equity - and those coming off fixed rate loans have less access to the widest selection of products on the market.

Falling property prices have made many mortgages more affordable, but only if you qualify for the loan under the tighter lending criteria the banks now impose. Nevertheless, buying a property remains an opportunity in a lifetime for a person to borrow substantial sums of money at a comparatively low cost.

For example, suppose you can afford to buy a property for €200,000 cash and once the market recovers (and it will some day) its price rises by 3% in real terms each year for the next 20 years.

At the end of that 20 years, the property will be worth €361,200 in real terms. You make a real profit of €161,200 (after accounting for inflation).

Now, suppose that instead of putting up the whole €200,000 yourself, you borrow €180,000, over 20 years and rent the property. We also assume that the rent you will receive from the property will be sufficient to repay the loan and also pay all interest charges, expenses and tax bills associated with the property over the next 20 years. Undertaking any property investment without a sound rental stream is not recommended - a warning so many ignored over the past decade.

After 20 years, your stake in the property will have gone up from €20,000 to €361,200 and your new profit is €341,200. Now, because your original investment was low, your stake has increased by a factor of 17 in real terms (€341,200 ÷ €20,000). That's a good investment by any standards.

The ups and downs of property prices

Property prices rose steadily over 30 years to 2007, but the increases, as the figures on page 46 show, were not always consistent. Since late 2006 the property bubble that blew up from 2001 has well and truly burst, both here in Ireland and around the world.

The following table illustrates how the average three bedroom semi-detached house in typical Dublin has increased in price over the past 30 years.

Average price of 3 bed semi-detached house in Dublin

Year	€
1981	€12,500
1991	€80,000
2001	€190,000
2011	€190,000

Commercial property

The value of commercial property is normally directly related to the rental income it can generate. In the table below, we highlight how rental income from commercial properties has been increasing at different paces over the years. This illustration outlines the average cost per square foot of commercial properties in the Dublin area over the past 30 years.

"Undertaking any property investment without a sound rental stream is not recommended"

Year	Average office rental cost per sq. ft.	Average retail rental cost per sq. ft. (shopping centres)	Average industrial rental cost per sq. ft.
1981	€4.75	n/a	n/a
1991	€13.00	€30.00	€3.75
2001	€22.50	€350.00	€10.50
2011	€30.00	€350.00	€6.50

(The above figures relating to property were provided by CBRE Research)

Rental Properties

Self employed individuals and company directors who purchase rental properties normally have substantial incomes so the rate of tax on rental income could be as high as 52% (41% tax plus PRSI and the universal social charge).

The rate of corporation tax on rental income is 25%. Rental income in a company which is not distributed is liable to a surcharge of 20% and the effective corporation tax rate can be as high as 40%.

Tax on disposal

When a property is sold the chargeable gain will normally be subject to CGT at 30%. So, if you own the property personally you retain proceeds less 30% CGT. If the property is owned by a company it also pays CGT at 30%. However, there will be a further personal tax liability if you wish to gain access to the cash within the company. If you access the cash by way of salary or dividend, the rate could be as high as 52% (income tax,PRSI and USC). The other option is to liquidate the company, which will give rise to a further 30% CGT liability.

Budget 2013

The rate of CGT is increased to 33% for disposals made after 5 December 2012.

Example

You set up "A" Limited ten years ago with ordinary share capital of €2. "A" Limited bought a property for letting for €130,000. "A" Limited sells the building now for €500,000. Here we assume indexation of 30% for CGT purposes and that the company has no other assets or liabilities. The tax position for you is also illustrated as if you bought the property personally.

	Personal purchase €	"A" Limited €
Sale proceeds	€500,000	€500,000
Less: Cost of property plus indexation	€130,000	€130,000
Taxable amount	€370,000	€370,000
CGT on €370,000 @ 30%	€111,000	€111,000
Available for distribution		€389,000
CGT on liquidation of A Limited €389,000 @ 30%		€116,700
Net personal proceeds	€389,000	€272,300
Total tax payable	**€111,000**	**€227,700**

Stamp Duty

For instruments executed on or after 8 December 2010 the rates of stamp duty are as follows;

Aggregate consideration	Rate of duty
First €1,000,000	1%
Excess over €1,000,000	2%

The rate of Stamp Duty on a non-residential property executed on or after 15 October 2009 is as follows:

"VAT should be deducted before calculating the charge or rate of stamp duty."

Market value	Houses / Apartments
Up to €10,000	Exempt
€10,001 - €20,000	1%
€20,001 - €30,000	2%
€30,001 - €40,000	3%
€40,001 - €70,000	4%
€70,001 - €80,000	5%
Over €80,001	6%

The stamp duty rate for non-residental properties is a flat 2% rate in respect of instruments executed after 6 December 2011.

Where VAT is included in the cost of the property, it should be deducted before calculating the charge or rate of stamp duty.

Income tax

Rents are taxed under Schedule D Case V on the basis of the actual year's income - e.g. rents arising in the year ending 31 December 2012 are assessed to tax in the income tax year 2012. The following expenses can normally be deducted from the gross rents for tax purposes.

- Interest paid on money borrowed to purchase residential property. From 7 April 2009 only 75% of mortgage interest paid on residential property can be offset against the gross rental income.

- Rent payable on the property.

- Rates payable on the property.

		€
	Residential Property Rental Income and Expenditure Account Y/E 31st December 2012 Name: _____ PPS No. _____ Y/E: _____	
	Rent received	€15,000
Less	**Allowable expenses**	
	Rates / ground rents payable	€100	
	Insurance on premises	€500	
	Repairs & renewals	€900	
	Light, heat and telephone	€400	
	Cleaning & maintenance	€1,000	
	Agency & advertising	€700	
	PRTB registration	€70	
	Interest on borrowed money (75%)	€6,500	
	Mortgage protection premiums	€300	
	Sundry expenses	€300	
	Total expenses	€10,770
	Net rental income	**€4,230**
Less	Capital allowances on fixtures & fittings	(€875)
	Taxable rental income after capital allowances	€3,355
	Income tax & levies - assuming a 41% rate of tax + 11% PRSI & USC	**€1,744.60**

- Goods provided and services rendered in connection with the letting of the property.

- Repairs, insurance, maintenance and management fees.

- Capital allowance of 12.5% per annum on the value of the fixtures and fittings.

- Mortgage protection premiums.

Be sure to keep all receipts, especially for repairs and maintenance, as your Inspector of Taxes may wish to examine these.

The Non Principal Private Resident (NPPR) charge for residential units is not an allowable expense in computing your taxable rental income.

In order to claim mortgage interest relief as an expense it is necessary to be registered with the PRTB (Private Residential Tenancy Board).

A typical rental income and expenditure account is shown on page 49.

Specified relief restrictions

From 1 January 2007 the amounts which "high earning" individuals can claim as a deduction in respect of "specified reliefs" was severly restricted. Specified reliefs include most Section 23 schemes, BES seed capital Employment investment incentive scheme and film investment schemes, tax exempt patent income and charitable donations.

Section 23 type reliefs and accelerated capital allowances

A surcharge effective from 1 January 2012 applies to individuals with gross incomes over €100,000. The surcharge applies at a rate of 5% on the amount of income sheltered by property reliefs in a given year.

This surcharge (essentially a higher rate of USC) applies to all investors regardless of whether they invested in Section 23 or accelerated capital allowance schemes with this level of gross income.

Residential owner-occupier relief is unaffected by these changes.

Private residential tenancy board

Entitlement to a deduction for interest paid on borrowed money used to purchase, improve or repair a rental residential property is now conditional on compliance with the registration requirements of the Residential Tenancies Act 2004. This change applies to interest paid by individuals during the year of assessment 2006 and subsequent years.

Persons who are required to register

The Act applies to the vast majority of private rented dwellings situated in Ireland but does not apply to;

- Business premises.

- Former rent controlled dwellings occupied by the original tenant or by their spouse.

- A dwelling let by a local authority or a voluntary housing body.

- A dwelling occupied under a shared ownership lease.

- A dwelling in which the landlord also resides (this would include the 'rent a room' scheme).

- A dwelling in which the spouse, parent or child of the landlord is resident and where there is no written lease or tenancy agreement.

- Holiday lettings.

A dwelling let by, or to, a public authority is also excluded. A "public authority" includes a recognised educational institution. Therefore, owners of student accommodation dwellings let to third level college for onward letting to students are excluded from the requirement to register. However, tenancies in dwellings that are let directly to students must be registered.

Registration requirements

Landlords are required to register details of all of their tenancies within one month of the commencement of those tenancies. Once it is registered it remains a registered tenancy for as long as the tenancy remains in existence. Once it is terminated, any new tenancy created in respect of the dwelling must be registered with the PRTB. If the tenancy has not previously been terminated it will be deemed to have terminated when it has lasted four years and a new tenancy will then be deemed to commence. This new tenancy must be registered with the PRTB and the appropriate fee paid.

The registration application form PRTB1 is available from the Private Residential Tenancies Board (PRTB) www.prtb.ie. The registration can also be completed online.

Non-principal private residence (NPPR) charge

Budget 2013

It was announced in Budget 2013 that the NPPR will apply for 2013 and will be abolished thereafter as it will be replaced by a Local Property Tax (LPT).

What is the Non Principal Private Residence (NPPR) charge?

The Local Government (Charges) Act 2009 introduced an annual €200 charge on non principal private residences, payable by the owner of the property to the Local Authority in whose area the property concerned is located.

What types of properties are liable for the NPPR charge?

Subject to certain exclusions the NPPR charges applies to every residential property owned by a person, which is not the principal or main residence of the owner. This includes any house, maisonette, flat, apartment or bedsit.

The main exemption from the charge is on your principal private residence (PPR).

While the exemption for a PPR covers one property only, a further limited exemption may apply where a person is moving house and temporarily owns two properties. This exemption covers a second residential property acquired within one year of the liability date where the first property is sold no less than six months after the liability date.

Additional exemptions include:

- A mobile home, caravan or vehicle.

- A newly constructed residential building that is unsold and has not yet been used as a dwelling, provided it forms part of the trading stock of a business.

- A residential property owned by an approved charity.

- A residential property occupied under a shared ownership agreement with a housing body or HSE.

- A residential property held in a discretionary trust;

- A residential property occupied rent free by a relative of the owner of the property provided the said residential property is located no more than 2km from the PPR of the owner. This would include a granny flat and other similar residences.

- A residential premises owned by a person who lives elsewhere by reason of physical or mental incapacity.

- A building liable to commercial rates.

- Where a decree of divorce or judicial separation has been granted and a spouse owns the PPR of the other spouse, then he/she will not be liable to the charge in respect of that property.

The payment of the NPPR charge for residential properties is not an allowable expense in computing taxable rental income.

"The NPPR late payment fee for each property amounts to €20 per month or part of a month."

Local property tax (LPT)

From 1 July 2013, residential property owners will be liable for an LPT based on the self-assessment market value of their property on 1 May 2013.

Property values are grouped into value bands. A rate of 0.18% will apply to the midpoint of the value band up to €1m. To calculate how much you will have to pay for 2013 select the value band appropriate to the market value of your property and read across in the table on page 54. For properties values at over €1m the LPT liability will be calculated as follows: 0.18% on the first €1m and 0.25% on the portion over €1m.

Local Property Tax rate bands

Valuation band	LPT in 2013 (half year charge)	LPT in 2014 (full year charge)
€	€	€
0 to 100,000	45	90
100,001 to 150,000	112	225
150,001 to 200,000	157	315
200,001 to 250,000	202	405
250,001 to 300,000	247	495
300,001 to 350,000	292	585
350,001 to 400,000	337	675
400,001 to 450,000	382	765
450,001 to 500,000	427	855
500,001 to 550,000	472	945
550,001 to 600,000	517	1,035
600,001 to 650,000	562	1,125
650,001 to 700,000	607	1,215
700,001 to 750,000	652	1,305
750,001 to 800,000	697	1,395
800,001 to 850,000	742	1,485
850,001 to 900,000	787	1,575
900,001 to 950,000	832	1,665
950,000 to 1,000,000	877	1,755
< 1m - assessed on the actual value at 0.18% on the first €1m and 0.25% on the portion above €1m		

Exemptions

Certain properties will be exempt from LTP. These exemptions largely correspond to exemptions from the Household Charge (see page 52). Exemptions will also apply to new and previously unused properties purchased from a builder or developer between 2013 and 2016, and to second-hand properties purchased in 2013 by a first time buyer.

Deferrals

A system of deferral arrangements for owner-occupiers will be implemented under specified conditions to address cases where there is an inability to pay the LPT (e.g. where the gross income does not exceed €15,000 for a single person and €25,000 for a couple). Some owner-occupiers may be eligible to apply for marginal relief, which will allow them to defer up to 50% of their LPT liability. It should be noted that interest will be charged on deferred amounts at a rate of 4% per annum.

Rent a Room Scheme

Where a room or rooms in a person's private principal residence is let as residential accommodation, gross annual rent of up to €10,000 will be exempt from income tax.

The Rent a Room Scheme is not available where the rent received was from a child who in turn is claiming rent relief.

Household charge

From 1 January 2012, a household charge of €100 applies. Only recipients of mortgage interest supplement and homeowners living on qualifying "ghost estates" are exempt. The new local property tax (LPT) introduced in 2013 replaced the household charge. Any outstanding arrears of the household charge will be added to the LPT due on the property and collected by the Revenue Commissioners through the LPT system.

Managed funds

As the name implies, "Managed Funds" are funds where investors pool their resources to create a common investment fund which is controlled by professional managers. The two main benefits of this collective approach are, more efficient and economical investment management, plus greater security to investors, as the risk is spread over a diverse range of investments. Managed Funds are normally marketed under a number of headings:

- Life assurance products.
- Investment bonds / Unit linked funds.
- Tracker bonds.
- Offshore investment funds.
- UCITS.

Life assurance products

With-profit investment plans also invest your money in various assets outlined on the previous page over a fixed number of years. However, instead of your money being subject to the daily movement of the investment markets, the company sets out future minimum guaranteed values, as profits are earned and annual bonuses are declared, and this will increase your overall guaranteed values. Once declared, these bonuses cannot be taken away. The aim is to pay a bonus that relates to market growth but one that can also be sustained if the market falls. Some companies pay a higher proportion of performance growth in the form of a final bonus than others. This can penalise policyholders who encash their policies early and reward those who stay the course of the contract.

The smoothing-out effect of the bonus system protects with-profit funds from the volatility that is part and parcel of the market place. However, with-profits policies cannot buck the market: The values that are paid out at maturity will reflect the overall growth achieved by these stocks, property, gilts and cash investments that have underpinned them.

Investment bonds

Aimed at the lump sum investor, bonds come in different guises, such as

- Unit-linked and with-profit bonds.
- Tracker bonds.
- Special Investment bonds.

Life assurance bonds are among the most widely sold. Nearly all require a minimum investment of €5,000 and at least a five year investment time frame. Ideally, these should be regarded as medium to long-term investments to allow a good maturity value to build-up. Entry costs are usually between 3%-5% and annual management charges are usually 0.75%- 1%.

Tracker bonds were considered a relatively safe, if expensive way of participating in international stock markets, such as the FTSE-100, the Dow and Japanese Nikkei, without many of the associated risks. Most tracker bonds have an investment term of three to six years and normally require minimum investments of €5,000. However, tracker bond fund managers are not buying actual stocks and shares, just the options on the performance of shares represented by a particular stock market index.

In order to guarantee the safety of the investor's capital - a strong selling point for tracker bonds - a large portion of your investment must be put on deposit.

A number of years ago many tracker funds guaranteed the return of virtually the entire capital so long as the investors left their money untouched. With interest rates so low, the cost of this guarantee has risen, and recent tracker bonds are poor performers compared to the returns achieved a decade ago.

Absolute return funds

Most conventional investment funds only reward investors when markets go up and penalise them when they fall. Absolute return funds seek to deliver positive returns whether markets are rising or falling. They use a wide variety of assets, such as equities, bonds, property and cash. They can also use advanced instruments, such as derivatives, to gain additional returns or guard against market falls.

Most fund managers work on the basis of benchmarking against a stock market index or average fund in its sector – relative return. Objectives can be achieved even in "negative" market.

Absolute return basically attempts to produce a "positive" investment return over a specific term, irrespective of whether markets are positive or negative.

Most absolute return funds work towards a specific target return, e.g. 'X'% above Euribor over 'Y' period.

Tax

The returns from life assurance product funds commenced before 1 January 2001 are paid tax-free. All taxes due on profits earned will have already been paid at source by the life assurance fund managers to the Revenue Commissioners.

For products issued after the 1 January 2001 no tax will be imposed within funds. However, the life assurance company is obliged to deduct an exit tax on any gains or investment income generated during the currency of the product, at the rate of 33% in 2012 (36% from 1 January 2013). This tax will be a final liability tax for Irish residents. No tax will be deducted from payments to a person who is neither resident nor ordinarily resident here provided they have complied with the Revenue declaration requirements.

Tax on death or disability

The proceeds payable on death or disability are liable to the same level of exit tax as if the product had been surrendered at that date.

Example - Lump sum investment

An individual invests €100,000 in an Investment Bond on 4 January 2004. They die on 13 March 2012 when the gross value of their bond is €150,000. They made no withdrawals from the investment over the term. The "taxable gain" is the reduction in the surrender value of the bond as a result of the payout i.e. €150,000 less allowable premiums paid.

Chargeable amount	=	€150,000 - €100,000	=	€50,000
Exit tax @ 33%	=	€50,000 x 33%	=	€16,500

Example 2 - Protection plan

You took out a long term savings/protection plan on 5 March 2009. Annual premiums €1,000, Life cover €30,000. This gross surrender value after 15 years is €20,000 (at 5 March 2024).

In the event of a full encashment, exit tax is charged on the difference between the surrender value (€20,000) and the total premium paid (€15,000). Assuming an exit tax rate of 36%, this would amount to €1,800. The net encashment value payable is €18,200

Death

Using the above example and assuming the individual dies on 5 March 2024, the life company would pay the life cover sum (€30,000) less the appropriate exit tax. This tax would be calculated as follows - the surrender value of the plan after the payout is nil. Therefore, the reduction in surrender value as a result of the payout is € 20,000. So, exit tax is calculated on the difference between total premiums paid and the reduction in the surrender value after the payment of the sum assured is agreed (€20,000 less €15,000 = €5,000). Assuming a tax rate of 36%, the tax payable on the individual's death would also be €1,800.

Offshore policies

Most Irish investment managers are as competent, professional and lucky (or unlucky) as their counterparts in the UK, America or Japan. Some concentrate solely on the Irish market. Others buy and sell equities and other assets in far flung parts of the world. Certainly all the larger investment companies here offer a selection of domestic and international equity funds (such as UK, American, Japanese, European, developing economies and sectoral funds) to their clients as well as fixed asset funds such as Government gilts or currency funds.

One of the perceived advantages of buying an investment from a larger player is that it will usually have considerably greater access to research and analytical resources, often directly on the ground in the country where the investments originate. This in-depth knowledge has produced mixed results for many of the big international players familiar to Irish investors, such as Fidelity, Gartmore, HKSB, Invesco and others, but the financial crisis has shown that few fund managers - or funds - have been able to escape unscathed.

UCITs

'Undertakings for Collective Investments in Transferable Securities' are very popular and tax efficient with investment mainly in equity funds. UCITS are highly regulated by EU authorities, the unit prices are highly transparent, as are charges. The tax treatment of UCITS means that there can be greater overall potential for growth. UCITS are sold by a number of different providers, including the low cost on-line bank Rabodirect.ie .

Tax

Every person acquiring an offshore policy or fund is obliged to make a tax return to the Revenue Commissioners no later than 31 October following the end of the relevant tax year. This return will detail;

- When and how the policy or investment was acquired.
- The description of the product including premiums payable.
- Name and address of the person through whom the offshore product was acquired e.g. an intermediary.

Alternative investments

The case for gold

High demand for commodities in developing economies has resulted in the creation of a huge range of managed investment funds, index funds and ETFs that represent either the commodities themselves, such as oil, coal, iron, steel, base metals of all kinds, 'soft' agriculture-based commodities as well as commodity-related companies.

Precious metals, like gold, silver and platinum have also become widely traded commodities over the past several years, not just because of their growing industrial applications, but especially in the case of gold, and increasingly, silver because of their historic role as a store of value in tumultuous financial times. Very simply, more and more people are learning that gold and silver is 'real money'.

"An ounce of gold could buy a Roman tribune a fine set of clothes 2000 years - as it can today."

Whereas paper currencies lose their value over time when their supply is increased by governments and central banks, gold keeps its intrinsic value: an ounce of gold could buy a Roman tribune a fine set of clothes 2000 years ago - as it can today. Thirty years ago, an ounce of gold could buy an adult Irish private health insurance policy; today, that same ounce can still buy a good adult private health insurance plan.

The average price of gold peaked in 1980 at $612.56 an ounce for that year and then more than halved in price until the end of the 1990s. It has risen steadily since 2001, when global central banks began reducing interest rates to historically low levels and flooded the financial markets with credit in order to offset the double effects of the dot.com crash and the 9/11 attacks.

Since 2001 the price of gold, in dollars, has risen from an average price of $271 an ounce to an estimated $1,650 an ounce in 2012, as the destruction of the global banking system unfolded due to decades of excessive money supply, fractional reserve banking and poor regulation. The price of gold soared in 2011 over 2010 as the Eurozone crisis intensified.

The attraction of including gold as a small part of an investment portfolio during inflationary periods or during times of political turmoil, is that it provides a safe harbour - a hedge - against the falling value of a currency and because even though physical gold is not a tradeable currency, it is a convertible asset of value.

Price of Gold

Year	London Market Price (British £[1718-1949] or U.S.$. [1950 - 2006] per fine ounce)
1973	$97.81
1974	$159.74
1975	$161.49
1976	$125.32
1977	$148.31
1978	$193.55
1979	$307.50
1980	$612.56
1981	$459.64
1982	$375.91
1983	$424.00
1984	$360.66
1985	$317.66
1986	$368.24
1987	$447.95
1988	$438.31
1989	$382.58
1990	$384.93
1991	$363.29
1992	$344.97
1993	$360.91
1994	$385.42
1995	$385.50
1996	$389.09
1997	$332.39
1998	$295.24
1999	$279.91
2000	$280.10
2001	$272.22
2002	$311.33
2003	$364.80
2004	$410.52
2005	$446.00
2006	$610.00
2007	$696.00
2008	$871.96
2009	$972.35
2010	$1,225.94
2011	$1,565.67
2012	$1,650.00

Gold prices are also now rising as a result of lower supply and higher demand from the governments of emerging economies, especially China and India that have large reserves of US dollars, and in the form of jewellery. 2012 was a year of rising, but volatile prices, mainly as a result of the dangerously weak fiscal position of a number of European countries like Greece, Ireland, Portugal and Spain and because of the extraordinary measures – quantitative easing – undertaken by EU and European Central Bank to prevent both bank and sovereign collapse.

The steadily rising price and demand for gold has been facilitated by easier ways to buy it: huge trading now takes place in gold Exchange Traded Funds (ETFs), which can be purchased by Irish investors like a share on a stock market and which track the price of an ounce of gold in US dollars. Another popular method is to buy gold coins and bullion and in certificate form by way of certificates issued by the Bank of Western Australia in Perth and sold by the Irish gold bullion dealers , Goldcore. (see www.goldcore.com) Goldcore has also introduced a regular gold saving programme which allows investors to buy between €150 to €500 a month worth of gold every month over 12 months. At the end of the year the value of the cumulative savings can be encashed for physical gold, Perth Mint certificates or the cash value of the gold purchased. Transaction costs vary between the different methods of purchase. The direct purchase of physical gold will include a transaction commission plus either a delivery/insurance charge or an annual storage fee.

Investors need to be clear about their motives for buying gold: are they strictly speculating on its price, or do they want to add gold as a longer term hedge against the risk of other assets falling in value?

Gold may keep its intrinsic value forever, but investors need to remember that it pays no dividends and its price - as the table on page 61 shows -is subject to market forces that can push it down as well as up.

The price of silver is more volatile than gold because it has industrial as well as historic monetary uses. In the spring of 2011 it rose to a high of $50 an ounce, only to fall back again to about $32 on average at year end. That is where it has mainly remained for most of 2012. Many commentators continue to believe that silver has fallen far outside its historical 1:16 sync with gold (whereby it took 16 silver ounces to buy one ounce of gold.)

4 Borrowing and managing debt

"Neither a borrower nor a lender be" may be sound advice, but few of us can afford to be so virtuous. Yet borrowing money, as so many people have discovered to their detriment, can be a perilous activity, since there are so many things that can go wrong when it comes to repaying the loan - illness, unemployment, other unexpected events, even happy ones like having a baby and having to interrupt a career.

It is becoming increasingly difficult to secure credit, but whether it be a term loan from the bank, a mortgage or even a credit card, you need to consider the following:

- The amount.
- The type of loan.
- The rate of interest charged.
- The duration of the loan.
- Your ability to pay, especially should interest rates rise.
- Your personal circumstances.
- Borrowing outlets.

Loans

Borrowing money for a long-term purpose, such as a mortgage or to finance a business is very different from borrowing to buy a car, household goods or even a holiday. For one thing, the interest rate you pay and the repayment period are going to be very different. So try and match the loan with the right lender from the start.

If you want to borrow money for a home, go to a building society or bank. If you want an overdraft that you dip in and out of, you must stick with the bank or building society with which you have your current account. The lending pool for personal loans widens to include finance houses, credit unions and even life assurance companies if you happen hold a valuable with-profits policy. But moneylenders, who are the keenest of all to lend, should be avoided by all but the most desperate because of the crippling interest rates they charge – up to 188% per annum.

Since 2012, most licensed moneylenders charging an Annual Percentage Rate (APR) of interest above 23% have to include a warning notice saying "This is an high-cost loan" in any agreement with customers.

"Credit card loans should be used sparingly and ideally by people who can pay off the amount borrowed each month."

The cheapest interest rates are provided by mortgage lenders, who are counting on you borrowing over a period of many years. The most expensive interest rates are charged by credit card providers and moneylenders whose lines of credit are designed to be paid off ideally in a short amount of time. Credit card "loans" should be used sparingly and ideally by people who can pay off the amount borrowed each month; that way they will incur no interest at all.

An upward change in interest rates will not normally change the amount most people pay back each month for personal short-term loans, even if the rate is a variable one. However any adjustments that have worked against you over the period will have to be settled up at the end - usually with a final balancing payment(s).

Variable rate mortgages don't work this way. Any rate hike or fall is usually applied to the homeowner's next repayment. If rates go up by a half percent, you will have to pay more each month until they go down again. Fixing your personal loan or mortgage interest rate is one way to avoid this kind of volatility, but it is difficult to predict interest rate movements: if you fix your rate and interest rates fall, you must continue to pay the fixed rate for the agreed term or incur penalties to break the contract.

Many term loan borrowers are keen to stretch their repayments over a longer number of years because the monthly repayment is smaller. But they sometimes forget that ultimately they will pay more interest on this loan. See example on page 65.

Term loans

Before you take out a term loan with a bank or building society you need to determine the real cost of the loan, the Annual Percentage Rate (APR) and the total repayments. The APR is the true interest rate and is calculated based on the duration of the loan and any fees that may fall due. The APR is inevitably higher than the published flat rate. Along with the APR rate you should also ask for the cost per thousand per month which will tell you how much every €1,000 borrowed will cost. You then multiply this amount by however many thousands of euro you borrow and by the number of months over which you are repaying the loan. This figure represents your total repayment.

Example

APR	Amount borrowed	Loan term	Repayment each month	Total to be paid back	Total cost of credit (total paid less original loan)
8.5%	€10,000	3 years (36 monthly payments)	€314	€11,304	€1,304
8.5%	€10,000	4 years (48 monthly payments)	€245	€11,760	€1,760
8.5%	€10,000	5 years (60 monthly payments)	€204	€12,240	€2,240

Overdrafts

Arranged on your current account, overdrafts are a way to arrange extra credit as you need it. Interest rates are usually higher than the personal lending rate, but not as high as a credit card rate, and payable only as you use the facility. If you exceed your overdraft limit without permission, the bank is entitled to charge extra interest and a "referral charge" which can amount to several euro per event.

Budget account

This is a type of overdraft which smoothes out the annual cost of running your current account. It allows you to borrow a multiple of your monthly pay cheque (paid directly into the account) to cover large once-off outgoings like school expenses in September, Christmas spending in December or the cost of a summer holiday. Interest is charged only as you draw down the facility.

Credit Union loans

Credit Unions do not seek collateral before lending money - your record as a regular saver and whether you are employed or not, is how they judge your ability to repay. The loan amount is usually a multiple of the value of shares you hold. Credit Unions tend to show more flexibility regarding repayment schedules than conventional lenders and calculate the interest on the diminishing balance basis. Loans are automatically insured by the Credit Union and cleared in the event of your death.

Life assurance

Life assurance companies may seem like an unusual source from which to borrow money, but there is provision for lending up to 80% of the cash value of a with-profits policy. Interest rates are usually competitive and borrowing against the fund value may be better than encashing the policy. Investment policies like this should always be allowed to run their course - since a significant part of the total value of the policy may be paid in the form of a final bonus which only comes into effect on the maturity of the policy.

Life assurance policies are frequently used as security against conventional loans eg - if you renege on your debt the bank will simply encash the policy.

Credit cards

These are among the most expensive but convenient forms of borrowing. Designed for short-term purchases, the APR can be as high as 22.7% or more for those cardholders who don't clear their monthly balances in full. The highest rates of interest charged immediately on cash withdrawals is now slightly lower at 21.3%. Disciplined cardholders can take full advantage of the 50 plus days of free credit available, but those who don't, can run up large balances very quickly. The most popular credit cards are Visa and Mastercard which now come in different guises - such as affinity cards for professional groups who can benefit from a slightly lower interest rate and a donation to their college or charity or in the form of a loyalty card with which you can build up cash discounts with a series of retailers. With penalty charges for spending over your credit limit or not paying your bill on time and other conditions and interest rates varying so much between card providers, you need to shop around for the best rate and conditions. - see comparison tables on the National Consumer Agency website, www.nca.ie

Debit cards

The Visa debit card is now being introduced by a number of banks to replace Laser cards. The new debit card is more widely accepted internationally by merchants and it carries more on-line security features. It does not replace a conventional credit card because the funds you spend will still be deducted from your current account.

Charge/store cards

These include the likes of American Express and Diners Club as well as popular store cards like Arnotts, Clerys or Brown Thomas. Charge cards may involve an annual membership and require you to clear your balance off monthly within a set time frame or face hefty interest penalties. Unlike store cards, however, American Express and Diners Club do not have spending limits. The store cards are handy and convenient but interest rates can be very high (sometimes higher than ordinary credit cards) if you do not clear your balance each month.

Consolidation loans

These loans were much in demand in recent years as borrowers discovered that they could reduce the size of their overall monthly loan repayments by consolidating their credit card, overdraft, car loan, hire purchase payments into a new single super-loan. Ideally, many people wanted to consolidate these debts as part of an existing mortgage, since home loans carry the lowest annual interest rates.

Type of loan	Amount you owe	Term left to run	APR	Monthly Payments	Overall cost of credit
Existing mortgage	€100,000	20 years	5.20%	€664	€59,360
Home improvement loan	€30,000	7 years	6.80%	€447	€7,548
Car loan	€22,000	5 years	9.80%	€461	€5,660
Personal loan	€13,000	3 years	7.20%	€401	€1,436
Total	€165,000			€1,973	€74,004
New re-finance mortgage	€165,000	20 years	4.95%	€1,075	€93,000
Extra cost of debt -consolidation loan					
Total (€93,000 less €74,004)					€18,996

Although your repayments fall from €1,973 a month to €1,075 a month, you will end up paying €18,996 extra over the life of the new loan.

However, the credit crisis has made it more difficult to arrange consolidated mortgage loans; the option then is to seek personal loan consolidation finance.

The danger of re-financing all your debt is that the total, final repayment could end up much higher if you stretch your new repayment over an extended period, even if your monthly payment appears lower than the total of all the individual ones. The table on page 68 from the Financial Regulator shows how this expensive affect can occur.

Budgeting and dealing with the recession

Whether you are single, married or a parent with family responsibilities, most of us need some help controlling our finances, especially in these difficult economic times.

The range of new taxes and Government cutbacks introduced in recent budgets, and future budgets under our agreement with the EU, ECB and IMF, are going to take their toll on how far your income will stretch in the coming year.

You need an annual budget, which sets out the household's income and outgoings and allows you to plan your immediate and longer term financial needs in an ordered and, hopefully, stress-free way. This exercise will also be useful if you need to approach MABS, the Money Advice and Budget Service for help in presenting a budget statement to a creditor from whom you are seeking debt restructuring.

Be careful about engaging a commercial debt manager or 'credit counsellor'. These unregulated firms advertise that they can assist you renegotiate your loans with your creditors, but they do this by charging upfront fees and then by taking a percentage or proportion of any annual restructured savings they achieve. Always seek the free assistance of MABS at the outset and only use a private service after you have shopped around and are fully aware of all the terms and conditions.

So where do you start?

Begin by setting aside a couple of uninterrupted hours for yourself or with your spouse/partner for the review. The time you spend sorting out all your bills, accounts and receipts will pay dividends for the rest of the year.

Step 1:   Buy a large copybook or ledger.

Step 2:   Gather all your financial documents together, such as pay slips and P60s, social welfare books, bank and credit card statements, loan statements, utility bills, insurance policies, savings books, investment and pension accounts/ statements. Copies of weekly grocery bills, for example, will also be useful to get a picture of how much you spend on food.

Step 3:   On one page, under the heading, "income" itemise all gross annual earnings and income coming into the household and then calculate the monthly, after-tax, figure. In addition to salaries and wages and/or pension income, this should include commissions and bonuses, share dividends, anticipated capital gains, rental income, etc. Don't forget to include any social welfare payments, such as monthly child benefit.

On the opposite page, under the heading "essential spending", list your annual outgoings, beginning with the amount of tax and PRSI and universal social charge (USC), property tax you pay and any automatic deductions from salary or direct debits for pension/PHI or health insurance contributions. Prioritise the rest of your spending according to value, usually beginning with mortgage or rent payments and childcare costs if they apply. Leave two spaces for the annual amount, and the monthly average. Next, mark down your annual/monthly food bill, not forgetting to include the amount spent in addition to the large weekly shopping visit to convenience stores. Your food bill may be higher during the Christmas season and perhaps a bit lower over the summer if you are away on holidays.   Utilities - gas, electricity, telephone/mobiles, television and solid fuel - are often the next largest outgoing, followed by on-going transport, essential clothing and insurance costs, annual education fees/costs. Bank charges on current accounts should also be included.

Step 4:   Underneath your list of "essential spending", mark down another heading, "non-essential spending" or "discretionary spending". This category should include occasional savings, personal loans, credit card balances, entertainment and hobbies, holidays and travel, miscellaneous shopping.

Discretionary spending

While most of us have a pretty good idea of the size of our essential outgoings, too often we underestimate how much we spend for discretionary purposes. The best way to get a clear picture of exactly how much you are overspending is to keep a spending diary for one month.

This diary should be small enough to fit into a handbag or inside jacket pocket so that your daily purchases - from newspapers and magazines, cigarettes and coffee, milk and bread, petrol and flowers, evening drinks at your local pub, can all be marked down.

Bigger spontaneous items you believe you can still afford can also be recorded in your ledger: those must-have shoes or top, the lunch out with a friend you've met in the street, the no-frills weekend flight to somewhere warm. Keeping a spending ledger will be an eye-opener. It will point out exactly why your income is not stretching as far as it should; it will probably reveal your spending patterns and triggers, especially concerning indiscriminate credit card or laser card usage. Ideally, it will make you more conscious of just how much you can afford for discretionary purchases.

Prepare your budget

You are now ready to create a budget for yourself or your family, to which you can refer as the year progresses. By knowing how much you spend for housing, utilities, food and transport, clothing and insurance, entertainment and holidays, you can try and make some savings by eliminating waste or unnecessary purchases.

For example, could you convince your existing lender to offer a better mortgage or personal loan rate; if not, is there another who will? Is there any cheaper credit card on offer? Are your savings enjoying the highest deposit rate on the market? Are you paying over the odds for motor, home, life or health insurance? You should refer to the surveys posted on the National Consumer Agency website, www.nca.ie for the best deals, or contact a good non-life broker to compare products and prices on your behalf.

Is there room to cut your food and waste charges bill, either by eliminating wastage or by switching to a better value grocery store? By only shopping with a list, and avoiding any impulse purchases, you could actually reduce your weekly bill. Are you and your family paying too much for telephone, internet and mobile phone bills? This is one area of expenditure that has exploded in recent years and deserves being carefully scrutinised. If you have children in the family a spending and time limit should be placed on internet usage. What about bank charges and interest repayments? Is your bank providing good value for its services and free banking? If not, check out other banks.

Once you have trimmed your expenditure page of wasteful and unnecessary spending you can now allocate to your budget all the different categories of spending events and purchases. Some will be pretty immutable: the mortgage, car loans, utilities and insurance. Others will be a moveable feast, depending on the month or season. For example, you may need to budget for higher spending in August and September to accommodate the children going back to school and in December for Christmas. The month in which a summer holiday is booked will eat into your (usually) fixed income more than ones in which the family stay home.

A good way to tackle this is to set up a payment plan at your bank or Credit Union, in which all your major outgoings are estimated. The bank then averages this expenditure over a year and arranges for an overdraft facility to cover those months when your expenses are higher than usual - but which have been budgeted for. Over the course of the year, your income and expenditure usually balance out, with only a small drawdown on the overdraft. Costs are kept to a minimum, and there are no monthly money crises to deal with.

Savings and investments

An important part of any personal budget exercise is the review of your savings and investments. Everyone needs a good savings account, into which you hold sufficient cash reserves to see you over any short-term financial emergency, such as illness, temporary unemployment. Ideally, such a fund should amount to between three and six months net income. It might take you some time to build up this fund, so start making steady contributions as soon as you can, ideally from the moment you start drawing your first pay cheque.

If you have achieved any savings over the year, you should prioritise how it can be allocated: expensive debt like credit card and store card balances should be paid off first. Paying off a higher portion of your mortgage each month will have a disproportionate, positive impact on the capital sum because of the effect of compound interest on long term debt.

"Everyone needs a good savings account into which you hold sufficient cash reserves to see you over a short-term emergency."

If debt is not an issue you can use your budget savings to increase your life insurance, if need be; to build up your emergency fund; to start a longer term investment fund or to even buy individual stocks and shares or some gold or silver.

An investment fund is aimed at longer term financial goals - the purchase of a house, to cover education costs for your children, early retirement. Stock market losses and continuing volatility has devastated pension funds and other savings, but carefully selected investments, over the longer term, have in the past outperformed deposits, which are so vulnerable to inflation. The best way to arrange such an investment is to learn for yourself about how markets work, why some stocks are 'value' and others, 'growth' stocks. Consider taking an investment course - check out www.investRcentre.com or talk to a good financial advisor about your financial goals. This person can help you establish your risk profile and how much you are willing to save and for how long. The advisor can then produce a list of appropriate options. Once you choose one, the amount you contribute can automatically be deducted every month and you can adjust your budget accordingly.

The recession here in Ireland means that many people, even those still in employment, have to make significant changes to their spending patterns and lifestyle. We need to also take into account factors like currency risk and Ireland's position within the wider eurozone.

Every year going forward, on your personal Budget Day, you should review the state of your savings/investments and occupational pension fund. If you are unhappy with its performance, find out why it has under performed and research the affordable alternatives.

Once your budget is in place, you can hopefully rest more easily: your income and expenditure is under control for the time being. You have reviewed the important financial contracts - mortgages, loans, insurance policies - and have made savings on other essential purchases like food, clothing, utilities and transport costs.   If you budget for an annual holiday and Christmas spending, there is less chance for mad overspending.

Children, of course, learn by example. When they see how you keep control of your spending, and having a responsible attitude towards debt and savings, chances are they will develop the same good habits. Their own savings account and a spending ledger could be one of the best gifts you give them this year.

What goes into your personal budget	
Annual Income	**€**
Salary	
Commissions	
Bonuses	
Pensions	
Part-time earnings	
Total Income	
Annual Expenditure - Essential Spending	
Income tax/PRSI/USC	
Mortgage/rent	
Childcare costs	
Pension contributions	
Utilities: Gas/oil	
Electricity	
Telephone	
Mobile	
Internet (ISDN/Broadband)	
TV and cable	
Household charge/Property tax	
Insurance: Life insurance	
Health	
Home and contents	
Motor	
Travel / pet	
Food: Grocery (weekly/daily)	
Clothing: Essential purchases and uniforms	
Transport: Bus or train tickets,	
Car tax, petrol and maintenance	
Bank account charges & loan repayments	
Charitable donations	
Christmas: Gifts	
Food	
Alcohol	
Entertainment	
Savings and investments	
Total expenditure	

Annual Expenditure - Non-essential or discretionary spending	€
Private education fees/expenses/donations	
Holidays: Transport	
Accommodation and food	
Travel insurance	
Entertainment	
Souvenirs	
Kennel fees	
Hobbies & Entertainment:	
Eating and drinking	
Entertainment	
Memberships and equipment	
Video's, DVD's, CD's	
Books, cinema, theatre, sports	
Tickets	
Collector's items	
Pets	
Gifts - birthday, weddings anniversary etc.	
Consumables: Clothing	
Jewellery	
Personal grooming products & services	
Electrical equipment	
Gadgets	
Newspapers & magazines	
Snacks, food, drink	
Total Non Essential expenditure	

5. Buying a home

Buying a home is a big investment and an anxious time. If property prices have not quite bottomed there is still a risk of negative equity where the size of your mortgage is greater than the value of your home. If they have hit bottom after the crash will they rise again?

Then there's the difficulty with credit. To buy a home today you need considerably more capital in the form of a deposit than you would have needed in previous years. Lending has been sharply curtailed and at least one lender is seeking a 20% downpayment. First time buyers in particular may need to find up to 15% deposits, with mortgage finance only available for loans between 85% and 92% of the value of the property.

Gone are the controversial 100%, interest only loans, and many buy-to-let borrowers are also discovering that interest-only terms are not being extended once their initial term expires.

The most competitive and good value mortgage on the market until now, the tracker mortgage, which 'tracks' the European Central Bank (ECB) rate, has been withdrawn. Borrowers who secured trackers will continue to enjoy its security: the cost of their loan is priced based on the ECB lending rate plus an agreed interest premium, typically an extra 1%. Under no circumstances should they amend their payment method if it means the loss of this valuable payment product.

Start saving

If an average new home costs in the region of €200,000, you would typically need a minimum of €16,000 - €40,000 as a downpayment. Many savers set up a good interest-yielding account in the Post Office, bank, building society or credit union to start the process, though up until recently you do not need to be saving with any particular institution in order to secure a mortgage from them at a later date.

Choosing a lender

Once you have the appropriate minimum capital and have found the home of your choice, you need to start shopping around for the best mortgage.

The property supplements in the major newspapers publish updated mortgage interest rates from all the leading lenders. These lists also include a column which shows the cost per thousand euro borrowed so that you can quickly calculate the monthly repayment of the mortgage you have in mind.

Large numbers of mortgage applications are still being refused, or discouraged, and you may want to use the services of a reliable mortgage intermediary to secure a loan.

Income conditions

All lenders require certain income conditions before they will give you a mortgage. Lending conditions may have been relaxed during the boom years, when credit was cheap and plentiful while property inflation was high. But the bursting of the property bubble and the collapse of the banks means conservative lending is back. Prospective first time buyers should not expect to be able to borrow the five, six, seven times multiple of income that banks had been extending, even with substantial down payments. All the old 'rules of thumb' have been thrown out and many commentators and lenders themselves are now conceding that as property prices revert to the mean - that is, are affordable to people on 'ordinary' incomes again - so are borrowing ratios, that is, perhaps three or four times combined incomes. A couple earning €60,000 and €35,000 - or nearly €100,000 combined - should not be too surprised to discover that they cannot borrow more than €250,000 to €300,000.

House purchase related costs

Other costs which may be connected with home purchase include: application or arrangement fees, legal and valuation fees, administration fees, indemnity bonds (which are now being required again by some lenders) and stamp duty as well as the cost of furnishing your new home.

Stamp duty

One of the most significant costs for anyone buying a home during the height of the property bubble was Stamp Duty. The Stamp Duty rate for all residential properties is;

● 1% on property values up to €1 million

● 2% on amounts over €1 million

Fees

Home buyers can expect to pay up to 1.5% of the purchase price of the property plus VAT. But competitive rates can be found with solicitors reducing their fees for this type of business, so you should shop around.

Lenders vary considerably in the way they apply charges. Some, for example, insist on charging you their legal costs, calculated as a percentage of the loan up to a maximum amount. It could amount to as much as €250 to €350. If a lender's fees seem low in comparison to another, take a good look at the interest rates being charged. Both in the first year when a discount of half to one percent may apply and over the longer term, when you will revert to the normal interest rate.

Mortgage interest relief

Mortgage interest relief or Tax Relief at Source (TRS) is available at source from your mortgage provider. This means that your mortgage provider will reduce your monthly mortgage repayments or make a direct payment into your bank account equal to the amount of tax relief you are entitled to.

A mortgage taken out between 1 January 2004 to 31 December 2012, used to purchase, repair, develop or improve your sole or main residence, situation in the State is eligible for mortgage interest relief until 31 December 2017. Mortgages taken out after 31 December 2012 will not be eligible for mortgage interest relief.

A qualifying loan, is a secured loan which was used to purchase, repair, develop or improve your principal private residence situated in Ireland. If you switch lender or mortgage type to get a better interest rate this is not considered to be a new qualifying loan. However, moving home and taking out a new mortgage for this home with a new or existing lender is eligible for relief.

You can also claim tax relief, subject to the maximum allowance, in respect of interest paid by you for your separated/divorced spouse or former partner in a dissolved civil partnership, and a dependent relative for whom you are claiming a dependent relative allowance.

For individuals who purchased their first principal private residence between 1 January 2004 and 31 December 2008, the rate of tax relief on the interest paid on the loan to purchase that property is 30% for the tax years 2012 to 2017.

Amount of mortgage interest relief /tax relief at source (TRS)

The ceilings or upper thresholds on the amount of interest paid that qualifies for tax relief are dependant on -

- the status of the individual, that is, whether he or she is married, in civil partnership or single; **and**

- whether he or she is a first time buyer

The ceilings are

	Married / civil partnership / widowed / surviving civil partner	Unmarried / Not in a civil partnership
First time buyer (First 7 tax years of entitlement to tax on relief on interest paid)	€20,000	€10,000
Non-first time buyers	€6,000	€3,000

The rates of tax relief on qualifying interest paid are;

	Rates of tax relief		
	Tax years 1 & 2	Tax years 3, 4 & 5	Tax years 6 & 7 (*)
First time buyer (First 7 tax years of entitlement to tax on relief on interest paid)	25%	22.5%	20%
Non-first time buyers	15%		

*Note: After year 7, the rates are those that apply to non-first time buyers.

How to claim mortgage interest relief (TRS)

Mortgage interest relief must now be claimed online at www.revenue.ie/en/online/mortgage-interest-relief.html.

You can contact the TRS Help Line on 1890 46 36 26 or by email at trsadmin@revenue.ie.   You can claim mortgage interest relief for previous years up to a maximum of four years.

De-registering your loan for mortgage interest relief (TRS)

If your property ceases to be your principal private residence, if you decide to rent the property and the mortgage is not paid off, or if your loan's qualifying percentage changes you must notify Revenue immediately. You can do this by using a TRS 4 form (available on www.revenue.ie) or by contacting the Revenue TRS help line on 1890 46 36 26.

Bridging loan interest

Additional tax relief is allowed for interest on bridging loans obtained to finance the disposal of your main residence and the acquisition of another residence. This relief is confined to a period of 12 months from the date the loan is obtained. It is subject to the same restrictions as mortgage interest. However, both relief's may be claimed at the same time.

Interest rates and the cost of borrowing

The cost of borrowing for a mortgage is still at historically low rates. However, some lenders have raised their rates by up to 4% in recent years as their need for capital has increased. And while the 2012 ECB base rate was at just 0.75%, current mortgage rates are not sustainable, certainly not over a typical 25-year repayment term. The important thing for every prospective homebuyer is to take account of as many unforeseen circumstances as possible.

Although many couples are dual earners, an unexpected event, like illness, redundancy or even the arrival of a new baby, can put considerable strain on a family budget. A typical €250,000 mortgage being repaid at 4.5% interest will result in monthly repayments of €1,267 over 30 years; if it rises to a rate of 5.5%, repayments will rise to €1,419.

A further 1% rise in interest rates to 6.5% will increase the payment to €1,580 month. It is for this reason that you need to ensure that your

"A loan for the purchase of an investment property does not qualify for mortgage interest relief."

mortgage repayment is stress-tested before you accept a loan offer.

Below we illustrate the typical monthly repayments on a €250,000 loan, assuming annual interest rates of 4.00%, 4.50%, and 5.50% and 6.5% p.a. over four lending periods:

* Repayments do not include mortgage interest relief

Monthly repayments - €250,000 loan *				
Rate	20 yrs	25 yrs	30 yrs	35 yrs
4.00%	€1,515	€1,320	€1,194	€1,107
4.50%	€1,582	€1,390	€1,267	€1,183
5.50%	€1,650	€1,461	€1,342	€1,262
5.50%	€1,720	€1,535	€1,419	€1,342
6.50%	€1,864	€1,688	€1,580	€1,510

The longer your mortgage term, the cheaper the monthly repayment will be. But when the total cost of interest and capital repayments are added up, an extra five or ten years will cost you thousands of extra euro over the entire term.

Example

Using the figures from the above chart you see that a €250,000 loan arranged over 25 years at 3.5% interest will cost €1,252 per month, but the same loan stretched out over a further five years will cost €1,123 a month, a "saving" of €129. The extra five year lending term, however, will amount to an extra €28,680 in mortgage payments overall.

Anyone who finds a lender that agrees to a 30 or even 35 year mortgage should try to accelerate their payments after a few years, when their income has increased and the high early costs associated with home ownership have diminished.

Mortgage lenders: choose carefully

Choosing a mortgage lender that offers the best, long-term interest rate, is very important. By carefully shopping around, you may be able to save yourself a considerable sum of money over the term of your loan.

Home equity release loans and annuities

Lifetime equity release loans and reversions - the selling of a share of the property - became hugely popular during the property boom. Established homeowners sought to raise another mortgage on a second or buy-to-let property and retired homeowners whose properties may have been worth a great deal, but whose pensions did not keep up with inflated property bubble values did likewise.

Due to the on-going credit crisis and the collapse of property prices, the market for equity release has practically dried up for anything other than genuine trading up applications: gone are the easy mortgage based loans which allowed the homeowner to extend the kitchen or buy a new car.

Only one branded equity release product for pensioners is now available on the Irish market. Seniors Money Over 60s equity release loan allows a proportion of the value of the property to be borrowed, relative to the owner's age. Seniors Money has capped the maximum amount they will allow to be borrowed, typically no more than €200,000. Check their website, www.seniorsmoney.ie for terms and conditions and availability.

Home reversion products, which involve the purchase of a portion of the house in exchange for a cash payment or a regular, guaranteed income were withdrawn from the market by their suppliers over the past year and are no longer available.

While the capital and interest payable on equity release loans for pensioners is only repaid after the death of the borrower or if the house is sold or is left uninhabited by its owner for six months or more, the longer term cost can be prohibitive if the value of the property drops significantly (as many properties have done over the past few years.)

At the end of 2012, Seniors Money's variable interest rate was set at 5.28%. If the borrower lives long enough to require sheltered or institutional care in their old age, they may find that the combination of

"Gone are the easy mortgage based loans which allowed the homeowner to extend the kitchen and buy a new SUV."

the higher interest rate and the falling value of their property leaves little equity left in their home if it needs to be sold.

Ideally, if you do arrange an equity loan, it should be one that allows you:

● To draw down the approved amount at your own pace, with interest charges applying only to the amount drawn down and not on the entire sum;

● To repay all or part of the loan, including interest, without penalty or charge;

● That charges competitive legal or arrangement fees;

● That provides an occupancy guarantee, regardless of the performance of property or investment markets.

(Source: Seniors Money)

Equity release borrowing limits					
Age	Loan limit	Age	Loan limit	Age	Loan limit
60	15%	73	28%	86	41%
61	16%	74	29%	87	42%
62	17%	75	30%	88	43%
63	18%	76	31%	89	44%
64	19%	77	32%	90	45%
65	20%	78	33%	91	45%
66	21%	79	34%	92	45%
67	22%	80	35%	93	45%
68	23%	81	36%	94	45%
69	24%	82	37%	95	45%
70	25%	83	38%	96	45%
71	26%	84	39%	97	45%
72	27%	85	40%	98	45%

Subprime mortgages

The subprime mortgage market, which extended finance to borrowers with impaired credit records, some self-employed people who were unable to produce three years of audited accounts or people with no credit record at all in Ireland has also ceased to operate in the Irish market.

This market was catered for by a number of sub-prime or 'specialist' lenders who were prepared to take on the greater credit risk - but at a price. All of the sub-prime lenders are either out of business or have suspended their lending. A large proportion of foreclosure cases appearing in the Commercial Court have been instigated by sub-prime lenders; their customers simply cannot afford to repay the much higher interest rates charged by these companies as their personal circumstances deteriorate and they are also unable to refinance with lower cost mortgage lenders.

Sub-prime mortgages were sold mainly through mortgage brokers who earned high commissions for the sale of these loans. The sale of these products has come under the aegis of the Central Bank Financial Regulator and extreme caution is always recommended for anyone who may wish to arrange such a loan in the future.

Mortgage repayment methods

Annuity based

The annuity method, also known as a repayment mortgage, is the most common way to pay off a mortgage. Annuity mortgages involve the payment each month of interest and some of the principal of the loan. In the early years, the bulk of the payment is interest, on which tax relief at source may be available.

As the years progress, you will pay less interest and more capital until eventually your entire loan will be cleared. A typical repayment mortgage will be repaid as illustrated on page 86, over a 30 year term.

Endowment mortgage

Endowment mortgages are rarely negotiated anymore, mainly because of high costs and their being reliant on the performances of investment markets.

Unlike conventional annuity mortgages, in which you repay both interest and capital each month, an endowment mortgage, also known as an 'investment' mortgage, involves only the repayment of interest and also an additional investment into a life-assurance based unitised or with profits funds. The interest payment attracts full mortgage interest relief subject to the normal limits (see page 80), but the high costs associated

Repaying a €250,000 annuity mortgage @ 4.5% x 30 yrs

End of Year	Annual repayments	Capital repaid	Cumulative capital repaid	Interest paid	Cumulative interest paid	Loan outstanding at end of year
€	€	€	€	€	€	€
1	15,201	4,033	4,033	11,167	11,167	245,967
2	15,201	4,218	8,251	10,982	22,150	241,749
3	15,201	4,412	12,663	10,788	32,938	237,337
4	15,201	4,615	17,278	10,586	43,524	232,722
5	15,201	4,827	22,105	10,374	53,898	227,895
6	15,201	5,049	27,154	10,152	64,050	222,846
7	15,201	5,280	32,434	9,920	73,970	217,566
8	15,201	5,523	37,957	9,677	83,647	212,043
9	15,201	5,777	43,734	9,424	93,071	206,266
10	15,201	6,042	47,776	9,158	102,229	200,224
11	15,201	6,320	56,096	8,881	111,110	193,904
12	15,201	6,610	62,706	8,590	119,700	187,294
13	15,201	6,914	69,620	8,287	127,987	180,380
14	15,201	7,231	76,851	7,969	135,956	173,149
15	15,201	7,564	84,415	7,637	143,593	165,585
16	15,201	7,911	92,326	7,289	150,883	157,674
17	15,201	8,274	100,600	6,926	157,809	149,400
18	15,201	8,655	109,255	6,546	164,355	140,745
19	15,201	9,052	118,307	6,148	170,503	131,693
20	15,201	9,468	127,775	5,732	176,235	122,225
21	15,201	9,903	137,678	5,298	181,533	112,322
22	15,201	10,358	148,036	4,843	186,376	101,964
23	15,201	10,834	158,870	4,367	190,742	91,130
24	15,201	11,331	170,201	3,869	194,611	79,799
25	15,201	11,852	182,053	3,348	197,960	67,947
26	15,201	12,397	194,450	2,804	200,764	55,550
27	15,201	12,966	207,416	2,234	202,998	42,584
28	15,201	13,562	220,978	1,639	204,637	29,022
29	15,201	14,185	235,162	1,016	205,653	14,838
30	15,201	14,838	250,000	364	206,017	0

with these types of mortgages have had the effect of eating into the investment fund, especially during periods of stock market volatility. Any performance shortfall has to be made up with higher endowment contributions either during the lifetime of the mortgage or at maturity in order to pay off the capital sum.

Pension mortgage

A pension mortgage is similar to an endowment mortgage, in that only interest is paid on the loan during the term of the contract. In this case, the investment vehicle which is used to pay off the capital is the homeowner's personal pension plan. Under Revenue rules, a quarter of the final pension fund value can be paid out as a tax-free lump sum up to a maximum of €200,000 from 1 January 2011, and it is this sum which is used to repay the mortgage capital. Pension mortgages are subject to the investment performance of underlying assets in the pension fund and should be regularly reviewed.

Variable or fixed rate?

Should you arrange your mortgage on a variable interest rate basis or fix the interest for a period of years? Nearly all new borrowers are offered a discounted fixed rate for the first year of their loan, which usually amounts to a saving of a couple of hundred euro. In year two, you immediately revert to the variable rate of interest, which can go up and down over the term of the mortgage.

A fixed interest rate can provide considerable peace of mind and protect the borrower from the volatility of world money markets, but you can also suffer financially - if rates fall and your rate is fixed at a higher level for a few more years. The cost of breaking a fixed rate mortgage can be very high. Some banks charge nearly the entire interest balance that they could have expected to earn if you had seen out the contract.

Trackers

A tracker mortgage, whereby the cost of the loan for the entire repayment term is linked to the current ECB bank rate plus a premium rate, typically 1%, has proved to be advantageous to those borrowers who were able to secure one before they were withdrawn by the main lenders. These loans are costly for the banks, and their policy is to discourage tracker customers from keeping them by recommending that in some cases they fix their loans instead, in an effort to avoid what may or may not be higher ECB rates in the future. No one should transfer their tracker to a variable rate loan unless the lender offers substantial capital write off. Always refer to the tracker lending terms in your mortgage contract.

Local property tax (LPT)

From 1 July 2013, residential property owners will be liable for an LPT based on the self-assessment market value of their property on 1 May 2013.

Property values are grouped into value bands. A rate of 0.18% will apply to the midpoint of the value band up to €1m. To calculate how much you will have to pay for 2013 select the value bank appropriate to the market value of your property and read across in the table in Chapter 3 page 54. The LPT liability for property valued at over €1m, will be calculated as 0.18% on the first €1m and 0.25% on the portion over €1m.

Exemptions

Certain properties will be exempt from LPT. These exemptions largely correspond to exemptions from the Household Charge (see page 52). Exemptions will also apply to new and previously unused properties purchased from a builder or developer between 2013 and 2016, and to second-hand properties purchased in 2013 by a first time buyer.

Deferrals

A system of deferral arrangements for owner-occupiers will be implemented to address cases where there is an inability to pay the LPT under specified conditions (e.g. where the gross income does not exceed €15,000 - single and €25,000 - couple). Some owner-occupiers may be eligible to apply for marginal relief, which will allow them to defer up to 50% of their LPT liability. It should be noted that interest will be charged on deferred amounts at a rate of 4% per annum.

Mortgage and home insurance

The monthly mortgage repayment is not the only one you have to make. Mortgage protection and buildings insurance are compulsory in most cases and can cost up to 10% of your gross monthly mortgage repayments.

Mortgage protection insurance is a life assurance policy that covers the value of the mortgage and ensures that your debt to the bank or building society is repaid in the event of your death or that of your spouse. Rates are based on age and sex and the premiums can be paid monthly or annually. You are not obliged to purchase the policy from the lender and you should shop around for the best market rate, especially if you are a smoker.

Many new home owners arrange serious illness cover as part of their mortgage protection policy, in order that the loan can be paid off not only if they die but also in the event of a life-threatening illness. The cost is higher, but can be mitigated against by arranging the policy on a decreasing term basis.

Example

You and your spouse have a mortgage of €250,000 over 30 years. You are both age 29 and non-smokers. The monthly cost of a conventional mortgage protection plan and a mortgage protection plan, which includes accelerated serious illness cover,(the benefit of which will pay out once on the earlier event of either serious illness or death), will work out approximately as follows:

Plan type	Monthly cost
Conventional mortgage protection plan	€21.36
Mortgage protection plan plus serious illness cover	€77.71

*   Based on rates at 3rd December 2012

**   The EU Gender Directive came into force on 21st December 2012. This means that insurers are no longer able to use gender to determine the price of a product.

Protect your mortgage repayments

If you are concerned about how your mortgage would be paid if you became ill or were made redundant, even for a short period of time, you may want to take out mortgage payment protection cover. Keep in mind that this type of insurance can work out very expensive and the widespread misselling of this insurance is under investigation since the summer of 2012 by the Central Bank.

Available from all the major lenders, it costs about €5 - €6 for every €100 cover required per month and pays out benefits if you become ill or disabled and are unable to work, or have been made redundant. You need to have been out of work for at least 30 days before your first claim can be made. Some firms impose up to a six month exclusion period, and

"Mortgage protection and building insurance are compulsory."

there is generally a 12 month payment limit per claim. You need to very carefully read the terms and conditions under which benefits are paid before you take out such a policy and if you already have permanent health insurance (PHI) or serious illness cover, this type of policy may be unnecessary.

Protect the building

Building insurance is also compulsory if you take out a mortgage. Again, the lender wants to protect their share of the property in the event of a fire or another disaster. The premiums are based not on the market value of the property, but on the cost of rebuilding. It is important that you have the property surveyed to ensure the rebuilding cost is correct and any changes in the cost of materials and labour are taken into account.

Most general insurance companies offer combined buildings and contents policies. Some automatically provide contents cover worth up to half the value of the building cover. Engage an independent financial advisor to help you find the right policy for you and to ensure you put a correct value on your fittings and personal belongings. Premium discounts may be available, which will depend on your age, whether the house is occupied during the daytime and if it is fitted with approved locks, fire and burglar alarms etc.

Coping with mortgage debt

Estimates vary about how far house prices have fallen in Ireland since 2007 – but it is now widely accepted that the national rate is approximately 50%-55%, with falls as high as 65% in certain areas of Dublin.

However, there were also been some signs of recovery during the summer of 2012, with price increases recorded in some Dublin neighbourhoods and among properties suitable for young families.

The most serious consequence of this extraordinary collapse in house values over the past five years is the number of borrowers who now find themselves in negative equity - where the balance of their mortgage is greater than the market value of their property. It is now estimated that nearly 130,000 households are in serious arrears of more than 90 days or in receipt of some form of mortgage forbearance measure, such as interest only repayments. A new government web-based information service was launched in 2012 – www.keepingyourhome.ie - in conjunction with the Money Advice Budgeting Service (MABS) to assist this growing number of distressed homeowners.

Negative equity, say some commentators, is not a problem if you have no intention or need to sell your home. House prices are cyclical and will eventually recover, but temporarily depressed house prices are only one aspect of a much wider and disturbing picture.

What if you happen to have a fixed rate interest arrangement that is maturing and your lender is adamant that you must pay a higher than average annuity interest rate? Negative equity means that you are now tied to your lender - other banks are not interested in taking on a customer with a property that may still be devaluing.

Negative equity becomes a personal financial disaster and not just an unfortunate financial setback, when the mortgage holder struggles to make their repayments or they lose their job. A build up of arrears, default and foreclosure can become a real possibility in such a scenario. The combination of negative equity and a stagnant property market means such a person doesn't even have the choice of selling up and moving into cheaper accommodation.

Code of conduct on mortgage arrears

Fortunately, the main retail lenders are not interested in foreclosing on customers who are experiencing difficulties caused by the recession as there is no demand for property and a great wave of For Sale signs will only further depress prices. The revised Central Bank Code of Conduct on Mortgage Arrears (CCMA) offers protection to mortgage holders in arrears once they agree to cooperate with the banks' Mortgage Arrears Resolution Process (MARP).

Other features of the revised Code include:

- Communication with borrowers have to be clear and consumer-friendly and the lender cannot initiate more than three unsolicited communications with a borrower, by whatever means, in a calendar month other than correspondence required by the CCMA or other regulatory requirements.

- A lender must not require a borrower to change from an existing tracker mortgage to another mortgage type, as part of an alternative arrangement offered to the borrower in arrears or pre-arrears.

- Lenders are required to set up an Arrears Support Unit (ASU) to assess arrears and pre-arrears cases;

- Borrowers can make an appeal in relation to the decision of the Arrears Support Unit and the lender's treatment of the borrower's case under the MARP process, to an internal Appeals Board which lenders are required to establish; **and**

- When a lender is determining the 12 month period it must wait before applying to the courts to commence legal action, it must exclude any time period during which a borrower is complying with the terms of an alternative repayment arrangement, making an appeal to the internal appeals Board or making a complaint to the FSO under the CCMA.

Not everyone in negative equity is in danger of losing their home, or in need of protection under this code. But if you are worried about the possibility of being unable to meet your mortgage and debt liabilities you should certainly think about the following exercise, with, or without the help of your local MABS office:

- Prepare an income and expenditure budget statement that takes into account all essential and discretionary spending;

- Reduce your food and drink budget; cut out all unnecessary purchases and contracts; shop around for cheaper utility and insurance products.

- Reconsider luxury purchases like holidays, the second family car, sports club membership, private school fees. Sell items if need be.

- Prioritise debt repayments by the cost of interest repayments.

- Consider renting a spare room in your home under the Rent-a-Room scheme which allows you to earn up to €10,000 per annum rent free.

- Prepare a realistic debt repayment schedule to your lenders and/or creditors for their consideration. Lenders are overwhelmed these days with arrears and debt cases and you may find them to be very receptive to your proposal.

6 Insurance

Everyone has something to protect - your wealth, your health, your life and those dearest to you. Insuring your own life against sudden serious illness or unexpected death relieves the financial burden on your dependents. Insuring your car, home and contents is yet another way for you to avoid financial disaster should anything unexpected ever happen to you.

The variety of insurance products available to you has increased considerably in recent years with the result that prices have now become very competitive. There are a number of different ways for you to arrange your insurance. You can either contact an insurance company of your choice directly or you can arrange insurance through your bank, building society, online or a service provider like a motor association. Alternatively, you can contact an independent financial advisor who can offer you independent advice on the type of insurance protection that best suits your needs and your budget and you can even buy insurance directly on-line. Keep in mind that the latter is usually an execution-only service and you need to do your own research.

Life assurance

The purpose of life insurance is to make sure that your dependents are financially secure in the event of your death. As a general rule, the younger you are, the better your health and the safer your lifestyle, the cheaper the cost of your insurance. You may not be able to obtain any life assurance cover at all if you are suffering from a serious illness. Alternatively, you could be offered insurance at a premium price - which, in insurance jargon is called 'loading'. For example, a 50% loading could mean you pay 50% more than the average insured person of your age for the same amount of life cover.

How much cover do you need?

Ten times the size of your net, after-tax, salary is a standard gauge for the amount of life insurance cover you should have. A good rule of thumb when trying to decide your total level of cover, is to aim to provide a fund to adequately replace your income in the event of your premature death. This means that your income, the number and ages of your dependents, your assets and outstanding loan commitments etc. all have to be carefully considered. You may find that you don't need as much 'stand-alone' life cover as you might initially think if your employment benefits package includes a 'death-in-service' benefit and a spouse's/dependent's pension, or if your mortgage is covered by mortgage protection insurance. This is invaluable advice that an independent financial advisor will be able to offer you.

When you meet an independent financial advisor they will tell you that basic life assurance is arranged for a fixed number of years and comes in a number of forms:

Level term cover

"Ten times the size of your net after tax salary is a standard gauge for the amount of life cover you should have."

This type of cover is relatively inexpensive, and it only pays out at death and has no underlying investment value. Quite simply, when you take out a term assurance plan, you agree to pay a specific or level premium over a pre-agreed number of years. Every year, as you get older, your risk of death increases so your level premium is based on the average risk of death.

'Averaging' means that in the early years of your plan you will pay too much in proportion to the actual risk of death involved, and this extra premium in the early years is used to 'subsidise' the cost of your life assurance benefit in later years. If your plan is discontinued, or in the event of an early claim before your pre-agreed number of years have elapsed, this surplus will not be repaid.

Convertible term cover

This is slightly more expensive than level term cover but it gives you the flexibility, without any further medical test or examination and regardless of any change in your health circumstances, to convert into another type of policy at any future date in your contract. This could include converting to a 'whole of life assurance plan' which could be a very valuable option for you to have because, regardless of any changes in your health, no unexpected 'loadings' are applied to your premium payable at conversion. Like all 'term' covers, this is a protection policy only and it will never acquire a cash value.

Decreasing term cover

This is a variation on the basic 'term' cover, which means that it is a protection policy only. Decreasing term cover is often taken out as a mortgage protection policy where both the requirement and the amount of cover decreases as your mortgage is repaid and your need for protection recedes.

Guaranteed 'whole of life' cover

Effectively 'whole of life' is a term cover protection policy which guarantees to pay a specific sum of money whenever you die, provided of course, that you continue to pay the premiums. Because of 'averaging', your premiums are relatively high at the outset, but they remain unchanged for the entire duration of your life. As you might expect, these policies do not have any residual or investment value but the cost is relatively cheap, particularly when you are young and healthy. They are very suitable if, for example, you are self-employed and don't have a pension plan but you want to provide long term financial protection to a dependent spouse or partner in the event of your death. They are also very useful if you have a disabled child or relative who will need financial protection after your death.

Monthly cost of a male, non-smoker, obtaining €350,000 life assurance cover (Different plan types)

Age next birthday	25	35	45	55
Decreasing Term over 20 yrs	€13.10	€19.74	€42.16	€111.85
Level Term over 20 yrs	€16.48	€26.48	€57.27	€161.89
Convertible Term over 20 yrs	€17.47	€27.80	€60.31	€170.76
Whole of life	€163.33	€254.30	€421.60	€732.95

Notes: The premiums quoted above include a 1% government life assurance levy.

* Based on rates at 3rd December 2012

** The EU Gender Directive came into force on 21st December 2012. This means that insurer's will no longer be able to use gender to determine the price of a product.

Unitised whole of life policies

Another type of whole of life policy is the unit-linked one, in which the life assurance company invests your premium in a managed fund that aims to grow at a certain rate and to increase in value over time.

The fund value is not guaranteed and it may grow by enough to pay for your life insurance throughout your life or, in some cases, it may fall short of the amount that is needed to pay for your life insurance. In that case, you may have to pay a higher premium to keep the sum assured at the agreed level. Whole-of-life policies have ongoing charges, such as yearly charges for managing the investment fund and sometimes monthly charges for handling your premium. These charges have the effect of reducing the value of the policy fund so the amount of any benefit paid out on your death is not guaranteed.

For a unitised whole-of-life policy to build up a cash lump sum over and above what is needed to pay for your life insurance, the investment fund will need to provide strong, steady growth. Too often, policy holders have found that their policy has little or no cash value at any time. A better arrangement is usually to de-couple life insurance from savings and buy separate policies.

Changing circumstances

There is a saying among life assurance professionals that 'a little life assurance can be a dangerous thing'. Effectively, what this saying means is that, all too often, the very fact that you know you have 'some kind' of a life assurance cover lulls you into a false sense of security. The years slip by without you ever feeling the need to check and make sure that your 'fixed' level of protection is still sufficient for your 'changing' requirements. It is always good advice to discuss your changing requirements with an independent financial advisor on a regular basis

"Too often, policy holders have found that their policy has little or no cash value."

Own life / joint life policies

If the policy is an 'own life' plan, effectively you are both the 'life assured' and 'the assured'. This means that the lump sum that is payable from the policy upon your death will form part of your estate and may be subject to inheritance tax. In the case of a joint-life policy, usually taken out by spouses, the death benefit is normally paid to the surviving spouse.

If your policy is arranged on an 'own life' basis, your legal representatives, (i.e. your 'executor' if you have made a Will) may be required to produce a grant of probate and proof of title before the insurance company can pay out the sum assured. However, if no Will exists, the policy benefits will be subject to the law of intestacy and the payments of the proceeds of the life assurance policy will be as set out in the legislation which may not be in accordance with your wishes.

If your life assurance policy is arranged on a 'life of another' basis, then, when you die, that other person becomes the owner of the policy. They can claim the encashment value of the policy from the insurance company by simply producing the policy document, together with your death certificate.

Life assurance under Trust

Setting up a life assurance policy under Trust is an increasingly popular way of making sure that your policy proceeds will not become part of your estate when you die. In addition, a Trust ensures:

- Quick and easy payment of the death benefit. The insurance company will pay the surviving Trustee(s), usually your spouse or children, on proof of death and the production of the policy document.

- By being a Trustee of the policy yourself you can maintain a degree of control over the policy during your lifetime. The Trust must be set up, by completing a standard Trust form and nominating Trustee(s) and the beneficiaries, before you commence the policy.

Exit tax

No tax relief is available for life assurance premiums unless it is set up as part of your pension scheme. The returns from life assurance products funds taken out before 1 January 2001 are paid tax-free. All taxes that were due on profits earned will have already been paid at source by the life assurance fund managers to the Revenue Commissioners.

For products issued after the 1 January 2001 no tax will be imposed within funds on certain 'chargeable events'. However the life assurance company is obliged to deduct exit tax on any gains or investment income generated during the term of the product. This tax will be a final liability tax, for Irish residents. With effect from 1 January 2012 the rate of exit tax is 33%.

Budget 2013

The rate of exit tax is increased to 36% from 1 January 2013.

Is anyone exempt from exit tax?

- Non-resident individuals.
- A life assurance company.
- An investment undertaking.
- A Revenue approved charity.
- A PRSA provider.
- A credit union.
- The court service.

What is a chargeable event

- A claim, maturity or the full surrender of a policy, including a payment on death or disability.
- A partial encashment, including an automatic income payment.
- An assignment of a life policy in certain circumstances.
- Every eight anniversary of the policy.

A credit will be given for the tax deducted in year eight against any tax payable on a subsequent chargeable event. Also, where the tax payable on a subsequent chargeable event is lower than the tax deducted on the 8th anniversary the customer will receive a refund of the "overpaid" tax.

Example

€25,000 invested on 1 March 2004.

Deemed encashment 8th anniversary i.e. 1 March 2012.

Cash value at 1 March 2012 is €37,000.

The policy is deemed to be "encashed" and so the gain of €12,000 is liable to exit tax @ 33%, is €3,960.

This amount deducted and paid to Revenue, so the value of the bond immediately after is €33,040.

The bond is then fully encashed on 1 March 2013 with a gross value of €37,750.

In order to calculate the 'chargeable gain' on the encashment, the gross policy value is first increased by the exit tax deducted on the deemed disposal i.e. €3,960.

The gain liable to exit tax of 36% is	€37,750 + €3,960 - €25,000 = €16,710
The exit tax at 36% is	€16,710 x 36% = €6,016
But the previous exit tax deducted of €3,960 is deducted	€6,016 - €3,960 = €2,056

The total exit tax on this policy is 6,016, which is comprised of the 8th anniversary plus €2,056 on the subsequent encashment.

Tax on death or disability

Prior to 15 February 2001 no exit tax was payable in respect of payment's made on death or disability. Under the new rules the proceeds payable on death or disability are liable to the same level of exit tax as if the product had been surrendered at that date.

Income protection insurance / disability insurance

Unlike life assurance, which only pays out benefits on death, disability or permanent health insurance (PHI) pay benefits, if you become ill or injured and cannot work. Its aim is to replace your current income - up to retirement age if necessary. It may also be included as part of your pension scheme.

If it is not provided as a benefit of your pension scheme - there is no obligation for employers to provide this benefit, though many workers think they do - you can buy PHI (or Income Protection Insurance as it is also known).

How much does it cost?

The cost varies with age, sex, occupation and with the 'deferred period', which is explained in more detail below. Occupation is also a crucial factor in determining the cost of the risk involved and people who work in higher risk jobs and more likely to have an accident or illness and less likely to return to work than those in more sedentary jobs normally have to pay more.

Case study

Jack, 40, is an accountant currently earning €85,000 per year. He has chosen to protect 50% of his salary i.e. €42,500 per year until his retirement at age at 65. He selects a 26 week period (deferred period) before benefit becomes payable and chooses to index link his benefit and premiums. Jack's benefit is €42,500 per annum (or €817.31 per week) and he pays a premium of €46.46 per month after tax relief based on a tax rate of 41% (gross €78.75), which includes the 1% government life assurance levy.

If Jack were to claim on his policy in two years time (aged 42) and his claim lasted for five and half years (benefits are typically paid for five and a half years) then the benefit payable to him would be over €265,513 including indexation. If he were unable to return to work before retirement then over that 23 year period the benefit payable to him would be total of €1,463,000.

"There is no obligation for employers to provide this benefit."

Deferment period

Most disability plans will not pay you any benefit until you have been out of work for at least thirteen weeks - the deferment period. The longer the deferment period, which normally ranges from 13 to 52 weeks, the cheaper the premiums. At the outset of your plan you can decide on the length of the deferment period that best suits your budget and financial protection requirements.

To ensure that you don't actually end up financially better off claiming benefit, which could leave these plans open to abuse, many disability contracts put a limit on the amount of benefit payable and this limit applies regardless of your maximum level of benefit insured. Normally, you will not be able to receive a benefit that is more than 75% of your average annual earnings in the year prior to your disablement. Many plans also include the value of State disability benefits within this 75% rule.

Tax relief

Disability or PHI premiums are eligible for tax relief at your highest rate of income tax. However, the amount of relief granted cannot exceed 10% of your total income. All disability and PHI benefits are taxed under PAYE.

Tax relief for PHI contributions made by PAYE taxpayers is given on a net pay basis i.e. the contributions are deducted from your gross salary prior to the application of income tax and PRSI. However employee contributions to a PHI scheme do not reduce the pay amount for USC purposes.

Loan protection insurance

If you ever lose your job, become ill and are unable to work, any outstanding personal loans that you are committed to will still have to be repaid. This is why most lenders offer you the option of taking out payment protection insurance with any personal loans or mortgages that they advance to you.

This insurance option is normally only available to you at the time of taking out the loan or mortgage and it covers your monthly loan repayments if you ever become redundant, sick or disabled. Payment protection insurance is included as part of your monthly loan repayments. Although it generally provides only 12 months of benefits per claim, the financial security and peace of mind that it brings can be invaluable and reassuring. However, this cover is very expensive - sales commissions are high - and the Financial Regulator and National Consumer Agency (see www.nca.ie) have warned against some excessive pricing in the market and the restrictive benefit conditions. If you already have a contingency savings account, this money should be used to meet your repayments; meanwhile income replacement insurance, (also known as Permanent Health Insurance) will pay a portion of your salary until retirement and will also help cover your loan repayments.

Optional payment protection insurance should not be confused with compulsory mortgage protection insurance. Mortgage protection insurance repays the mortgage in the event of death only.

If you already have adequate PHI cover, you may feel that it is unnecessary for you to take out payment protection insurance as well. After all, the whole purpose of PHI is to provide you with a replacement income so that you can meet your regular outgoings and other financial commitments. Keep in mind, however, that most PHI policies only pay benefits after an average of 26 weeks have elapsed, while many payment protection plans pay out benefits after just one month of redundancy, illness or disability.

Serious illness insurance

Serious illness insurance that is linked to a mortgage pays your entire loan if you contract any one of a defined number of serious illnesses.

It is designed to alleviate the financial burdens of anyone who suffers a serious life threatening illness or condition. It does this by paying you a tax-free lump sum on official diagnosis of a serious illness. This lump sum can be used to meet your day-to-day living requirements, pay off your mortgage or even meet the cost of health care.

Illnesses and conditions

The main illnesses and conditions include cancer, heart attack, stroke, kidney disease, multiple sclerosis. However most policies will also pay out for organ transplants, rare ailments like motor neurone disease and CJD, and in the rare chance that you contract HIV by accident or injury. The better policies also pay out benefits in the event of permanent and total disability (PTD) (including loss of limbs, hearing or speech, Alzheimer's disease, etc.), and offer cash benefit options if you are hospitalised.

Every insurer includes a slightly different list of conditions so it is always prudent for you to check these in advance with an independent financial advisor. Although the lump sum benefit is tax-free, there is no tax relief available on serious illness policy premiums.

More recent hybrid serious illness policies now offer other options that can be added to serious illness insurance, such as hospital cash. This is a daily amount that will be paid to you for each complete period of 24 hours you are hospitalised. This limit is usually capped at approximately €200 per day.

Also accident benefit may be an option offered to you by the insurer at an extra cost. Accident benefit is similar to income protection but is only payable if you are temporarily disabled as a result of an accident and are unable to carry out your occupation. It is a weekly amount that is tax free and usually capped at approximately €400 p.w. The deferred period before the benefit is payable, is shorter than income protection, usually about 2 weeks but the benefit will only be payable for a maximum of 52 weeks.

Mortgage protection

Serious illness cover is becoming an increasingly popular part of mortgage protection policies, and both the level of cover and the premium payments can be arranged either on a level or decreasing premium basis.

In the latter case, your cover decreases in value with the decreasing value of your outstanding mortgage. The drawback to this, however, is that although your benefits will clear your outstanding mortgage, there will be no extra cash available to ease any other financial burdens you may face. By arranging your cover on a term basis, you will be guaranteed a lump sum (the size of the original mortgage) throughout the entire duration of your loan.

Serious illness policies are often arranged by companies for key members of staff or directors. In this context they are known as "keyman" insurance and the benefits are paid, not to the individual but to the company or partners, to lessen any financial burden that they may face because of the absence of that key employee or director.

Mortgage protection case study

Conor and Sinead have a mortgage of €300,000 over 30 years.

They are both age 29 and non-smokers. The monthly cost of a conventional mortgage protection plan and a mortgage protection plan, which included serious illness cover, will work out approximately as follows:

Plan type	Monthly cost
Conventional mortgage protection plan:	€25.18
Mortgage protection plan plus serious illness cover:	€92.74

Health and medical insurance

Nearly two million people have private health insurance in Ireland, mainly in response to their concerns about delays in accessing specialist consultants for diagnosis and long hospital waiting lists. Health insurance still attracts standard rate tax relief, credited at source by the insurer, but in the past year a levy of €205 per adult and €66 per child has been imposed by the Department of Health and Children in order to subsidise the VHI, its wholly owned subsidiary because it is unable to meet the rising cost of its older, more expensive members, a legacy from when the VHI was a state monopoly.

As a result of the levy, the continuing high cost of medical treatment and rising public hospital charges that VHI, Aviva Health and Layla Healthcare are obliged to pay, the cost of private health insurance is becoming increasingly expensive and many members now have little choice, but to switch to lower cost plans, providers or are dropping their cover altogether as their personal finances come under pressure.

There are now over 200 different health insurance plans provided by the three main providers (the Gardai and ESB have their own, private schemes) - and they all offer plans that include not just access to out-patient and in-hospital benefits, but a growing range of other services like health information help lines with 24 hour access to a nurse or general practitioner and travel insurance.

All Irish health insurance plans include core, minimum benefits such as in-hospital treatment and the plans are "community rated" which mean that policyholders cannot be discriminated against, either on a cost or benefits level, because of their age. All members can ask for the corporate equivalent of individual plans, at some savings.

There are no penalties for switching health providers, and there is no age restriction for joining a health insurance plan. However, if you decide to switch to a higher benefit plan with your existing provider or a different provider and you have a pre-existing medical condition, you may be subject to a period in which benefits will not be paid for that condition. Be sure to check all terms before you switch.

The price and terms of the three private health insurance plans can be compared on the Health Insurance Authority website, www.hia.ie or you can hire a specialist, fee-based health insurance advisor to do the comparison for you (see www.healthinsurancesavings.ie).

Hospital cash benefit plan

Sold by non-profit, charitable-status, companies like The Hospital Saturday Fund (HSF) pay tax-free cash payments to members who need hospitalisation or a range of out-patient treatments.

Premiums, which can be as low as a few euro a week, are age related, but they provide reduced benefits for dependents at no extra cost. Benefits are also paid for routine optical, dental and alternative medical treatments that are not covered by the private health insurers. Daily cash benefits are not paid for routine maternity in-patient stays, but new mothers are paid upon delivery.

Hospital cash schemes are usually arranged on a group or company basis, but can also be purchased by individuals. There is no tax relief available on these premiums.

Insuring your home and its contents

Your home and its contents are among your most valuable possessions. Insuring them against fire, theft and other damage should be an important priority. If you have a mortgage you will have been required to take out compulsory buildings insurance, which varies in price depending on the value of your property, the size, location and rebuilding cost of your property. Your lender requires this insurance, not for your benefit, but for theirs. Their major concern is to protect their financial interest vested in your property. You should take great care, therefore - especially once your mortgage is paid off - to ensure that your building and contents are properly valued and insured.

Proper valuation

The minimum insurance you require is the cost of rebuilding your home in the event of its destruction. Your rebuilding costs are not the same as your mortgage amount, or the market value of your property and rebuilding costs have fallen sharply in recent years. If you have any doubt about the rebuilding cost of your property you should arrange for an independent valuation or survey and check the chartered surveyors annual survey which is available from the Society of Chartered Surveyors at 5 Wilton Place, Dublin 2.

Also, take care not to under insure your home or contents because most home insurance policies include what is known as an "averaging" clause which determines that if you under insure your property, for example, by 50%, the insurer is only obliged to pay you 50% of your claim.

Nowadays, the cost and the scope of benefits available in home and contents insurance policies vary widely. But with annual premiums rising by as much as 20% it pays to shop around to make sure that you get the best available value in terms of level of claim excesses, exclusions, discounts and risk cover. A good general insurance broker can help you assess the value of your buildings and possessions and carefully choose the right policy for your needs and budget.

The National Consumer Agency (www.nca.ie) produces bi-annual home insurance surveys with several examples of different home values. If in doubt, seek out the best professional advice available.

As we said at the outset of this chapter, your wealth, your health, your life and those nearest to you are important priorities when it comes to financial protection. Likewise, your home and its contents are among your most valuable possessions. That is why it makes such good sense for you to seek out the best available independent professional advice before making your final decision about what policies and protection arrangements suit your requirements best.

Keep in mind that as you get older, married, or your family commitments change, your protection requirements will change too. So you should regularly check your existing arrangements to ensure that they are still adequate to meet your changing needs and, indeed, to ensure that you are not 'over protecting' yourself in any areas, for example, as your children grow up and become financially independent.

7 Income tax

Individuals whose income is taxed under the PAYE system are obliged to make a return when requested to do so by their Tax Inspector. Self employed individuals and proprietary company directors must submit a return on or before the 31 October for the tax year ending the previous 31 December, whether they are requested to do so or not, under the self assessment system.

If your main income is taxed under the PAYE system and you have other income e.g. rental, dividend income, foreign pension etc., you may be regarded as a "chargeable person". This means that you are required to submit and pay your taxes under the "self assessment" system.

Chargeable person

An individual who is in receipt of income chargeable to tax under the PAYE system but who is also in receipt of substantial gross income from other sources, such as trading, professional or rental income, will be regarded as a "chargeable person" under the self assessment system unless the gross income from all non-PAYE sources is less than €50,000 and the net assessable income is less than €3,174 and the income is coded against PAYE credits.

Proprietary director

A proprietary director is a director of a company who is the beneficial owner of, or is able either directly or indirectly to control more than 15% of the ordinary share capital of the company. All proprietary directors are "chargeable persons".

Classification of income

Income is classified under a number of headings. These headings are known as schedules and the income falling under each is as follows:

Schedule C:

Those who have deducted income tax from certain payments are assessed under this schedule e.g. banks.

Schedule D:

Case I: Profits from a trade.

Case II: Profits from a profession.

Case III: Interest not taxed at source and all foreign income.

Case IV: Taxed interest income not falling under any other case or schedule.

Case V: Rental income from properties in Ireland.

Schedule E:

Income from offices or employments together with pensions, benefits-in-kind and certain lump sum payments arising from an office or employment.

Schedule F

Dividends and other distributions from Irish-resident companies.

Tax credits

	2011	2012	2013
Single person	€1,650	€1,650	€1,650
Married couple or couple in a civil partnership	€3,300	€3,300	€3,300
Widowed person or surviving civil partner			
Without dependent children	€2,190	€2,190	€2,190
In year of bereavement	€3,300	€3,300	€3,300
One-parent family	€1,650	€1,650	€1,650
Widowed Parent			
First year after bereavement	€3,600	€3,600	€3,600
Second year after bereavement	€3,150	€3,150	€3,150
Third year after bereavement	€2,700	€2,700	€2,700
Fourth year after bereavement	€2,250	€2,250	€2,250
Fifth year after bereavement	€1,800	€1,800	€1,800
Home carer's credit - max	€810	€810	€810
PAYE credit	€1,650	€1,650	€1,650
Age credit			
Single/widowed/surviving civil partnership	€245	€245	€245
Married/civil partner	€490	€490	€490
Incapacitated child credit	€3,300	€3,300	€3,300
Dependent relative credit	€70	€70	€70
(Income Limit)	€13,837	€13,837	€13,837
Blind Credit			
Blind person	€1,650	€1,650	€1,650
Both spouses/civil partners blind	€3,300	€3,300	€3,300

Computation of your income tax liability

Income tax is payable on your taxable income, i.e. your total assessable income for a tax year, less deductions for any, non standard rate allowances (not tax credits) to which you may be entitled.

Tax bands and rates

2012	2013
Single/Widow(er) or surviving civil partner First €32,800 @ 20% Balance @ 41%	**Single/Widow(er) or surviving civil partner** First €32,800 @ 20% Balance @ 41%
One Parent Family First €36,800 @ 20% Balance @ 41%	**One Parent Family** First €36,800 @ 20% Balance @ 41%
Married or in civil partnership - two incomes Note 1 + 2 First €65,600@ 20% Balance @ 41%	**Married or in civil partnership - two incomes** Note 1 + 2 First €65,600 @ 20% Balance @ 41%
Married or in civil partnership - one income First €41,800 @ 20% Balance @ 41%	**Married or in civil partnership - one income** First €41,800 @ 20% Balance @ 41%

1. Transferable between spouses up to a maximum of €41,800 in 2012 and 2013 for any one spouse.

2. Subject to the lower earning spouse having income of at least €23,800 in 2012 and 2013.

Individualisation

In 2013 the standard rate tax band for a married couple, where both spouses have income, can be increased by the lower of;

- €23,800

  or

- the income of the lower earning spouse.

The maximum standard rate band available to either spouse is €41,800.

Income exemptions limits

A person over the age of 65 whose income does not exceed the following limits, is completely exempt from income tax.

	2011	2012	2013
	€	€	€
Person age 65 years or over:			
- Single / Widow(er) / surviving civil partner	€18,000	€18,000	€18,000
- Married / in a civil partnership	€36,000	€36,000	€36,000

Increased exemption/dependent children

If you have dependent children, the exemption limit can be increased, by €575 for the first and second child and €830 for the third and subsequent qualifying children.

Marginal relief

Marginal relief is available for those whose total income exceeds the exemptions limits, but is less than twice the relevant limit. It restricts the tax payable to 40% of the difference between your income and the appropriate exemption limit.

Example

A married man aged 70, has total income for 2012 of €40,000. His tax liability would normally work out as follows:

		€
	Total Income	€40,000
	Taxable	€40,000
	€40,000 @ 20%	€8,000
Less:	Tax Credits	
	Personal	(€3,300)
	PAYE	(€1,650)
	Age	(€490)
	Net tax payable	**€2,560**

However, marginal relief will restrict the overall tax liability to €1,600. (€40,000 - €36,000) x 40% = €1,600

Tax credits

An individual who is resident, ordinarily resident and domiciled in the State, is liable to income tax in respect of their total income, wherever it arises. They are entitled to claim certain tax credits and deductions.

Single credit

This credit is granted to the following

- Individuals who are single

- Married couples or civil partners who opt for single/separate assessment - both partners receive a single tax credit

- Separated couples who have not opted for joint assessment.

Married credit

This credit, which is double the single credit is granted to couples in a marriage or civil partnership who;

- Are assessed to tax under joint assessment (See Chapter 15 - Marriage on page 301)

  or

- Are living apart but one partner is maintaining the other and is not entitled to claim tax relief on the maintenance paid (for more details on this see Chapter 16 - Separation and Divorce on page 309).

One parent family credit

This credit is granted to a parent or guardian, of a qualifying child who is not entitled to the married person's credit. However, it is not available to an unmarried couple who are living together as man and wife.

Qualifying child

To qualify a child must:

- Have been born in the tax year

  or

- Be under the age of 18 years at the commencement of the tax year

  or

- If over 18 years of age be receiving full-time education or be undergoing a full time training course for a trade or profession for a minimum of two years or be permanently incapacitated by reason of mental or physical infirmity and if over 21 years of age, be incapacitated before reaching that age.

Widowed parent credit

An additional credit is granted to widowed parents for the five tax years following the year of bereavement. The credit is €3,600 in year one, €3,150 in year two, €2,700 in year three, €2,250 in year four and €1,800 in year five.

Home carer's credit

The Home Carer's credit of €810 may be claimed by a couple who are married or in a civil partnership, where one partner cares for one or more dependent people.

If the carer has income in their own right of less than €5,080 the full home carer's credit may still be claimed. If they have income between €5,080 and €6,700 for the tax year they may claim a reduced credit. Only one credit is due irrespective of the number of dependents.

In order to qualify for the credit the following conditions must apply;

- The couple must be jointly assessed to tax - it does not apply where couples are taxed as single persons.

- The Home carer must care for one or more dependent persons. A dependent person is:

    - A child for whom child benefit is payable.

      or

    - A person aged 65 years or over;

      or

    - A person who is permanently incapacitated by reasons of mental or physical infirmity.

A dependent person does not include a spouse/partner.

- The dependent person(s) must normally reside with the couple for the tax year.

You can also claim the carer's credit for a dependent relative who is cared for outside the home provided they live in a neighbouring residence or within two kilometres of the carer.

If your income exceeds €6,700 in the tax year you can still claim the Home Carer's credit, provided, the allowance was granted for the immediately preceding tax year and the other conditions for claiming the tax credit are met.

A couple cannot claim both the Home Carer's credit and the increased standard rate cut off point for dual income couples. However, they can claim whichever of the two is more beneficial. In practice, the tax office will grant the more beneficial treatment.

Incapacitated child credit

Incapacitated child credit can be claimed where an individual proves that they have living with them at any time during the tax year a child who is permanently incapacitated either physically or mentally from maintaining themselves and is maintained by the claimant.

"If the Home Carer has income in their own right of less than €5,080 the full Home Carer's credit can be claimed."

- The child must have become incapacitated before reaching 21 years of age;

  or,

- If over 21 years had become permanently incapacitated while still in full time education or full time training for a trade or profession for a minimum of 2 years.

For the tax year 2013 the tax credit is €3,300.

Age credit

A credit is available if you or your spouse/civil partner are over 65 years of age in the relevant tax year. In the case of a couple, married or in a civil partnership, the credit for 2013 is €245 and for a single or widowed person it is €490.

Dependent relative credit

This credit is granted to claimants who prove that they maintain at their own expense any person who is:

- A relative, who is incapacitated by old age or infirmity from maintaining themselves.

- Their or their spouse/civil partner's widowed mother or father, whether incapacitated or not.

- A son or daughter who resides with them and whose services they depend on by reason of old age or infirmity.

The credit of €70 p.a. in 2013, is reduced by the amount by which the income of the person whom the claim is made for exceeds the maximum rate of old age contributory pension payable to a single person over 80 (€13,837 in 2013). If two or more people help maintain the relative the credit is divided between them in proportion to the amounts contributed by each.

Incapacitated person (employing a carer)

This allowance can be claimed if you employ a person to take care of yourself or a family member who is totally incapacitated, owing to old age or infirmity. The amount of this allowance is the net cost of employing the carer up to a maximum of €50,000.

This allowance is granted at your marginal rate of tax.

Blind person's credit

A credit of €1,650, is available during the tax year if you are blind. If both you and your spouse/civil partner are blind, a credit of €3,300 in may be claimed.

Mortgage interest relief

Interest payments are divided into two categories:

- Loans on main residence.

- Other loans.

Loans on main residence

Mortgage interest relief in respect of interest on money borrowed for the purchase, repair, development or improvement of your sole or main residence is now granted at source. Your monthly repayments are reduced by the amount of your tax credit. This relief may also be claimed for interest paid on a loan to purchase a residence for a former or separated spouse or a dependent relative if this accommodation is provided by you rent-free. Your dependent relative must be one in respect of whom you claim the dependent relative credit

A mortgage taken out from 1 January 2004 to 31 December 2012 used to purchase, repair, develop or improve your main residence is eligible for mortgage interest relief.

Mortgage interest relief will no longer be available to house purchasers who purchased after the end of 2012 and will be fully abolished by the end of 2017.

Amount of mortgage interest relief (TRS)

The ceilings or upper thresholds on the amount of interest paid that qualifies for tax relief are dependant on -

- the status of the individual, whether they are married, in civil partnership or single; **and**

- whether they are first time buyers

	Married / civil partnership / widowed / surviving civil partner	Unmarried / Not in a civil partnership
First time buyer (First 7 tax years of entitlement to mortgage interest relief)	€20,000	€10,000
Non-first time buyers	€6,000	€3,000

The ceilings are

	Rates of tax relief		
	Tax years 1 & 2	Tax years 3, 4 & 5	Tax years 6 & 7 (*)
First time buyer (First 7 tax years of entitlement to mortgage interest relief)	25%	22.5%	20%
Non-first time buyers	15%		

The rates of tax relief on qualifying interest paid are;

*Note: After year 7, the rates are those that apply to non-first time buyers.

Increased mortgage interest relief

Notwithstanding the rates of tax relief mentioned above, for individuals who purchased their first principal private resident between 1 January 2004 and 31 December 2008, the rate of tax relief on the interest paid on the loan to purchase that property will, for the tax years 2012 to 2017, be 30%.

A loan used for the purchase of an investment property does not qualify for mortgage interest relief. You can however, claim 75% of the mortgage interest paid as an expense against the gross rent received. (See page 48 for more details) If part of your mortgage is used to finance non-qualifying expenditure such as a holiday or a car, only the percentage applicable to your principal private residence qualifies for mortgage interest relief.

Example

A married couple have a €350,000 mortgage at a rate of 5.25%, are 41% tax-payers and pay mortgage interest of €18,375 in the tax year. Their mortgage interest relief (TRS) will work out as follows;

	2012	
	A	**B**
	Less than 7 years mortgage holders	More than 7 years mortgage holders
Mortgage interest paid	€18,375	€18,375
Maximum interest allowed for tax purposes	€20,000	€6,000
Tax credit €18,375/€6,000 @ 25%/15%	€4,594	€900

A   Assumes they are first time buyers.

B   Assumes they are not first time buyers.

Note: This tax relief will be granted at source by your bank or building society.

Bridging loan interest

Additional relief is available on bridging loan interest. A bridging loan is a loan to finance the disposal of your sole or main residence and the acquisition of another residence for use as a sole or main residence. The position on bridging loan interest is as follows:

● It is subject to the same restrictions as mortgage interest. However, both reliefs may be claimed for the relevant period.

● The additional allowance is for a period of 12 months only from the date on which the loan was granted. If the bridging period falls partly in one tax year and partly in another, the allowance is apportioned on a time basis according to the number of months falling into the respective years.

● No tax relief is granted for bridging loan interest which exceeds the limit of 12 months.

If after the end of the 12 month period the old home is still unsold, interest will continue to be allowed in the normal way if it is occupied as the sole or main residence. If the old residence is unoccupied, no interest deduction is allowed after the end of the 12 month period.

Other loans

There are no restrictions on the amount of interest on which tax relief may be claimed in the following circumstances.

- Interest paid out for business purposes under Case I and II of Schedule D.

- Interest on money borrowed to pay death duties.

- Interest on money borrowed to acquire an interest in a company or partnership or in granting a loan to a company or partnership provided the loan was taken out before 7th December 2010. No relief is available for loans taken out after this date.

Relief for interest paid on existing loans is being phased out over a four year period so that only 75% of the interest paid in 2011, 50% of the interest paid in 2012, and 25% of interest paid in 2013, qualifies for relief. For the tax year 2014 and subsequent years the relief will be abolished.

No tax relief is available for interest on loans taken out to acquire an interest in property rental companies.

PAYE credit

If your income is subject to PAYE, e.g. wages, salary, occupational pension, social welfare benefit or benefit in kind, you can claim the PAYE credit. The PAYE credit is €1,650 in the 2013 tax year. If you are married or in a civil partnership and both spouses/partners pay PAYE, each is entitled to a PAYE credit of €1,650.

The following PAYE income does not qualify for a PAYE credit:

- Income paid to a proprietary director or a spouse/civil partner of a proprietary director.

- Income paid by an individual or a partner, to their spouse/civil partner.

A proprietary director is a director who controls, either directly or indirectly, 15% or more of the ordinary share capital of the company.

The PAYE credit is available to children of proprietary directors and the self employed, provided they work full-time in their parent's business and their annual salary exceeds €4,572. (may be apportioned on a time basis).

Payments made under deeds of covenant

A deed of covenant is a legally binding written agreement made by an individual to pay an agreed amount to another individual, without receiving any benefit in return. To be legally effective, it must be properly drawn up, signed, witnessed, sealed and delivered to the individual receiving the payments. Any amount can be paid under a Deed but only covenants in favour of the following individuals qualify for tax relief.

- People over 65 up to a maximum of 5% of the covenantor's total income;

- Permanently incapacitated individuals.

Payments by a parent to a son or daughter under 18 do not qualify for tax relief even if incapacitated.

If you pay tax at the higher rate you may reduce your tax liability and increase the disposable income of the covenantee. In addition, if the covenantee pays tax at a lower rate or is exempt from tax, a tax advantage may be gained.

Example

You have an income of €58,000 in the 2012 tax year and pay tax at 41%. Your spouse has no income. In 2012 you wish to supplement your widowed mother's (aged 81) income by €2,000 p.a. Your mother's income is a pension of €12,896 p.a.

You can do this in one of two ways:

- Hand over €2,000 to your mother each year.

  or

- Complete a Deed of Covenant for €2,500 (it gets a little complicated here!) You deduct tax at the standard rate (20%) from this gross amount and pay the balance of €2,000 to your mother.

We have illustrated both positions on the pages 122 and 123. When all the paperwork is completed, under a Deed of Covenant you will be better off by €525 p.a. and your widowed mother is better off by €500 p.a.

A note of caution; if your mother's pension is a non-contributory pension, the covenant income will be taken into account for means-test purposes and may affect the amount of pension she will receive.

Retirement annuity pension contributions

Income tax relief is available for premiums paid to an approved personal pension scheme, to provide income in your retirement between the ages of 60 and 75 on non-pensionable earnings.

Relief is restricted as a percentage of net relevant earnings (NRE) as follows;

Up to 29 years	15%	50 to 54 years	30%
30 to 39 years	20%	55 to 59 years	35%
40 to 49 years	25%	60 and over	40%

Notes:

- Net relevant earnings are limited to €115,000 in 2012 and 2013.

- Relevant earnings consist of income from non-pensionable employment or from self-employment. A husband and wife have separate relevant earnings, which cannot be aggregated for retirement saving purposes. Income from a claim under a Permanent Health Insurance (PHI) policy is considered to be relevant earnings for retirement saving purposes. Investment earnings are not treated as relevant earnings and cannot be taken into consideration in calculating your maximum allowable pension contributions. Net relevant earnings consist of relevant earning less capital allowances, trading losses and certain other charges e.g. covenants and mortgage interest, for which you can claim tax relief.

Your position as the Covenantor

		2012 Tax Year	
		Without Covenant €	With Covenant €
A	Total Income	€58,000	€58,000
	Less: Deed of Covenant	–	(€ 2,500)
B	Taxable	€58,000	€55,500
	Tax payable		
	€41,800 @ 20%	€ 8,360	€ 8,360
	€16,200/ €13,700 @ 41%	€ 6,642	€ 5,617
		€15,002	€13,977
	Tax on Covenant €2,500 @ 20%	n/a	€500
	Total Tax	€15,002	€14,477
	Less: Tax Credits		
	Personal	(€ 3,300)	(€ 3,300)
	PAYE	(€ 1,650)	(€ 1,650)
C	Net Tax Payable	€10,052	€ 9,527
D	Direct payment to Mother	€ 2,000	€ 2,000
	Net Income	**€45,948**	**€46,473**
		A-(C+D)	A-(C+D)

Your Mother's position as the covenantee

		2012 Tax Year	
		Without Covenant €	With Covenant €
A	Deed of Covenant	Nil	€2,500
B	Pension	€12,896	€12,896
	Total Income	€12,896	€15,396
	Taxable Income (Income Under Exemption limit)	Nil	Ni
	Tax Payable	Nil	Nil
C	Tax Refund Due (tax paid by you)	Nil	€500
D	Payment from you	€2,000	€2,000
	Disposable Income	**€14,896**	**€15,396**
		B+D	B+(C+D)

Medical insurance

Tax relief is granted at source (TRS) at the standard rate of tax on the full amount of the subscription paid for medical insurance.

Tax relief is also available at the standard rate for insurance premiums paid to cover the cost of non-routine dental care.

An employee who's medical insurance premium are paid by their employer will not have been allowed TRS. Any tax relief due in this case should be included on the employees tax credit certificate or claimed on their annual tax return.

Medical expenses

Relief is available at the standard rate of tax, for qualifying health expenses paid by you in respect of any individual. You cannot claim relief for any expenditure that has been or will be reimbursed by any body such as VHI, Layla Healthcare, Aviva Health Insurance, HSE, or where a compensation payment is or will be made.

Health expenses relief are granted at the standard rate for expenses incurred from 1 January 2009 with the exception of nursing home expenses.

Health expenses cover a wide variety of matters and include :

- Doctors' and consultants' fees.

- Diagnostic procedures carried out on the advice of a practitioner.

- Drugs or medicines prescribed by a doctor, dentist or consultant.

- Maintenance or treatment in a hospital or nursing home provided the expenses are necessarily incurred in connection with the services of a practitioner or refer to diagnostic procedures carried out on the advice of practitioner.

- Supply, maintenance or repair of any medical, surgical, dental or nursing appliance used on the advice of a practitioner.

- Physiotherapy or similar treatment prescribed by a practitioner.

- Orthopaedic or similar treatment prescribed by a practitioner.

- Speech and language therapy carried out by an approved Speech and Language Therapist for a qualifying child.

- Transport by ambulance.

- Educational psychological assessments for a qualifying child, carried out by an Educational Psychologist who is registered with the Minister for Education and Skills.

- Certain items of expenditure in respect of a child suffering from a serious life threatening illness.

- Kidney patients' expenses, (up to a maximum amount depending on whether the patient used hospital dialysis, home dialysis or CAPD).

- Specialised dental treatment.

- "In vitro" fertilisation.

- Maternity care and IVF.

- Glucometre machine for a diabetic.

- The cost of food products manufactured specifically for diabetics is an allowable expense for the purpose of a health expense claim.

- The cost of gluten free foods for coeliacs. As this condition is generally ongoing, a letter instead of prescriptions, from a doctor

"Tax relief for medical expenses is granted at 20%."

stating that the taxpayer is a coeliac suffer is acceptable. Receipts from supermarkets in addition to receipts from a pharmacist are acceptable.

- Nursing care and, in certain circumstances, maintenance paid to a nursing home, for a dependent relative.

Where qualifying care is only available outside Ireland, reasonable travelling and accommodation expenses can also be claimed. In such cases the expenses of one person accompanying the patient may also be allowed where the condition of the patient requires it.

Certain non routine dental treatment also qualify for tax relief.

Health expenses carried out outside the State also qualify for tax relief provided the practitioner is qualified to practice in the county.

Dental treatments which qualify for standard rate tax relief are as follows;

- Crowns which are permanently cemented to the existing tooth tissue.

- Veneers/rembrant type etched fillings.

- Tip replacing where a large part of the tooth needs to be replaced and the replacement is made outside the mouth.

- Posts which are inserted in the nerve canal of a tooth to hold a crown.

- Inlays which are smaller versions of a crown. Relief will only be available if they were fabricated outside the mouth.

- Endodontics - root canal treatment: This involves the filling of the nerve canal and not the filling of teeth.

- Periodontal treatment which includes, root planing, curettage and debridement, gum flaps and chrome cobalt splint.

- Bridgework consisting of an enamel retained bridge or a tooth supported bridge.

- Orthodontic treatment which involves the provision of braces and other similar treatments.

- Surgical extraction of impacted wisdom teeth when undertaken in a hospital or dental surgery.

Health expenses carried out outside the State also qualify for tax relief provided the practitioner is qualified to practice in the county.

Exclusions

Health care specifically excludes expenses relating to routine ophthalmic treatment and routine dental treatment.

Routine ophthalmic treatment

This means sight testing and advice as to the use of spectacles or contact lenses and the provision and repair of spectacles or contact lenses.

Routine dental treatment

This means the extraction, scaling and filling of teeth, bridgework and the provision and repairing of artificial teeth and dentures.

How to claim

Relief for any income tax year is normally given by repayment i.e. a refund after the relevant 31 December. You can claim tax relief

- Online using Revenue's PAYE anytime service. See www.revenue.ie.

- By completing a Med 1 form and submitting it to your local tax office.

- If you complete a Form 11 each year you can claim relief for health expenses on this form. There is no need to complete a separate Med 1 form.

A claim for relief for the cost of dental treatment other than routine dental treatment must be accompanied by a certificate (Form Med 2 -this will be provided by your dentist) signed by a qualified practitioner.

Guide dog

A standard €825 per annum is allowed as medical expenses where a blind person maintains a trained guide dog and is the registered owner with the Irish Guide Dog Association.

Permanent health insurance (PHI)

Permanent health insurance (PHI) protects your income against accidents or illness for up to 75% of your normal earnings. After a specific period has expired, the benefits are paid for the duration of your incapacity or to a specific age, whichever is the earlier. Income tax relief may be claimed on the contributions made to a PHI scheme.

Contributions to a PHI scheme by PAYE tax payers are on a 'net pay' basis i.e. the contribution is deducted from your gross salary prior to the application of tax and PRSI. However employee contributions to a PHI scheme do not reduce the pay amount for USC purposes.

The amount of relief granted cannot exceed 10% of your total income for the year of assessment in which the premiums are paid. All receipts from a PHI plan are taxable, regardless of whether or not the relief is claimed on premiums paid.

Rent relief for private rented accommodation

A tax credit is available to tenants paying rent for private rental accommodation. However claimants who were not renting on the 7th December 2010 and who subsequently enter into a rental agreement are not entitled to rent relief. The amount of this credit in the 2012 and 2013 tax year for a single person is €320 and for a couple who are married, in a civil partnership or a widowed person / surviving civil partners the credit is €640. If you are over 55 and paying rent for private rental accommodation, the credit in 2012 and 2013 is €640 for a single person, and €1,280 for a couple who are married, in a civil partnership or a widowed person / surviving civil partner.

Relief for rent credit is being withdrawn on a phased basis over the next 7 years.

Job assist

An additional allowance is available over three tax years to any person who has been long term unemployed and who is returning to work.

You can opt to claim the allowances in the tax year you commence work, or if you prefer, you can commence your claim in the year of assessment following your return to work.

	Year 1 €	Year 2 €	Year 3 €
Additional personal allowance	€3,810	€2,540	€1,270
Child tax allowance	€1,270	€850	€425

Long term unemployed means that you have been continuously unemployed and in receipt of Jobseekers Benefit, Jobseekers Allowance or One parent family payment for the 12 months prior to taking up employment.

People with disabilities who have been in receipt of Disability allowance or Blind persons payment for at least 12 months can also claim the additional tax allowance.

Budget 2013

A new scheme called the "One Plus Initiative" will replace the Job assist.

Fees paid to private colleges

Tax credit is available at the standard rate of tax on college fees paid for yourself or a dependent relative. The following courses apply;

- Tuition fees paid for certain full time and part time undergraduate courses of at least 2 years duration. The relief applies to fees up to €7,000 including the student contribution from 2011.

- Tuition fees paid for certain training courses in the area of Information Technology and Foreign Languages. The relief applies to fees ranging from €315 to €1,270.

- Tax relief is also available on certain postgraduate courses.

- For the year 2011 and subsequent years the first €2,000 of each claim is disregarded for relief, where any one of the students in respect of whom the claim is being made is a full-time student.

- In the case of a claim for relief where all the students concerned are studying part-time, the first €1,000 of the claim for relief is disregarded.

Donation/gifts

Tax relief is available in respect of donations/gifts made to certain approved bodies/charities as follows:

- Donations made to an "approved body" to teach "approved subjects".

- Gifts for education in the Arts.

- Gifts to, or for the benefit of, designated schools. Relief is granted at the standard rate on aggregate gifts in a single year of assessment.

- Gifts made to third level institutes.

- Donations to designated charities The minimum donation is €250.

If you are paying PAYE you are not entitled to claim tax relief on donations made to charities. The relief is given on a "grossed up" basis to the eligible charity. This means that the donation is treated as being received by the charity net of income tax. The charity can then reclaim the deemed tax deduction. If you are self-employed you are entitled to claim a tax credit on charitable donations.

- Donation of heritage items limited to 80% of the market value of heritage item donated.

- Donation of gifts or money to the State which are used for any purpose or towards the cost of which public moneys are provided.

- Donation made to the Scientific and Technological Education (Investment) Fund.

Budget 2013

Budget 2013 announced a simplification of the scheme of tax relief available for donations to charitable and other approved bodies, including the introduction of a blended rate of relief of 31% and an annual donation limit of €1 million per individual.

Donations from all individual donors under the scheme will be treated in the same manner, with the tax relief at the blended rate in all cases being repaid to the charity. This would mean that self-assessed individuals would no longer be able to claim a deduction on their tax returns for donations made under the scheme.

Employment Investment Incentive (EII)

The Employment Investment Incentive (EII) is a tax relief incentive scheme that provides tax relief for investment in certain corporate trades. The scheme has replaced the Business Expansion Scheme (BES).

The scheme allows an individual investor to obtain income tax relief on investments up to a maximum of €150,000 per annum in each tax year up to 2014. Relief is initially available to an individual at 30%. A further 11% tax relief will be available where it has been proven that employment levels have increased at the company at the end of the holding period (3 years) or where evidence is provided that the company used the capital raised for expenditure on research and development. An investor who cannot obtain relief on all their investment in a year of assessment, either because their investment exceeds the maximum €150,000 or their income in that year is insufficient to absorb all of it, can carry forward the unrelieved amount to following years, subject to the normal limit of €150,000 on the amount of the investment that can be relieved in any one year.

Budget 2013

The EII scheme will be extended to 2020.

Relief for investment in the film industry

Special tax incentives are available for investment in the film industry. In order for a film to qualify for the relief, the film must be given a certificate by the Minister for Transport, Tourism and Sports and it is also necessary that a certain amount of the production work be carried out in Ireland.

Tax relief is available at your highest rate of tax, on your investment up to a maximum investment of €50,000 per annum. A couple married or in a civil partnership can claim tax relief on their investment up to a maximum investment of €100,000, provided each has sufficient income.

An investor who cannot obtain relief on all their investment in a year of assessment, either because their investment exceeds the maximum of €50,000 or their income is insufficient to absorb all of it, can carry forward the unrelieved amount to following years, subject to the normal limit of €50,000.

Budget 2013

The film tax relief scheme is extended to 2020.

Childcare services relief

Where an individual minds no more than three children in their own home, no tax will be payable on the childminding earnings received provided the gross amount is less than €15,000 per annum. If the childminding income exceeds this amount the total amount will be taxable, as normal, under self assessment. An individual will be obliged to return their childminding income on their annual tax return.

Universal social charge (USC)

The universal social charge was introduced from 1 January 2011. It is payable on gross income including notional pay, after relief for certain trading losses and capital allowances, but before pension contributions.

All individuals are liable to the USC if their gross income exceeds €10,036 per annum or €193 per week.

The rate of USC for 2012 and 2013 are as follows;

USC Thresholds 2012 and 2013		
Income up to €10,036	Income from €10,036 to €16,016	Income above €16,016
2%	4%	7%

The reduced rates of USC for 2012 and 2013 are as follows;

USC Thresholds			
2012		2013	
Individuals aged 70 years or over. Individuals who hold a full medical card (regardless of age)		Individuals aged 70 years or over whose aggregate income for the year is €60,000 or less. Individuals (aged under 70) who hold a full medical card whose aggregate income for the year is €60,000 or less.	
	Rate		Rate
Income up to €10,036	2%	Income up to €10,036	2%
Income above €10,036	4%	Income above €10,036	4%

Note1:   "Aggregate" income for USC purposes does not include payments from the Department of Social Protection.

Note 2:   A "GP only" card is not considered a full medical card for USC purposes.

The exempt categories of USC are as follows;

- Where an individual total income for a year does not exceed €10,036,

- All Department of Social Protection payments

- Income already subject to DIRT.

8 PAYE made easy

The Pay As You Earn (PAYE) system applies to you if you have income from employment or a pension that is taxed at source.

Tax credits

Tax credits are allowed at the standard rate of tax only, regardless of whether you are a higher rate tax payer or not. This means that tax credits benefit each individual by the same amount.

Tax credit system

Tax is calculated at the appropriate tax rates on gross pay and this tax is then reduced by any tax credits due, in order to arrive at the net tax payable.

Before the start of the new tax year, around December your tax office will issue a notification of determination of tax credits and the standard rate cut off point.

The notification of determination of tax credit and standard rate cut off point will show the following information;

● Standard rate cut off point.

● Tax credit due to you.

● Your rate(s) of tax.

Standard rate cut off point

This is the amount of income you can earn at the standard rate. The amount will depend on whether you are married, in a civil partnership, single or widowed. Also if you have any allowances which are allowed at the higher rate of tax e.g. pension contribution, this will increase your "standard rate cut off point".

Standard rate band

	2013 €
Single person	€32,800
Married couple(one spouse working)	€41,800
Married couple(*both spouse working - maximum)	€65,600
One parent family	€36,800

*   Subject to lower earning spouse having an income of at least €23,800.

The tax credits and standard rate cut off point will vary depending on the circumstances of each individual.

Income tax is calculated for each pay period by applying the information supplied by the notification against the gross pay as follows;

The standard rate of tax (20%) is applied to your gross pay up to the standard rate cut off point for that week or month. Any balance of income over that amount in the pay period is taxed at the higher rate (41%). This gives the gross tax payable. The gross tax payable is reduced by the amount of tax credits as per the notification sent by your tax office, to arrive at the net tax payable.

Example

A married individual has gross earnings of €50,000, their spouse has no income. For 2013 a notice of determination of tax credits and standard rate cut off point issues showing;

Standard rate cut off point of €41,800 per annum of €803.85 per week.	Based on a standard rate band of €41,800 for a married couple - one spouse working.
Standard rate of tax is 20%	Based on standard rate of tax of 20%
Higher rate of tax is 41%	Based on a higher rate of 41%
Tax credits of €4,950 per annum or €95.19 per week	Personal €3,300 PAYE credit €1,650 Total €4,950

Income tax would be calculated as follows for the first week

Gross pay	€961.52	(€50,000/52)
Tax on €803.85 @ 20%	€160.77	(Standard rate up to a maximum of €803.85 which is the standard rate cut off point as advised by the tax office)
Tax on €157.67 @41%	€64.64	(Higher rate of tax in excess of income over the standard rate cut off point)
Gross tax	€225.41	Total of higher rate and standard rate tax.
Less: Tax Credits	€95.19	Tax credits as advised by the tax office
Total Tax due for this week	€130.22	Total tax less tax credit

Non standard rated reliefs

If you have deductions from income tax which qualify for tax relief at the higher rate of income tax, your tax credits will be increased by the amount of the relief at the standard rate of income tax and the standard rate tax band will also be increased by the amount of the relief in order to arrive at the standard rate cut off point.

Example

A married individual has a gross income of €50,000. Their spouse has no income. Personal and PAYE tax credits amount to €4,950. They have a standard rate tax cut off point of €41,800 and their rates of tax are 20% and 41%. They also pay €2,000 into a personal pension scheme, tax relief on which is allowed at the higher rate of tax. Their tax credit will increase by €400 (€2,000 @ 20%). Their standard rate tax band will also increase by €2,000 in order to arrive at the standard rate cut off point.

Calculation of tax credits	
	2013 €
Married	€3,300
PAYE	€1,650
Total	€4,950
Increased by pension	€400
Net tax credits	**€5,350**

Calculation of standard rate cut off point	
	2013 €
Standard rate band (married couple one spouse working)	€41,800
Increased by pension	€2,000
Standard rate cut off point	**€43,800**

Income tax would be calculated as follows for the first week

Gross pay	€961.52	(€50,000/52)
Tax on €842.31 @ 20%	€168.46	(Standard rate up to a maximum of €842.31 which is the standard rate cut off point as advised by the tax office)
Tax on €119.21 @41%	€48.88	(Higher rate of tax in excess of income over the standard rate cut off point)
Gross tax	€217.34	Total of higher rate and standard rate tax.
Less: Tax Credits	€102.88	Tax credits as advised by the tax office
Total Tax due for this week	€114.46	Total tax less tax credit

Summary

Tax credit system

- Gross pay is taxed at the appropriate tax rate(s) to give the gross tax.

- The tax office will advise you of the standard rate cut off point for each pay period. The standard rate of tax is applied to pay up to that limit. Any balance of pay over that amount in any pay period is taxed at the higher rate.

- The gross tax is reduced by a tax credit as advised by the tax office to arrive at the tax payable.

PAYE emergency tax

The emergency tax operates when:

- Your employer has not received a notification of determination of tax credits and standard rate cut off point for you for the current year or your Form P45 for the current tax year.

  or

- You have given your employer a completed form P45 with "E" written on it.

For the year 2013 the PAYE emergency tax credit for the initial period of employment and the rates at which tax will be deducted are set out below.

If paid weekly:

	2013	
	Tax credit €	**Rate** %
Weeks 1 - 4	€31.73 (1/52 of single persons tax credit)	20% up to €631 (1/52 of single persons standard rate cut off point) Balance @ 41%
Weeks 5 - 8	Nil	20% up to €631 (1/52 of single persons standard rate cut off point) Balance @ 41%
Week 9 onwards	Nil	41%

If you do not supply your employer with your PPS Number, your employer must deduct tax at the higher rate on your gross pay (less superannuation and permanent health contribution if applicable). No tax credits are due.

Tax refund during unemployment

If tax has been deducted from your pay since 1 January last, and you are now unemployed, you may be entitled to a tax refund. If you have not paid tax, you cannot claim a refund on becoming unemployed.

How do I apply

You should complete Form P50 and send it to your local tax office together with Form P45 (parts 2 & 3) given to you by your former employer. You may also be able to claim this refund online if you are registered for PAYE anytime, see www.revenue.ie

PAYE refund after the year end

It is simpler to make a claim during the course of the tax year. By doing so you ensure that any refund due can be made by your employer during the year and avoid the need for further contact with the tax office at the end of the year.

If you have not made your claim before the end of the tax year you should submit the following to your local tax office;

- Form P60 (and, if relevant, a Form P60 for your spouse) for the tax year. Form P60 is issued to you by your employer at the end of the tax year.

- Details of your claim for e.g. medical expenses, rent relief, service charges and trade union subscriptions.

- If your claim relates to medical expenses you will also need to complete a Form Med 1.

PAYE anytime?

This is the Revenue On-Line Service for employees. It is an interactive systems which allows individuals who pay tax under the Pay As You Earn (PAYE) system, a quick, secure and cost effective method to manage their taxes online.

To register for PAYE anytime log onto www.revenue.ie, and from the "PAYE anytime" logo, click on the register button.

Once registered, you can:

- View your tax record.

- Claim a wide range of tax credits.

- Apply for refunds of tax including health expenses.

- Declare additional income.

- Request a review of tax liability for previous years.

- Re-allocate credits between yourself and your spouse.

- Track your correspondence submitted to Revenue.

Changes requested are reflected in your PAYE record in two days. There is no need to submit paper claims when a transaction is submitted through PAYE anytime, however you are obliged to retain receipts for six years as Revenue may ask to view them at a later stage.

The PAYE anytime system is for PAYE employees only. If you are self-employed you should register instead for ROS. (see page 168)

Time limited for claiming tax refunds

There is a four year time limit for claiming income tax refunds. PAYE tax payers seeking an income tax refunds for 2009 must submit their claim to Revenue by 31 December 2013.

What is a P21

A P21 is a PAYE balancing statement of your total income tax credits and tax paid for a particular tax year.

I need to get a P21 to apply for a grant, how do I get one?

You may need to send a PAYE balancing statement (Form P21) to your Local Authority, Bank, Building Society etc., as proof of earning for the purpose of obtaining an education grant, a house or a loan. A P21 gives details of your total income, tax credits and PAYE tax paid for a particular tax year. It also shows whether you have overpaid or underpaid tax for the year. If you have overpaid tax, a cheque for the amount overpaid will be attached. If you have underpaid tax your district office will indicated if, and how the underpayment will be collected - usually by reduction of your tax credits for a subsequent tax year.

Allowable deductions incurred for your employment

For expenses to be allowable for tax purposes they must be incurred for your employment and must be "wholly, exclusively and necessary" for the purpose of performing the duties of your employment. This rule is very strictly interpreted.

Motor and travelling expenses

A mileage allowance agreed between you and your employer for the use of your car for business purposes is not taxable provided it does not exceed the civil service mileage rate. However, you are not entitled to claim the cost of getting to or from work but only expenses incurred in the actual performance of your occupation.

For employers who use their cars in the normal course of their duties the rates are as follows;

Cars (effective from 5 March 2009)

Official motor travel in a calendar year	Rates per kilometre		
	Engine capacity: Up to 1200 cc	Engine capacity: 1201 - 1500cc	Engine capacity: 1501cc & over
Up to 6,437 km	39.12	46.25	59.07
6,438 km & over	21.22	23.62	28.46

Motorcycles (effective from 5 March 2009)

Official motor travel in a calendar year	Rates per kilometre			
	Engine capacity: Up to 150 cc	Engine capacity: 151 - 250 cc	Engine capacity: 251 - 600 cc	Engine capacity: 601 cc or more
Up to 6,437 km	14.48	20.10	23.72	28.59
6,438 km & over	9.37	13.31	15.29	17.60

Flat rate expenses

Special flat rate allowances are allowed to certain categories of workers such as teachers, nurses, journalists and building workers for expenses. The amounts are agreed from time to time between trade unions and professional bodies and the Revenue Commissioners. (Details of these expenses are listed on www.revenue.ie)

Round sum expenses

If you get round sum expenses from your employer they will be regarded as part of your salary and taxed accordingly, unless you can demonstrate that the expenses were incurred "wholly, exclusively and necessarily" in the performance of your duties. If your expenses actually exceed the sums reimbursed, you are entitled to an expense allowance for the excess.

Employee tax-efficient benefits

Here we list benefits which may be paid to you tax-free or tax efficiently by your employer:

1. If an employee is working away from normal base, daily and overnight allowances to cover the cost of lunch, evening meal, bed & breakfast etc. may be paid tax free provided it does not exceed the following limits.

    Salary levels corresponding to the following classes;

    A - Salary exceeds €67,960 (full PRSI)
    €64,565 (modified PRSI)

    B - Salary exceeds €36,620 (full PRSI)
    €34,790 (modified PRSI)

    Normal rate - up to 14 nights

    Reduced rate - next 14 nights

    Detention rate - next 28 nights

    Special rules apply to absences over 56 nights

From 5 March 2009

Class of allowances	Night Allowances			Day Allowances	
	Normal Rate €	Reduced Rate €	Detention Rate €	10 hours or more €	5 hours but less than 10 hours €
A Rate	€108.99	€100.48	€54.48	€33.61	€13.71
B Rate	€107.69	€92.11	€53.87	€33.61	€13.71

2. Canteen meals and refreshments, provided these are available to all employees or luncheon vouchers up to 19c per working day.

3. Rent-free or low rent accommodation provided this is necessitated by the job.

4. Non-cash personal gifts for reasons not connected with work but including retirement presents.

5. Share in an employer's Revenue-approved profit sharing scheme (subject to certain limits). (see page 158).

6. Staff entertainment and outgoings at a reasonable cost.

7. Pool transport to place of work.

8. Mileage allowance agreed between the employer and employee for the use of the employee's car for business purposes. The rate cannot exceed the civil service mileage rate. (see page 141)

9. Scholarship income and bursaries.

10. Lump sum payments on retirement or removal from an employment within certain limits. (see page 250).

11. Payments under the Redundancy Payment Act 1967. (see page 247)

12. Payments made on account of injury or disability.

13. Working clothes, overalls and tools provided by the employer.

14. Employer's contributions to a statutory or Revenue-approved pension scheme.

15. Cost to the employer of providing life assurance cover of up to eight times the employee's salary.

16. Employees can receive an annual benefit up to a value of €250 tax free.

17. Cost of providing sick pay/permanent health insurance.

18. Cost of providing contributions for medical insurance premiums paid to authorised insurers (higher rate tax payers will suffer BIK penalties)

19. Monthly/annual bus/rail travel passes provided by employers to their employees.

20. The provision of bicycles and associated safety equipment by employers to employees who agree to use their bicycle to travel to work, will be treated as a tax exempt benefit in kind, up to a limit of €1,000 per employee. This exemption may only apply once in any five year period in respect of any employee.

Employee benefits & shares

If you receive a benefit from your employer, then subject to certain exemptions PAYE, PRSI and USC will be applied by your employer on the taxable benefit (notional pay) received.

Normally any PAYE, PRSI or USC due in respect of the taxable benefit must be paid to the Collector General for the month in which the benefit is received. In the case of the benefit in kind (BIK) on a company car or van, the provision of accommodation or a preferential loan the annual notional pay amount can be spread out over the full tax year.

Best estimates

In order for the employer to calculate the PAYE/PRSI on benefits provided, they must make a "best estimate" of notional pay in respect of certain benefits.

However, in many cases e.g. on the provision of vouchers, the employer will be aware of the exact value of the benefits provided. This is called the "notional pay" amount.

Valuation rules

Except where there are specific rules e.g. company car (see page 145), the amount of the taxable benefit (i.e. the notional pay), which will be liable to PAYE/PRSI will be the higher of:

- The expense incurred by the employer in connection with the provision of the benefit to the employee

  or

- The value realisable by the employee for the benefit in money or money's worth.

  Less any amount made good to the employer by the employee.

Insufficient wages/salary to cover benefit

Where the amount of salary paid to an employee is insufficient to collect the full amount of PAYE, PRSI and USC due on the "notional pay", the employer must pay any shortfall to the Collector General.

Any shortfall, paid by an employer must be recovered from the employee. Any amount not recovered by the 31 March following the end of the tax year in which the benefit is received, is treated as a taxable benefit in the following year and liable to PAYE and PRSI, resulting in a double charge to tax.

Small benefits

Where an employer provides a benefit of less than €250 per annum to employees no PAYE/PRSI will apply. If the value of the benefit exceeds €250, PAYE/PRSI will apply to the full benefit.

Company cars

Where a company car is available for the private use of an employee, the employee is liable to PAYE, PRSI and USC in respect of the car.

A car is defined as all cars and includes crew cars and jeeps.

The "notional pay" to which PAYE, PRSI and the USC applies, is on the cash equivalent of the car. This cash equivalent is normally calculated at 30% of the "original market value" (OMV) of the car supplied. This calculation is applied regardless of whether the car is acquired new or second hand. However, this 30% can be reduced for high business mileage as follows;

Travel to and from work is considered private use.

For cars first provided for employees in the tax year 2008 or earlier the percentage's are as follows;

Annual business mileage	
24,000 km or less	30%
24,000 km - 32,000 km	24%
32,000 km - 40,000 km	18%
40,000 km - 48,000 km	12%
48,000 km or over	6%

If you receive a company car any time after 1 January 2009 your benefit in kind is based on the CO_2 emissions of the car as well as your business mileage.

Higher charges apply for cars with higher emission levels.

Lower limit	Upper limit	Category A, B, C	Category D and E	Category F and G
Kilometres	Kilometres			
0	24,000	30%	35%	40%
24,001	32,000	24%	28%	32%
32,001	40,000	18%	21%	24%
40,001	48,000	12%	14%	16%
48,001		6%	7%	8%

Vehicle Category	CO_2 Emissions (g/km)
A	0 to 120
B	> 120 to 140
C	> 140 to 155
D	> 155 to 170
E	> 170 to 190
F	> 190 to 225
G	> 225

Calculation of notional pay

Step 1:   Find out the original market value of the car.

The 'OMV' of the car is usually the list price of the car including duties, VRT and VAT. If a discount was received when the vehicle was bought the list price may be reduced by the discount provided the discount would normally be available on the open market when buying a single vehicle.

Step 2:   Ascertain the business mileage for the year or the CO_2 emission levels, and calculate the cash equivalent using the chart on page 146.

Example

You are provided with a company car on 1 January 2012. The OMV of the car is €35,000, and your business mileage is less than 15,000 a year, its falls into category C based on the CO_2 emission levels of the car. You make no payments towards the running costs of the car.

Your "notional pay" in respect of the company car would be calculated as follows;

$$€35,000 \times 30\% = €10,500$$

If you are paid weekly, €201.92 "notional pay" (€10,500 / 52) will be added to your normal salary and income tax, PRSI and USC will be applied to this amount.

Step 3:   Deduct amounts paid by the employee to the employer in respect of the car. Taking the above example, but assuming you make a payment directly to your employer of €1,000 in respect of the running cost of the car, you also pay all your own private fuel. Your BIK would work out as follows:

Notional pay as per previous example	€10,500
Less: The running expenses paid directly to your employer	€1,000
Notional pay amount	€9,500

There is no deduction for the private fuel, as you did not make this payment directly to your employer.

In some cases an employee will pay a lump sum contribution towards the purchase of a company car. In this case, the lump sum is deducted from the "notional pay" in the first year the car is provided. This deduction is only allowed in the first year.

20% reduction in BIK for low mileage

Your BIK charge can be reduced by 20% provided all of the following conditions are met:

- You spend 70% or more of your time away from your place of work.

- Your annual business mileage exceeds 8,000 kilometres p.a. but does not exceed 24,000 kilometres p.a.

- You work an average of at least 20 hours per week.

- You keep a log book, detailing the mileage, nature and location of business and amount of time spent away from your employer's business premises. This log must be available for inspection by your Inspector of Taxes, if requested, and must be certified by your employer as being correct.

Chauffeur driven cars

In the case of a chauffeur driven car two separate charges arise:

- A benefit in kind charge in respect of the provision of the car

    and

- A benefit in kind charge in respect of the expenses incurred by the employer in the provision of a chauffeur

Charge for the chauffeur benefit is the total expenses incurred by the employer in the provision of the chauffeur (e.g. chauffeur's salary) less any amount made good by the employee.

End of year adjustment

The exact business mileage for an employee cannot be determined until the end of a tax year. So during the year employers should make a best estimate of the business mileage for the year, based on available information and records. However, prior to the end of the tax year this best estimate should be reviewed to ensure that it is correct. Any necessary adjustment should then be made before the end of the tax year.

Company car available for less than a full year

Adjustments will be necessary where a car is not available for the full year, e.g. where

- An employee receives a car after the start of the tax year.

- An employee gives up a car before the end of the tax year.

Equally an adjustment will be required where a car is for some other reason not available for private use for part of the tax year, for example, where an employee is working abroad for an extended period. In this case, a car provided to an employee will not be regarded as available for private use for that part of the year which the employee is outside the State for the purpose of performing the duties of the office or employment, provided the following conditions are met:

- The employee travels abroad without the car.

- The car is not available for use by the employee's family or household during the employee's period of absence outside the State.

Where a car is not available for part of a year, the business mileage thresholds and the percentage cash equivalents used should be calculated by reference to the following calculation;

"The exact business mileage for an employee cannot be determined until the end of a year."

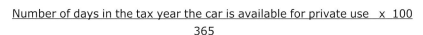

Number of days in the tax year the car is available for private use   x 100

365

Company car or mileage allowance?

Many people now look at the option of using their own car for business and taking a mileage allowance for business travel instead of a company car.

To see which option is best for you, first work out how much your car costs.

Motoring costs

Each year the AA publishes a leaflet entitled "Motoring Costs" in which they divide motoring costs into two distinct categories:

- Standing charges.

- Operating costs.

A standing charge is any fixed annual cost which remains the same regardless of your annual mileage. An operating cost, on the other hand, is a cost which is directly related to your mileage, for example, petrol.

Of course, your overall motoring costs depend to a large extent on the type of car you drive, your age, driving experience etc., but to make everything as straightforward as possible, we have outlined below what the AA estimated were the average standing charges for the different CO_2 emission bands A - G. You can check your car CO_2 emissions on www.ratemycar.ie. Now that you can identify the standing charges, we next outline what the AA estimated were your operating costs in June 2012 expressed in cents per kilometre.

By referring to these two tables, you can see that if you own a car in the co_2 emission band C, drive 16,000 kilometres per annum between standing charges and operating costs, the AA estimates it will cost you an average of €11,817 p.a.or €227.25 p.w.. The corresponding figure for a car win the band E emission level is €14,896 p.a. or €286.46 p.w.

Operating costs per kilometre (in cents)

Standing charges

CO2 Emissions Bands	Band A €	Band B €	Band C €	Band D €	Band E €	Band F €	Band G €
Motor tax	104	156	302	447	630	1,050	2,100
Insurance	730	885	986	1,065	1,232	1,422	1,834
Driving licence	3	3	3	3	3	3	3
Depreciation	1,415	1,691	2,445	2,996	3,613	5,412	8,247
Interest costs	112	138	189	223	283	424	446
Garage /parking	3,990	3,990	3,990	3,990	3,990	3,990	3,990
NCT test	18	18	18	18	18	18	18
AA subscription	149	149	149	149	149	149	149
Total charges	**6,522**	**7,030**	**8,082**	**8,900**	**9,918**	**12,468**	**16,787**

Cost per kilometre (in cent)

Engine capacity	Band A €	Band B €	Band C €	Band D €	Band E €	Band F €	Band G €
8,000	82.07	88.97	101.65	112.71	125.97	157.22	182.63
16,000	41.03	44.03	50.82	56.35	62.98	78.61	91.31
24,000	27.36	29.66	33.88	37.57	41.99	52.41	60.88
32,000	20.52	22.24	25.41	28.18	31.49	39.30	45.66

Operating costs per kilometre (in cents)

Engine capacity	Band A €	Band B €	Band C €	Band D €	Band E €	Band F €	Band G €
Petrol	9.87	11.17	12.13	14.15	15.73	16.98	21.90
Oil	0.10	0.13	0.16	0.18	0.20	0.21	0.25
Tyres	0.05	1.72	1.82	2.50	2.73	2.72	5.29
Servicing	1.56	2.05	2.23	2.61	2.70	2.72	3.43
Repairs	6.08	6.36	6.70	7.63	8.77	9.43	13.15
Total	17.66	21.43	23.04	27.08	30.12	32.07	44.03
* Petrol based on 151.70 per litre (unleaded) for each cent more, or less, add or subtract							
	0.07	0.08	0.09	0.11	0.12	0.13	0.15

Total costs per KM - based on 16,000 km

Engine capacity	Band A €	Band B €	Band C €	Band D €	Band E €	Band F €	Band G €
Standing charges	41.03	44.49	50.82	56.35	62.98	78.61	91.31
Operating costs	17.66	21.43	23.04	27.08	30.12	32.07	44.03
Cents per kilometre	58.70	65.91	73.86	83.43	91.11	110.68	135.34

Civil service mileage rates

The civil service mileage rates for cars and motor bikes are shown on page 141.

Provided your employer agrees and provided you do not charge an amount in excess of the civil service mileage rates, these charges will be tax free into your hand.

Evaluating which is best for you in your particular circumstances can be a complex exercise and we suggest that you go about it as follows:

● First estimate your annual standing charges (A).

- Estimate your operating costs per kilometre (B).

- Estimate your total annual mileage (C).

- Calculate how much of your total annual mileage is for business purposes.

From A, B and C you can calculate your total annual cost. By applying the civil service mileage rate to your annual business mileage you can calculate the value of reimbursements your employer may pay you tax-free.

Taking a salary increase instead of a company car

Another consideration is salary in lieu of a company car. For example, if you do relatively low business mileage and are considering the option of giving up the company car in favour of a salary increase coupled with the ability to claim a small mileage allowance. The question you must ask yourself is "Will I lose money"? The example below will help you to answer this question.

Example

You have a company car with an original market value of €30,000, which falls into category C for CO_2 emissions. Your total mileage is 13,000 km per year of which 8,000 km are business miles. Assuming you pay tax at 41%, your BIK will work out as follows with a company car.

	€
Original market value of car	€30,000
BIK @ 30%	€9,000
Your increased tax bill (€9,000@ 52%) (Income tax @ 41%, PRSI & USC @ 11%)	€4,680

The estimated cost of running your car is €9,602 per annum.

You have the option of giving up your company car, taking a salary increase of €3,000 and a mileage allowance of €4,246. Should you take it?

Your position

	€
Running cost of car	€9,602
Salary increase of €3,000 (Net of Tax @ 41%, PRSI & USC @ 11%)	(€1,440)
Mileage allowance	(€4,246)
Net annual cost of car	**€3,916**

The cost to you of the company car is €4,680 per annum i.e. your additional tax bill. If you provided your own car and you got an increase in salary of €3,000 and mileage allowance of €4,246, the net cost of running your car will work out at €3,916. A saving of €764 per annum.

Car pools

Cars included in car pools are treated as not being available for an employee's private use and no tax liability arises on the provision of a car from a car pool provided all of the following conditions are met:

- The car is made available to, and actually used by, more than one employee and in the case of each of them it is made available to them by reason of their employment, but is not normally used by any one of the employees to the exclusion of the others.

- Private use by each employee is incidental to other use.

- The car is not normally kept overnight at, or in the vicinity of, any of the employee's homes.

Company van

If an employee has the use of a company van for private use the Benefit in Kind is calculated at 5% of the OMV of the van.

No BIK will be charged on company vans were the following conditions are met:

- The van is supplied to the employee for the purposes of the employee's work.

- The employee is required by the employer to bring the van home after work.

- Apart from travelling from work to home and back to work, other private use of the van by the employee is forbidden by the employer and there is no other private use.

- In the course of their work, the employee must spend at least 80% of their time away from the premises of the employer to which they are attached.

Business mileage involving travel direct from/to home

Where an employee proceeds on a business journey directly from home to a temporary place of work (rather than commencing that business journey from their normal place of work) or returns home directly, the business mileage should be calculated by reference to the lesser of :

- The distance between home and the temporary place of work

  or

- The distance between the normal place of work and the temporary place of work.

Payment of medical insurance

Tax relief for medical insurance premiums paid to an authorised insurer is granted at source (TRS). Subscribers pay 80% of the gross premium, which is the same as giving tax relief at the standard rate of 20%. If your employer pays medical insurance on your behalf you will not have been given the tax relief at source and so you will have to reclaim this directly from the tax office.

Claiming relief

You can claim this relief.

- On www.revenue.ie through the Revenue PAYE Anytime service facility, if you have registered for this service with the Revenue.

- By phoning your local tax office

- Or completing Form IT5 which is available on www.revenue.ie

Preferential loans

A preferential loan is a loan made to an employee by their employer (directly or indirectly) on which they pay no interest or interest at a rate lower than the specified rate.

The Benefit in Kind for tax purposes is the difference between the interest paid (if any) and interest calculated at the specified rate. However, the amount of interest assessed to tax will qualify for mortgage interest relief as "deemed interest" providing it is a qualifying loan subject to the normal limits.

In 2012 the specified rate for home loan is 5%. For non-home loans the specified rate is 12.5%.

Budget 2013

The specified rate for home loans is reduced from 5% to 4% and for non-home loans is increased from 12.5% to 13.5% from 1 January 2013.

Example

You are married and joined the bank in January 2010. In April 2010, you were granted a preferential house purchase loan of €60,000 @ 3% p.a. You pay tax at 41%, your position is as follows for 2012.

		2012 €
	Preferential house purchase loan	€60,000
	Interest paid €60,000 @ 3%	€1,800
	Benefit-In-Kind (BIK) €60,000 @ 5%	€3,000
Less:	Interest paid	€1,800
	Taxable BIK	€1,200
	Interest relief for tax purposes	
	Interest paid	€1,800
	Deemed interest paid	€1,200
	Total	**€3,000**

Accommodation

If your employer provides you with accommodation rent free or at a reduced rate and this accommodation is not necessary for your employment, then a taxable benefit arises. This benefit is normally the market rate of the annual rent which could be obtained on a yearly letting of the accommodation.

Any amounts paid by the employee to the employer by way of rent are deductible from the taxable benefit.

Relocation costs - relating to employment

Strictly, the cost of relocating your home is a personal expense. However, if it is a requirement of your job that you move home and certain procedures are followed, your employer may compensate you for these costs in a tax free manner.

The types of expenses covered are:

- Auctioneer's fees, solicitor's fees and stamp duty arising from moving home.

- Furniture removal costs.

- Storage charges.

- Insurance of furniture and items in transit.

- Cleaning stored furniture.

- Travelling expenses on removal.

- Temporary subsistence allowance while looking for new accommodation.

Formal requirements

- The cost must be borne directly by the employer in respect of actual expenses incurred by you.

- The expenses must be reasonable.

- The payments must be properly controlled.

Receipts must be provided (apart from temporary subsistence), and your Inspector of Taxes must be satisfied that moving home is necessary for your job.

Share schemes

More and more employers are looking at share schemes as a way of rewarding their employees. Some, of these schemes attract favourable tax treatment provided certain conditions are met, although these have been reduced in the past couple of years.

Approved profit share scheme

An approved profit sharing scheme allows a full or part time employee or a full time director to receive shares tax free from their employer up to an annual limit of €12,700 provided certain conditions are met.

A Trust is set up by the company, this Trust must purchase shares in the company on behalf of the employees with funds received from the company. The Trust must hold the shares for two years before transferring them to the employee, who must then hold the shares for three years after receiving them. If the shares are disposed of by the employee before the end of the three year period income tax is charged on the lower of:

● The market value of the shares at the date they were initially apportioned to the employee

   or

● The sale proceeds from the sale of the shares

However, if the employee/director ceases employment or reaches retirement age within the three year period, income tax will be payable at 50% of the lower of the above.

Approved profit sharing schemes are tax efficient for both the employee and employer as the employee can receive shares tax free up to an annual limit of €12,700 and the employer can offset the cost of the shares against the company's profits.

Shares appropriated to employees on or after 1 January 2011 under Revenue approved profit sharing schemes will continue to be exempt from income tax but will be subject to PRSI and the universal social charge (USC).

Employee share ownership trusts

Employee share ownership trusts (ESOT's) were first introduced in the Finance Act 1997.

A company can place shares for a maximum of 20 years in an ESOT. They are designed to work in conjunction with profit sharing scheme as shares can be released from the ESOT each year into the company's profit sharing scheme.

The €12,700 tax free limit which applies to a profit sharing scheme can be increased to a once-off €38,100 after 10 years in respect of shares previously held in an ESOT provided;

- The shares have been transferred to the Trustees of an approved profit sharing scheme by the trustees of an ESOT;

  and

- In the first five years of the establishment of the ESOT, 50% of the shares retained by the Trustees were pledged as security on borrowings.

- No shares which were pledged as security for borrowings by Trustees of the ESOT were previously transferred to the Trustees of a profit sharing scheme.

Stock options

A stock option arises where a company grants to its employees or directors, an option to subscribe for shares in the company, at a preferential price. A taxable benefit arises when the predetermined share price is less than the market value.

The amount liable to tax is the difference between the market value of the shares at the exercise date and the price you actually pay. This liability arises at the date you exercise the option.

If the options are capable of being exercised more than seven years after they were granted, income tax may also arise on the date the option is granted. The amount liable to income tax is the difference between the market value of the shares at the date the option was granted and the option price. Any tax paid at this early stage can be offset against the total tax liability when the option is eventually exercised.

Capital Gains Tax may also be payable on the shares if they increase in value from the date you exercise the option. Any amounts assessable to income tax are deemed to be part of the cost for Capital Gains Tax purposes.

Example

You are granted an option in August 2008 to purchase 2,000 shares in your employer's company at a future date for €7 per share. When you exercise your options in August 2012 the share price was €9 per share.

The amount liable to income tax in 2012		€
	Market value of shares in August 2012	€9 x 2,000 = €18,000
Less:	Option price	€7 x 2,000 = €14,000
	Benefit liable to income tax	€4,000

This tax would be payable 30 days after the date of exercise of the stock options.

Stock options and non resident

If you were granted an option, prior to 5 April 2007, before you became resident in Ireland, but exercised it after your arrival here no income tax liability would arise in Ireland, provided there was no connection between the Irish employment and the granting of the option and no tax planning or avoidance scheme was involved.

For options granted on or after 5 April 2007, income tax will be charged if you exercise stock options while resident in Ireland, even if you were not resident at the date the option was granted.

Returns by employers

Employers must provide certain information to the Revenue Commissioners about the stock options granted and exercised by employees.

Stock options and self-assessment

If you receive stock options from your employer, you are liable to tax under self-assessment in respect of the profit arising from the stock options.

Income tax is payable 30 days from the date of exercise of any stock options. The amount payable is 41% of the net cheque received i.e. 41% of the difference between the sale price of the shares less the option price. You should complete Form RTSO1 and forward it together with a cheque for the income tax due to the Collector General. You should also submit details of the share options received on your annual tax return - Form 11. The USC and PRSI may also apply to stock options.

Relief for new shares purchased by employees/share subscription schemes

When an employee or director of a company subscribes for new shares in a company, they are entitled to a deduction from their total income, up to a maximum lifetime deduction of €6,350, provided certain conditions are met.

- The individual subscribes for new ordinary shares in the company.

- The deduction is granted for the tax year in which the shares are issued.

- The company in which the shares are issued must be resident and incorporated in Ireland and must be a trading or a holding company.

- If the employee sells the shares within three years of the date of acquiring the shares any income tax relief granted is withdrawn by reference to the tax year in which it was originally given.

- The relief will not be withdrawn where the employee ceases employment with the particular company, or where the employee ceases to be a resident for tax purposes or ceases to be a full time employee.

- When the shares are sold the amount of the tax deduction granted is excluded from the base cost of the shares when calculating the Capital Gains Tax liability on the sale of the shares.

This scheme is terminated where shares are subscribed for on or after 8 December 2011.

Save as you earn scheme (SAYE)

Under an approved SAYE scheme a company grants options over shares to its employees. The share options are granted at a price which is fixed by the directors at the time of the grant. This may be at the full market price value or at a discount of up to 25% on the market value.

SAYE schemes operate by allowing the employee to save between €12 and €320 per month out of their net income for a three or five year period in order to finance the purchase of the shares. The employee must save in a special savings scheme which has been set up for SAYE schemes, with a qualifying savings institution. Any interest or bonus paid on the savings contract will be exempt from tax including deposit interest retention tax.

Example

5 Years Saving Contract	€
Monthly savings	€50.00
Share price at grant	€3.33
Discounted option price (75% of market value)	€2.50
Savings on maturity	€3,000
Interest on maturity	€250
Total savings & interest	**€3,250**
Options granted for 1,300 shares	

Normally when an employee exercises a share option, a charge to income tax will arise based on the excess value of the shares over the option price regardless of whether or not the shares are retained. However, options granted through a SAYE scheme approved by the Revenue Commissioners will not be liable to income tax on either grant or exercise provided the option is not exercised before the third anniversary of the grant. After this time any disposal of the shares will trigger a charge to capital gains tax based on the excess of the net sales proceeds over the actual option price.

Example

As part of a share incentive scheme, you save €200 per month from January to June 2012. At the end of 6 months you have saved €1,200.

Shares in your employer's company are €10 per share at June 2012. You buy 140 shares at 30 June 2012 at €8.50, at 15% discount, total cost of €1,190. You keep the shares until November 2012 when you sell them for €2,100.

	€
Income tax liability at 30 June 2012 - (Date Shares Acquired)	
Market value of shares acquired (140 x €10)	€1,400
Price paid (140 x €8.50)	€1,190
Taxable benefit	**€210**

A liability to Capital Gains Tax may arise when the shares are sold in November 2012, if the market rate at the time of sale exceeds €1,400.

Any gain on options that were granted and/or exercised under SAYE approved share option schemes on or after 1 January 2011 will continue to be exempt from income tax but will be subject to PRSI and the universal social charge (USC).

Share incentive schemes/employee share purchase plans (ESPP)

These are schemes whereby a fixed amount is deducted from your salary every month. After the end of a fixed period, say six months, you purchase shares in your employer's company at a discounted price.

This discount is a taxable benefit for you and is liable to income tax. If you sell the shares immediately on acquiring them no further liability to tax arises. However, Capital Gains Tax may be payable if you keep the shares and sell them at a profit at a later stage.

As share incentive schemes are designed to encourage employees to invest in their employer's business, many schemes prohibit the sale of shares immediately after they are acquired. Where the employee is prohibited from disposing of the shares for a number of years, the Revenue will allow an abatement in the income tax charge depending on the number of years of the prohibition on the disposal.

The abatement is as follows:

No. of Years	Abatement
1 Year	10%
2 Years	20%
3 Years	30%
4 Years	40%
5 Years	50%
Over 5 Years	55%

Restricted stock units (RSU's)

A Restricted Stock Unit is a grant (or promise) to an employee to the effect that, on completion of a 'vesting period', they will receive a number of shares. A restricted stock unit is, generally, evidenced by way of a certificate of such entitlement.

The 'vesting period' is the period of time between the date of the grant of the shares and the date on which the vesting condition is satisfied. Vesting periods are usually satisfied by, for example, the passage of time or by the individuals' employment performance

Tax treatment of RSU's

An RSU is not a share option but rather is a taxable emolument of the employment.

Timing of taxation of awards of RSU's

The income tax liability of the shares arises either:

- On the date of vesting (rather than on the date of the grant) of a restricted stock unit; or

- Where the shares pass to the employee on a date prior to the date of vesting, on that prior date.

Payment of dividend equivalents

In some instances, employees granted an RSU may be entitled to amounts equivalent to the dividends accruing to the shares promised under an RSU. Such dividend equivalents are taxable emoluments.

9 Self-employment

If you are self-employed or if you are in PAYE employment but have non-PAYE income the tax on which cannot be recovered by restricting your tax credits under the PAYE system you will be regarded as a "chargeable person" and liable to self assessment.

Proprietary directors are also subject to the self assessment system even if all their income is taxed under PAYE. A proprietary director is one who holds more than 15% of the share capital of the company.

Under the self-assessment system, you are required to ;

- Pay your preliminary tax on the due date in the year of assessment e.g. your preliminary tax for 2013 is due on the 31 October 2013.

- Submit your completed Income Tax Return - (Form 11) to your Inspector of Taxes on/before the 31 October following the year of assessment e.g. your 2012 tax return must be submitted on/before the 31 October 2013.

Preliminary tax

Preliminary tax is your estimate of income tax payable for the year. It is payable by the 31 October in the year of assessment e.g. on 31 October 2013 you pay your Preliminary Tax for 2013.

The amount payable is the lower of;

- 90% of your final liability for the current year,

  or

- 100% of your liability for the previous year

Payment by direct debit

If you choose to pay your preliminary tax by direct debit, your payments will be based on 105% of your final tax liability for non PAYE income in the pre-preceding year e.g. if your final tax liability for non PAYE income in 2011 was €8,000 - your 2013 preliminary tax liability can be paid by 12 monthly installments of €700 (€8,000 x 105% ÷ 12).

Surcharge

If you don't submit your tax return by the 31 October, a surcharge will be added to your tax bill. The amount of the surcharge will depend on when your tax return is eventually submitted.

A surcharge of 5% of the total tax due (up to a maximum of €12,695) is added where your tax return is submitted before the 31 December following the year of assessment or 10% (up to a maximum of €63,485) where the return is submitted after the 31 December following the year of assessment.

Relevant dates

Pay preliminary tax	31 October in year of assessment e.g. 31 October 2012 pay preliminary tax for tax year 2012.
File tax return	31 October following the end of the tax year e.g. tax return for 2012 (year ended 31 December 2012) must be filed by the 31 October 2013.
Pay balance of tax	31 October following the return filing date. Balance of tax due for 2012 (year ended 31 December 2012) must be paid by 31 October 2013.

ROS

If you pay your income tax and file your tax return using Revenue Online Service (ROS) you can avail of an extension to the 31 October deadline. In 2012 ROS filers had until 15 November 2012 to file their returns and pay their tax.

Contract of service vs contract for service

If you work for an employer for more than eight hours a week you are entitled to a contract of employment. This contract gives you the benefit of protective legislation, including the Holiday's Act 1973, the Unfair Dismissal Acts 1977 and 1993, the Minimum Notice and Terms of Employment Act 1973 and many others. As an employee you pay PAYE and PRSI.

As a contractor you have an independent business and your contract for work is a contract for services so you are not protected under the employment legislation mentioned earlier.

Setting up as a contractor

There are a number of issues you must face as a contractor. These include, do you operate as a Sole Trader / Partnership or Limited Company, VAT is also another consideration.

Limited company

Limited companies prepare audited accounts annually, which may be more costly than preparing accounts as a sole trader.

Paying corporation tax

The self assessment system 'Pay and File', applies to companies.

Preliminary tax is payable in one instalment and this amount is payable not later than the 21 day of the month preceding the end of the accounting period - e.g. for a company whose accounting period ends on 31 December 2012 the company must pay its preliminary tax by 21 November 2012.

The total amount of preliminary tax paid must be equal to or greater than 90% of the company's final tax liability for the accounting year.

Corporation tax is charged on company's profits at a rate of 12.5%. The taxable profit is computed in the same way as the taxable profit for a sole trader. A companies tax return form CT1 should be submitted to the Inspector of Taxes within nine months of the company's year end. If this date is 21 days after the ninth month the filing date is brought forward to the 21st day.

If you operate as a company, you, as a director, can decide the level of salary you will receive under the PAYE system.

From a pension point of view, a company can make more generous pension contributions to your retirement fund and have these contributions offset against its taxable profits.

If a director owns a car and pays their own car insurance, motor tax and petrol costs, they can claim a mileage allowance for any business miles they travel on behalf of the company in accordance with the civil service mileage rates (see page 141) and have this cost offset against the profits of the company.

Start up companies

A relief from corporation tax was introduced for new companies commencing to trade in 2009. The relief was extended to cover companies starting to trade in 2012, 2013 and 2014. The exemption is granted in respect of the profits of a new trade and chargeable gains on the disposal of any assets used for the purposes of a new trade.

The exemption is granted by reducing the total corporation tax (including the tax refereable to capital gains) relating to the trade to nil. Full relief is granted where the total amount of corporation tax payable by a company for an accounting period does not exceed €40,000. Marginal relief is granted where the total amount of corporation tax payable by a new company for an accounting period amounts to between €40,000 and €60,000. No relief applies where corporation tax payable is €60,000 or more.

"As a sole trader you are liable to income tax at 20% or 41% on the profits earned by the business each year."

For accounting periods beginning on or after 1 January 2011 the value of the relief is based on the amount of the employer's PRSI paid by a company in an accounting period, subject to a maximum of €5,000 per employee and an overall limit of €40,000.

Budget 2013

It was announced in Budget 2013 that the scheme is being enhanced to allow and unused relief arising in the first three years of trading, due to insufficiency of profits to be carried forward for use in subsequent years.

Sole trader

As a sole trader you are liable to income tax at 20% or 41% on the profits earned by the business each year, regardless of the actual cash you withdraw from the business. Tax is due for payment on 31 October each year. You are also liable to PRSI and the universal social charge.

Cars

As a sole trader the cost of running a car can be apportioned between your business and private use on a basis agreed with your Tax Inspector.

VAT

If you provide a service and your sales are in excess of €37,500 p.a. you must register for VAT. If you provide goods this VAT limit is increased to €75,000.

The implications of VAT registration are as follows;

- VAT must be charged on all invoices.

- VAT on business expenses (other than entertainment and motor expenses can be reclaimed).

- Proper VAT records must be kept and VAT returns completed

In order to register for VAT you should complete a Form TR1, if you are an individual or partnership, or a Form TR2 if you are trading as a company.

Insurance

If you are operating a business from your own home , you need to be aware your home is also now a business premises and can be treated as such for insurance purposes.

Insurance companies have become increasingly aware of the dual use of private homes and expect clients to inform them when their home is being used for business purposes. This may not necessarily result in a higher annual insurance premium, but it may affect your right to make a successful claim if equipment is stolen or damaged or if somebody is injured on your premises.

Registering for income tax

In order to register for taxes as a sole trader you should complete Form TR1, which is available from your local tax office or on www.revenue.ie. If you are setting up a company you should complete form TR2 tax registration form for companies. Registration can also be completed online.

Capital gains tax (CGT)

Using your house for business purposes means you can claim some of the running costs against your annual income tax bill. These can include electricity, gas, telephone, insurance, etc. However, on the sale of your home you may face a CGT bill for the part of your home which was used as a business.

Calculation of your profit

Income tax is charged on taxable profits. Taxable profits are your gross income less expenses which are allowed for income tax purposes.

The following expenses are specifically disallowed:

- Any expenses which are not wholly and exclusively made for the purpose of the trade.

- Entertainment expenses - this would include the provision of accommodation, food or drink or any other hospitality for clients. Entertainment provided for staff, within reason would be an allowable expense.

- Personal expenses.

- Capital expenditure incurred on improvements to the business premises.

- Any debt except bad debts and doubtful debts that are not expected to be recouped.

- Where the car is leased and the list price of the car exceeds €24,000 a portion of the lease expenses is disallowed. The disallowed lease expense is calculated as follows:

$$\frac{\text{Leasing charges x List price of car limit}}{\text{List price of car}}$$

Capital allowances

Depreciation, as such, is not allowable for tax purposes but Capital Allowances in the form of wear and tear allowances are allowed for plant and machinery, fixtures and fittings and motor vehicles which are used for the trade or profession. The rate of wear and tear allowance for plant and machinery and motor vehicles is 12.5% p.a. for eight years. For taxis and short term hire vehicles the annual rate of wear and tear is 40% each year. Accelerated capital allowances may be claimed for expenditure incurred on certain energy efficient equipment bought for the purpose of the trade.

Capital allowances on business cars can only be claimed on an amount up to €24,000. If the business car costs in excess of this amount, the capital allowances can only be claimed on €24,000.

A revised scheme of capital allowances and leasing expenses for cars used for business purposes was introduced for cars purchased or leased on or after 1 July 2008. The revision links the availability of such allowances expenses to the CO_2 emission levels of vehicles. Cars are categorised by reference to CO_2 emissions with the emissions bands being broadly consistent with the VRT system, as follows;

Cars with CO_2 emission levels in category A/B/C above will benefit from

Category A vehicles	Category B/C vehicles	Category D/E vehicles	Category F/G vehicles
0-120g/km	121 -155 g/km	156 - 190g/km	191 g/km [+]

capital allowances at the current car value threshold under the existing scheme of €24,000, regardless of the cost of the car. Cars in the category D/E will receive allowances of 50% of the current car value threshold or 50% of the cost of the car, if lower. Cars in category F/G will not qualify for capital allowances.

Leasing expenses for cars in category A/B/C will be increased or reduced, as the case maybe, in proportion to which the specified amount of €24,000 bears to the cost of the car. Such cars may benefit from a proportionately higher deduction than the actual leasing expenses if the cost of the car is less than €24,000. Cars in the category D/E will get 50% of the leasing expenses . Cars in category F/G will not qualify for a deduction for leasing expenses.

Keeping books and records

If you are self employed you must keep full and accurate records of your business from the start. You need to do this whether you send in a simple summary of your profit/loss, prepare the accounts yourself, or have an accountant do it. It is important for you to remember that the figures which are contained in your accounts, and your tax returns, must be correct. The records you keep must be sufficient to enable you to make a proper return of income for tax purposes.

You should bear in mind that you may need to keep accounts for reasons unconnected with tax. For example, your bank may want to see your accounts when considering an application for a business loan.

You must keep your books and records for a period of six years unless your Inspector of Taxes advises you otherwise.

Witholding tax on payments for professional services

Tax at the standard rate - is deducted by Government departments, State bodies, HSE, etc. from payments made for professional services.

The tax deducted can be claimed in the year in which it is withheld, i.e. tax withheld in 2012 can be offset against your tax liabilities for 2012 and any excess can be reclaimed.

Basis of assessment - new business

When you commence your business you are liable to income tax on your profits as follows;

First year

Actual profits from commencement to following 31 December.

Second year

(i)   If there is one set of accounts made up to a date within that tax year and these accounts are for 12 months, these accounts will form the basis period for the second year of assessment.

(ii)   If the accounts are for less than one year or if there is more than one set of accounts ending within the tax year, then the basis of assessment is the full amount of the profits for the 12 months ending on the latest of these dates.

(iii)   In all other cases, the actual profits for the tax year.

If the actual profits of the second year are less than the profits for the first 12 months of trading the difference can be used to reduce the income for the third year of assessment.

Third and following years

Profits for accounts for 12 months ending in the actual tax year.

Basis of assessment - cessation of business

When you cease your business your profits are assessed to tax as follows;

Final   Actual profits from the 1 January to date of cessation.

Penultimate Where the actual profits (1 January to 31 December) of the penultimate tax year exceed the profits assessed for that tax year, the assessment will be increased to the amount of the actual profits.

Partnership

A partner is assessed on the share of the partnership profits as adjusted for tax purposes, by reference to the profit sharing ratio in force during the period.

Capital allowances on plant and equipment are split between the partners according to their profit sharing ratio in the tax period.

The profits of a trade or profession carried on by a partnership are not assessed for income tax on the partnership as such, but each partner is deemed to be carrying on a separate trade and, each is assessed for tax individually.

Relevant period

For trades or professions carried on by a partnership, there is what is referred to as the "relevant period". This begins when two or more persons commence to carry on a trade or profession in partnership, continue as partners or join or leave the partnership, provided at least one person who is a partner before a change in the partnership remains on after the change. The relevant period ceases only in any of the following circumstances:

- The cessation of a trade.

- Where all the partners but one retire.

- Where a completely new group of partners replaces the old partners.

When the relevant period commences, the partners are assessed on the basis that they have set up new trades and each partner is assessed for tax under the commencement rules for Cases I and II. For the duration of the relevant periods, the partners are treated as continuing these separate trades and are assessed for tax accordingly.

Completing your income tax return

Under Pay and File you must file your 2012 Tax Return and pay your liabilities on or before 31 October 2013. On that date you must also pay your preliminary tax liability for 2013 and any balance of Income Tax due for 2012. It is your responsibility to calculate your own tax liabilities.

If your tax return is submitted after 31 October a surcharge (5% where the return is submitted within two months, otherwise 10%) may be added to your tax liability.

If you submit your tax return and also pay your tax liability online via Revenue Online Services (ROS), the 31 October deadline will be extended. In 2012 ROS filers had until 15 November 2012 to pay and file their tax return.

Revenue On-Line Service (ROS)

As an alternative to completing a paper tax return, you can file your return electronically through the Revenue On-Line Service (ROS).

ROS (Revenue Online Service) is an internet facility which provides customers with a quick and secure facility to file tax returns, pay tax liabilities and access their tax details, 24 hours a day, 7 days a week, 365 days a year

The main features of ROS include facilities to:

- File returns online.

- Make payments by laser card, debit instruction or by online banking.

- Obtain online details of personal/clients Revenue Accounts.

- Calculate your tax liability.

- Conduct business electronically.

- Claim repayments.

ROS will provide you with an instant calculation of your tax liability, letting you know how much to pay on 31 October.

You can access ROS through Revenue's website www.revenue.ie

What information should I submit with my tax return

You should not submit any supporting documentation with your tax return unless expressly asked to do so; for example where you have a genuine doubt about any item in the return you should make a note of this on the tax return by way of "expression of doubt" and enclose a covering letter setting out the point at issue. Supporting documentation, including business accounts, must be retained for six years as it may be requested by Revenue for the purpose of an audit.

Do not enter terms such as 'per attached', 'as before', etc on your tax return. You must enter the requested information.

Incomplete returns will be sent back to you for proper completion and you might incur a surcharge if the corrected return is submitted late.

Before submitting your return, ensure you sign and date the declaration on the front page of the return. If you are filing the return as an executor, guardian or administrator, or as an authorised agent, state the capacity in which you are signing the return and for whom you are acting.

"Incomplete returns will be sent back to you for proper completion.. .. you might incur a surcharge."

Revenue audit

A revenue audit is a cross-check of the information and figures shown by you in your tax returns against those shown in your business records

A revenue audit covers the following types of tax returns;

- Income tax, corporation tax, or capital gains tax returns and/or

- The returns submitted in respect of VAT, PAYE/PRSI, or relevant contracts tax (RCT).

How are taxpayers selected for audit?

Revenue uses three methods of selection. These are;

Screening tax returns

The vast majority of audit cases are selected in this way. Screening involves examining the returns made by a variety of taxpayers and reviewing their compliance history. The figures are then analysed in the light of trends and patterns in the particular business or professional and evaluated against other available information.

Projects on business sectors

From time to time, projects are conducted to examine tax compliance levels in particular trades or professions. The returns for a large number of taxpayers in a particular sector are screened in detail and a proportion of these are selected for audit.

Random selection

This is in addition to the first two methods. It means that all taxpayers have a possibility of being audited. Each year, a small proportion of audit cases are selected using this method.

The self-employed and PRSI

With few exceptions, all self-employed people between the ages of 16 and 66 must pay PRSI contributions on their reckonable income, if their gross income exceed €5,000 in a year. Reckonable income can be both earned and unearned and includes the following:

- Income from a trade or profession.

- Income from which tax has been deducted at source such as annuities, bank interest or building society interest and dividends.

- Irish rents and income from foreign property.

Self-employed individuals including propriety company directors pay PRSI under Class S.

PRSI is charged at 4% on all income or a minimum of €253 whichever is the greater.

Budget 2013

From 1 January 2013 the minimum annual PRSI exemption for people with annual self-employed income over €5,000 will increase to €500.

However, the following are excluded for PRSI purposes:

- Any sum received by way of benefit, pension allowance or supplement from the Department of Social Protection.

- Any sums received from FÁS for training courses.

- Any payments received by way of occupational pension, also income continuance plans payable in the event of loss of employment due to ill health where the scheme has been approved by the Revenue Commissioners.

- Redundancy payments (either statutory or non-statutory), "golden handshake" type payments and early retirement gratuities. However redundancy payments with the exception of statutory redundancy are liable to the universal social charge (USC).

- Health Board payments by way of Infectious Diseases Maintenance Allowance or Mobility Allowance.

- Payments received by a person in respect of the following offices; income related to a member of the Dáil, An Seanad or the European Parliament, the judiciary, public offices under the State such as Labour Court members, the Comptroller and Auditor General, Harbour Commissioners etc.

- Prescribed relatives i.e. certain relatives who help out a self-employed person in the running of a family business, assuming they are not partners in the business.

Paying PRSI

If you pay income tax directly to the Collector General, you also pay your PRSI contributions to the Collector General.

Class "S" benefits

Self-employed people paying Class "S" PRSI will generally be entitled to the following benefits, assuming they have paid the minimum qualifying contributions:

- State Contributory Pension.
- Widow's/Widower/Surviving Civil Partner's Contributory Pension.
- Orphan's contributory allowance.
- Maternity and Adoptive Benefits.
- Bereavement Grant.

Universal social charge (USC)

The universal social charge was introduced from the 1 January 2011. It is payable on gross income including notional pay, after relief for certain trading losses and capital allowances, but before pension contributions.

All individuals are liable to the USC if their gross income exceeds €10,036 per annum or €193 per week. The rate of USC are as follows;

USC Thresholds 2012 and 2013		
Income up to €10,036	Income from €10,036 to €16,016	Income above €16,016
2%	4%	7%

A reduced rate of USC applies for the over 70's and medical card holders which are as follows;

USC Thresholds			
2012		2013	
Individuals aged 70 years or over. Individuals who hold a full medical card (regardless of age)		Individuals aged 70 years or over whose aggregate income for the year is €60,000 or less. Individuals (aged under 70) who hold a full medical card whose aggregate income for the year is €60,000 or less.	
	Rate		Rate
Income up to €10,036	2%	Income up to €10,036	2%
Income above €10,036	4%	Income above €10,036	4%

Note1:   "Aggregate" income for USC purposes does not included payments from the Dept of Social Protection.

Note 2:   A "GP only" card is not considered a full medical card for USC purposes.

Exempt categories

- Where an individual's total income for a year does not exceed €10,036
- All Department of Social Protection payments.
- Income already subjected to DIRT.

10 Working abroad / Foreign income

Generally, your liability to Irish Income Tax on foreign income depends on:

- Whether you are resident in Ireland.
- Whether you are ordinarily resident in Ireland.
- Whether you are domiciled in Ireland.

Residence

You will be regarded as being resident here for tax purposes in the current tax year:

- If you spend 183 days or more here

  or

- If the combined number of days you spend here in the current tax year and the number of days you spent here in the last tax year exceeds 280. In applying this two year test, a period of less than 30 days spent in Ireland in a tax year will be ignored.

Your presence in Ireland for a day, means at any time during the day.

Electing to be resident

If you come to Ireland and are not regarded as resident here for tax purposes but you can show that you intend to remain and be resident here next year, you may elect to be treated as resident for tax purposes from the date of your arrival.

Electing to be non-resident

This is not possible in any circumstances.

Ordinarily resident

The term "ordinarily resident" as distinct from "resident", relates to your normal pattern of life and denotes residence in a country with some degree of continuity.

When does ordinarily residence begin?

If you have been resident here for three consecutive tax years, you become ordinarily resident from the beginning of the fourth tax year.

When does ordinarily residence cease?

If you have been ordinarily resident here, you will cease to be ordinarily resident at the end of the third consecutive year in which you are not resident. For example, if you are resident and ordinarily resident here in 2009 and leave the State in that year, you will remain ordinarily resident up to the end of the tax year 2012.

Domicile

Domicile is a complex legal concept. It is generally the country which you consider to be your natural home. When you are born, you obtain a domicile of origin which is normally the domicile of your father.

Resident & domicile

If you are resident and domiciled in Ireland you are liable to Irish income tax on your worldwide income. If you have foreign income on which you have paid foreign tax you are normally liable to Irish tax on the gross amount of this income. You may be able to claim a credit against your Irish tax liability for the foreign tax paid or to a refund or partial refund of the foreign tax and a credit for the balance, provided a Double Taxation Agreement is in place between Ireland and the foreign country.

Resident/not domiciled or ordinarily resident in Ireland.

If you are resident but not domiciled or ordinarily resident in Ireland, you are liable to Irish income tax in full on your income arising in Ireland and on your foreign employment income only if you perform the duties of this employment in Ireland. Any foreign non-employment income is only liable to Irish tax if it is remitted to Ireland.

Income arising in the UK was liable to Irish tax in full up to 31 December 2007. From 1 January 2008 it is deemed to be foreign income for the purposes of the remittance basis of tax.

Not resident but ordinarily resident and domiciled

If you are not resident but ordinarily resident and domiciled in Ireland you are liable to Irish tax on your world wide income. The only exception to this is income from a trade, profession or employment no part of which is carried out in Ireland, apart from incidental duties. If you have other foreign income it will not be taxed in Ireland provided the amount is less than €3,810.

Individual not resident and not ordinarily resident

If you are not resident and not ordinarily resident in Ireland, in general, you are liable to Irish income tax only on income arising in Ireland. In addition a non resident individual is generally not entitled to personal tax credits and relief's. They are liable to tax at the standard rate and the higher rate.

If , however, you can prove to the Revenue Commissioners that you are

- A citizen of Ireland

    or

- Resident outside of Ireland because of your health or the health of a member of your family and that before such residence outside Ireland you were resident in Ireland

    or

- Entitled under a double taxation agreement to the same personal allowances and relief's as an Irish citizen not resident in Ireland

    or

- An EU citizen

You will be entitled to that portion of the personal tax credits and relief's which would have been available to you if you were resident in Ireland that your income liable to Irish tax bears to your worldwide income including income which is not subject to Irish tax.

If you are a resident of another EU country and if at least 75% of your total income is liable to tax in Ireland then you are entitled to receive full personal tax relief's in Ireland.

Remittance basis of taxation

Prior to 1 January 2006 an individual who was resident but not domiciled in Ireland (e.g. a citizen of Germany, working in Ireland) was liable to Irish income tax in full on their income arising in Ireland and the UK but on 'foreign income' only to the extent that it was remitted to Ireland. This was known as the remittance basis of taxation.

From 1 January 2006 the remittance basis of tax no longer applies to employment income if that income relates to the performance of the duties of the employment in Ireland.

The remittance basis of tax continues to apply to "foreign" non-employment income as well as to "foreign" employment income provided the duties are exercised outside Ireland.

Employers must now deduct or account for PAYE on all remuneration which relate to the performance of the duties of the employment in Ireland.

Where only part of an employees earnings are chargeable to tax under Schedule E and the part which is not chargeable is unknown at the time, the employer can apply to Revenue for a direction as to the proportion of pay on which PAYE is to operate. In the absence of a direction, the employer must operate PAYE on the whole amount.

Temporary assignees

Revenue will not require an employer to operate PAYE on temporary employees working in Ireland from abroad, where the following conditions are met :

- The individual is resident in a country with which Ireland has a double taxation agreement and is not resident in Ireland for tax purposes for the relevant tax year;

- There is a genuine foreign office or employment;

- The individual is not paid by, or on behalf of, an employer resident in Ireland;

- The cost of the office or employment is not borne, directly or indirectly, by a permanent establishment in Ireland of the foreign employer;

  and

- The duties of that office or employment are performed in Ireland for not more than 60 working days in total in a year of assessment and, in any event, for a continuous period of not more than 60 working days.

Tax summary

Individual	Liability To Irish Income Tax
Resident and domiciled in Ireland	On worldwide income from all sources.
Resident but not domiciled or ordinarily resident in Ireland	On all Irish income and non Irish income remitted to Ireland
Ordinarily resident but not resident here in the relevant tax year.	On worldwide income. However, employment or income from an employment trade or profession which is exercised wholly abroad or income from other sources which does not exceed €3,810 will be ignored for tax purposes. Double taxation agreements may exempt some foreign income.
Not resident or ordinarily resident	Taxed on income arising from Irish sources.

Double taxation

Generally, Irish residents are liable to Irish income tax on worldwide income and non-residents are liable to Irish income tax on income arising in Ireland. As similar provisions apply to residents of other countries, this can give rise to double taxation. The purpose of double taxation agreements is to prevent this double taxation of income. This may be achieved either by:

- Exempting certain income from tax in one country,

   or

- By offsetting the tax paid on income in one country against the tax liability arising on that same income in another country.

Full personal tax credits and reliefs

- If you are a resident here, you are entitled to full personal tax credits and full tax reliefs.

- If you are not resident here but are resident in another Member State of the European Union and 75% or more of your worldwide income is taxable here, you will also be entitled to full personal tax credits and full tax reliefs here.

Partial personal tax credits and reliefs

- If you are a citizen of Ireland or a citizen, subject or national of another member state of the European Union

  or

- If you are a former resident of the State who is now resident outside of this country because of your health or because of the health of a member of your family resident with you,

  or

- If you are a resident or national of a country with which Ireland has a double taxation agreement which provides for such allowances.

If any of the above applies and you are non-resident here for tax purposes you will be entitled to a certain proportion of personal tax credits and tax reliefs. The exact proportion of these allowances is determined by the relationship between your income which is subject to Irish tax and your income from all other sources.

Example

In 2012 a single man who is an Irish citizen not resident here, had the following sources of income:

	€
Rental income in Ireland	€10,000
US Dividends	€3,000
Rental Income in UK	€4,000
Total Income	**€17,000**

As the individual is not resident here, they are liable to Irish tax only on income arising in Ireland and entitled to partial personal tax credits as follows;

	€
Irish Income	€10,000
Taxable €10,000 @ 20%	€2,000
Less: Tax Credits €1,650 x €10,000 / €17,000	€970
Net tax payable	**€1,030**

Year of arrival / return

If you return to Ireland but you are not already resident here for tax purposes and if you can show that you intend to remain here and to be resident here for tax purposes next year, you may elect to be treated as a resident here for income tax purposes from the date of your arrival and your tax position will work out as follows:

Example

You returned to Ireland on 1 September 2012 after spending three years abroad. Your earnings in Ireland from 1 September 2012 to 31 December 2012 were €18,500.

	€
Irish Income	€18,500
Tax Payable €18,500 @ 20%	€ 3,700
Less: Tax Credits	
Personal	(€1,650)
PAYE	(€1,650)
	(€3,300)
Net tax payable	€ 400

You will be liable to Irish tax on any foreign income which may accrue to you after the date of your return, subject to any relevant double taxation agreement.

Year of departure / split year treatment

If you are resident in Ireland during the tax year you leave and you will be non resident for the following tax year you will be deemed to be non resident from the date of departure. This means that your employment income will be exempt from Irish tax from that date. In order to avail of this arrangement (known as split year treatment) it is necessary that you satisfy your local tax office of your intention not to be resident in Ireland for the tax year following your departure.

Example

You leave Ireland on the 30 September 2012 to take up a two year contract in the USA. From the 1 January 2012 to the date of departure you earn €40,000 in Ireland and pay PAYE of €8,759. Your income in the USA from 1 October 2012 to 31 December 2011 will be €21,000. Your position in 2012 will be as follows:

	Split Year Treatment €
Salary - Ireland (up to Sept 2012)	€40,000
Taxable	€40,000
Tax Payable	
€ 32,800 @ 20%	€6,560
€ 7,200 @ 41%	€2,952
	€9,512
Less: Tax Credits	
Personal Credit	(€1,650)
PAYE Credit	(€1,650)
Tax Liability	€6,212
Less: PAYE Paid	(€8,759)
Refund Due	**(€2,547)**

Residence and married couples

Your spouse's resident status is not governed by your residence status. If the residence status of your spouse differs from yours, you may choose to be treated as single people for tax purposes if it is to your advantage to do so.

Right of appeal

If you disagree with your Tax Inspector's decision relating to your taxation in the year of your arrival or departure or to the special tax relief's applicable to foreign assignments, you have a right to appeal the decision to the Appeal Commissioners.

Renting while abroad

Many homeowners going abroad for a limited period will rent their homes while they are abroad. This income is taxable in Ireland regardless of residence status.

Example

You rent your home for €1,200 p.m. while you work abroad. You have a mortgage of €85,000, mortgage interest of €4,800 p.a. and outgoings (agency fees, insurance, repairs etc.) of €1,600.

		€
	Gross Rental Income	€14,400
Less:	Mortgage Interest (75%)	(€ 3,600)
	Outgoings	(€ 1,600)
	Taxable Income	**€ 9,200**

In order to claim mortgage interest relief as a rental expense it is necessary to register the tenancy with the Private Residential Tenancies Board (PRTB). From 7 April 2009 only 75% of mortgage interest paid on a loan to buy/improve or repair a rental residential property can be deducted as a rental expense against the gross rents received.

Rent paid to non-resident landlord

If you work abroad and rent your home, your tenant is obliged to deduct tax at the standard rate from the rental income and pay this tax over to the Revenue Commissioners. At the end of the year the tenant must give the landlord a completed Form R185 (available from your local tax office or on www.revenue.ie), showing the amount of tax withheld by the tenant from the gross rent paid, and confirming that this tax has been paid over to the Revenue Commissioners on behalf of the landlord. When you complete your Irish tax return, you will get credit for this tax against your liability to tax on the rent. If you have no liability you can claim a refund of the tax deducted by the tenant.

This obligation on your tenant to deduct tax from your rental income is removed if you appoint an agent resident in Ireland to look after your tax affairs here in Ireland while working abroad. The agent would then be liable as collecting agent for the landlord and must submit a tax return in relation to the rents and pay any tax due on the rent to the Collector General on behalf of the landlord.

Capital gains tax (CGT)

When you sell your main residence, it is normally exempt from CGT. However, if you have rented your main residence for a number of years, at the date of sale, the CGT exemption will be restricted on a time basis.

For CGT purposes, certain periods of absence are regarded as periods of occupation e.g.

● The last 12 months of ownership.

● Any period of absence throughout which you worked in a foreign employment or any period of absence not exceeding four years during which you were prevented from occupying the residence because of employment, provided you occupy the residence before and after the period of absence.

Example

You bought your home in January 2000 for €250,000. You rented it out from 1 January 2008 to 31 December 2011 while you worked abroad. You sold it in December 2012 for €350,000. Your CGT liability will be calculated as follows:

Period of Ownership:	
1 January 2000 - 31 December 2007	8 Years Principal Private Residence (PPR)
1 January 2008 - 31 December 2011	4 Years Rented
1 January 2012 - 31 December 2012	1 Year Deemed PPR - last 12 months of ownership
Total Period of ownership	13 years
Non Principal Private Residence	4 Years

		€
	Sale Price	€350,000
Less:	Selling Costs	(€5,000)
		€345,000
	Purchase Price Jan 2000	€250,000
	Indexation @ 1.193	€298,250
	Capital Gain	€46,750
Less:	Capital Gains Exemption	(€1,270)
	Taxable Gain	€45,480
	Tax @ 30%	**€13,644**

"If you work abroad and rent your home, your tenant is obliged to deduct tax at the standard rate from the rental income."

However, you may claim CGT exemption for the eight years while the property was your main private residence, together with the last 12 months of ownership which is deemed to be your Principal Private Residence. So, your CGT liability will be €3,934 (€46,750 x 4/13 - €1,270 @ 30%).

You could also claim total exemption from total CGT, provided you returned and lived in your former home for a period before you sold it.

Foreign earnings deduction

From the tax years 2012, 2013 and 2014, employees who carry out part of the duties of their employment in Brazil, Russia, India, China or South Africa may claim a tax deduction known as the Foreign Earnings Deduction.

Qualifying conditions

The basic condition is that, within a period of 12 months (part of which is in the tax year to which the claim relates), the employee has worked in one or more of the relevant states for a minimum period of 60 "qualifying days".

Exclusions

The Foreign Earnings Deduction does not apply to public servants nor does it apply to income -

- From an employment to which the remittance basis of taxation applies

- To which the key employee research and development tax relief applies

- To which the "split year" residence rules applies

- To which the cross border relief applies; **or**

- To which relief under the new special assignee relief programme (SARP) applies.

Budget 2013

With effect from 1 January 2013 the number of states has been extended to include Algeria, Democratic Republic of Congo, Egypt, Ghana, Nigeria, Senegal and Tanzania.

Coming to live in Ireland

If you become resident in Ireland, you will only be liable to Irish income tax from the date of your arrival, provided you were non-resident here in the previous year. Even though you will only be taxed in Ireland on income for part of the year, you will receive a full year's tax credits. If you arrive in Ireland and are not resident here for tax purposes, any income arising in Ireland will be liable to Irish tax. However, you will only receive tax credits for the portion of the year that you are actually here.

Emergency tax

If your employer does not receive either a certificate of tax credits and standard rate cut off point or a P45 for you, they will be obliged to deduct tax on an emergency basis from your salary. Under emergency tax, a temporary tax credit is given for the first month of employment. See page 138 for more details. In order to get a tax credit and standard rate cut off point certificate you must first get a Personal Public Service Number (PPS).

Obtaining a PPS number

In order to obtain a PPS number, you must present yourself at your local social welfare office together with some form of ID e.g. your passport, you will then be issued with a PPS Number. You must then complete a Form 12a which is available in any tax office. When your employer receives a tax credit and standard rate cut off point certificate for you, you will receive a refund of any tax which you may have overpaid.

You can expect to pay tax on all income, which may include:

- Gross salary.

- Bonuses and commissions.

- Cash allowances for housing, school fees, cost of living , etc.

- Benefit-In-Kind (BIK).

- Share incentives, though various rules apply depending on the scheme.

If you have earnings from other sources, such as rental income, share dividends or deposit interest, it will also be subject to tax, whether it has been earned here or abroad.

Capital gains tax (CGT)

Once you are resident here, any assets you still hold abroad but dispose of, could be subject to Irish Capital Gains Tax at a rate of 30% (33% from 6 December 2012), though this would not include your principal private residence. An annual CGT exemption of €1,270 applies in Ireland. The amount of tax you will have to pay will also be affected by whether or not you are domiciled here and how much, if any, of the gain from assets outside of Ireland is brought into Ireland.

Leaving Ireland

When you leave Ireland, providing you had been resident here for tax purposes, you will be taxed on your income up to the date of your departure, though you can offset a full years tax credits against this income. Depending on when you leave Ireland you may be entitled to a refund upon departure.

In order to claim a refund, you must complete a Form 12, and submit it to your tax office together with your P45 and details of all your tax credits, e.g. home carers allowances, service charges etc.

Relief for trans border workers

This allowance is aimed mainly at Irish residents who commute to work in Northern Ireland. However, it also applies to individuals who travel to the UK and elsewhere to work and return to Ireland at the weekends. It applies to individuals who commute daily or at weekends to work outside Ireland, to a country with which Ireland has a Double Taxation Agreement.

The relief means that such residents will not pay tax in Ireland on income from the foreign employment. Tax however, may be payable in the foreign country in which the individual is working.

To claim this relief you must comply with the following conditions;

- The work must be outside the State in a country with which Ireland has a double tax treaty.

- Employment must be held for a continuous period of 13 weeks.

- The duties of the employment must be performed wholly outside the State.

- The income must be taxed in the other country.

- The employee must be at least one day per week in the State.

- The employment must not be with the Government or an authority set up by the State.

UK double taxation agreement

The double taxation agreement between Ireland and the UK covers income tax, corporation profits tax, corporation tax, capital gains tax.

The purpose of double taxation agreements is to prevent the same income from being taxed twice. This is achieved either:

- By exempting the income from tax in one of the countries; **or**

- By setting off the tax payable on the income in one country against the tax payable on the same income in the other country.

"The purpose of the double taxation agreement ... is to prevent the same income being taxed twice"

Rental income

Rents may be taxed both in the country in which the property is situated and in the country of residence of the individual in receipt of the rent. A credit is given against the tax payable in the country of residence, for the tax paid in the other country.

Dividends

Dividends are taxed both in the country in which the recipient individual is resident and in the country of payment i.e. the country in which the company paying the dividend is resident. An Irish resident individual in receipt of UK dividends is taxed on the amount of the net dividend received. They do not receive any tax credit for any tax, which may have been deducted from the UK company paying the dividend.

Interest

Interest received is, in general, liable to tax only in the country of residence. Any tax deducted in the country of payment can be recovered in full.

Salaries, wages, directors fees and other similar remuneration derived by or received by a resident individual of one country from an employment exercised in the other country may be taxable in both countries. A credit is given against the tax payable in the country of residence for the tax payable in the other country.

Pensions

A pension (other than a governmental pension to which the provisions of Article 18 apply see below) or an annuity paid in one country to an individual resident in the other country in consideration of past employment is taxable only in the country of residence under the Agreement.

Income from governmental functions

Remuneration paid by a government or a local authority of one country to an individual resident in the other country in respect of services rendered in the discharge of governmental functions will be taxable only in the country of payment unless the individual is a citizen of the country of residence or did not become resident of the other country solely for the purpose of rendering the service.

For example, a UK citizen resident in Ireland who receives a pension from the UK Government is liable only to UK tax on the pension.

Payments to students

Payments to students or business apprentices who are resident in one country, but who are present in the other country solely for the purpose of education or training, will not be taxable in that other country provided that the payments:

- Are made for the purpose of maintenance, education or training;

  and

- Are made from sources outside that other country.

U.K. tax rates

	2010/11	2011/12	2012/13
Starting rate for savings: 10%*	£0 -£2,440	£0 - £2,560	£0 - £2,710
Basic rate: 20%	£0-£37,400	£0 - £35,000	£0 - £34,370
Higher rate: 40%	£37,400 - £150,000	£35,001 - £150,000	£34,371 - £150,000
Additional rate : 50%	Over £150,000	Over £150,000	Over £150,000

* The 10% starting rate applies to savings income only. If, after deducting your Personal Allowance from your total income liable to Income Tax, your non-savings income is above this limit then the 10% starting rate for savings will not apply. Non-savings income includes income from employment, profits from self-employment, pensions, income from property and taxable benefits.

UK-personal income tax summary tax allowances

	2010/11	2011/12	2012/13
	Stg. £	Stg. £	Stg. £
Personal Allowance			
Under 65	£6,475	£7,475	£8,105
Income limit for personal allowances	£100,000	£100,000	£100,000
65 to 74 Note 1 & 2	£9,490	£9,940	£10,500
75 and over Note 1 & 2	£9,640	£10,090	£10,660
*Married couple's allowance - Note 1 minimum amount	£2,670	£2,800	£2,960
75 and over Note 2 & 3	£6,965	£7,295	£7,705
Blind person's allowance	£1,890	£1,980	£2,100
Income limit for age-related allowances	£22,900	£24,000	£25,400

Note 1   From the 2010-11 tax year the personal allowance is reduced where the income is above £100,000 by £1 for every £2 of income above the £100,000 limit. This reduction applies irrespective of age.

Note 2   These allowances reduce where the income is above the income limit for age-related allowances by £1 for every £2 of income above the limit. For the 2010-11 tax year the Personal Allowance for people aged 65 to 74 and 75 and over can be reduced below the basic Personal Allowance where the income is above £100,000.

Note 3   Tax relief for the married couples allowances is given at the rate of 10%.

Average rates of exchange between Ireland and the U.K.

Tax year ending	€
31/12/11	Stg. £0.86788

11 Capital gains tax

Capital Gains Tax (CGT) is a tax on gains arising from the disposal of capital assets.

Persons chargeable

All persons resident in the State for tax purposes are liable to Capital Gains Tax (CGT). Individuals who are resident and domiciled in Ireland are chargeable on all gains wherever arising, while those who are resident and non-domiciled are liable in respect of all Irish gains and other gains to the extent that the gains are remitted to Ireland.

Non-Irish residents are liable only in respect of gains made on the disposal of assets related to Irish property, or mining/exploration rights.

Chargeable assets

All forms of property are assets for CGT purposes including options, debts and foreign currencies, except those specifically exempted.

Disposal

A disposal for CGT takes place whenever the ownership of an asset changes. This includes a part-disposal and also even where no payment is received e.g. a gift or exchange. An exception to this latter rule is on death. In the case of death, no chargeable disposal takes place and the person who receives the asset is treated as acquiring it at the market value at the date of the death.

Married couples

Transfers between spouses do not give rise to a CGT charge - the spouse who received the asset is deemed to have acquired it on the date and at the cost at which the other spouse acquired it.

Capital gains tax rates

For disposal made on or after 7 December 2011 a rate of 30% applies to most chargeable gains including gains from the sale of development land.

The due dates for payment of CGT are as follows;

- For disposals occurring between 1 January - 30 November , CGT is due to be paid by 15 December in the same year.

"Transfers between spouses do not give rise to a CGT charge."

- For disposals occurring in December, the payment date will be the following 31 January.

Budget 2013

For disposals made after 5 December 2012 the CGT rate is increased to 33%

Exemptions and reliefs

Annual allowance

The first €1,270 of chargeable gains arising to an individual in each tax year is exempt. This is an individual allowance and is not transferable between spouses.

Principal private residence (PPR)

No CGT arises on the disposal of your main residence and grounds of up to one acre, provided it has been occupied by you throughout the entire period of ownership. You are still deemed to occupy the residence where you are absent for any period of employment abroad or during absence of less than four years imposed by conditions of your employment, provided you live in the house before and after the period(s) spent abroad. If your house was not your principal private residence for the entire period of ownership e.g. if you rented the house for a period, any gain arising on the sale of the house will be apportioned between the period when it was your principal private residence (PPR) and the period when it was not. The gain when it was your PPR is exempt and the balance of the gain is liable to CGT.

Tangible moveable assets

A gain arising to an individual on the disposal of tangible moveable assets is exempt if the total consideration received does not exceed €2,540.

Life assurance policies/deferred annuities

Disposals of these contracts are exempt from CGT in the hands of the original beneficial owner. A chargeable gain can arise on the disposal of such contracts by a person who is not the original beneficial owner if they acquire them for a consideration of money or money's worth. A rate of 40% applies on disposal of certain foreign life assurance annuitised offshore funds.

Irish government securities

Exempt.

Site from parent to child

The transfer of a site from a parent to a child is exempt from CGT, provided it is for the construction of the child's principal private residence, the market value of the site does not exceed €500,000, and it is less than one acre in size. A parent can transfer one site to each child for the purpose of this exemption.

However, if the child subsequently disposes of the site without having occupied a principal private residence on the site for at least three years, then the capital gains which would have accrued to the parent on the initial transfer will accrue to the child. However, the gain will not accrue to the child where they transfer an interest in the site to his or her spouse.

Retirement relief - Disposal of business or farm or shares in a family company.

Where an individual aged over 55, having owned a farm or business for more than 10 years, disposes of a farm or business for a consideration of less than €750,000, the disposal is ignored for CGT. Where the proceeds exceed €750,000 the CGT arising is restricted to the lower of, half of the difference between the proceeds and €750,000, or the CGT as computed in the normal way.

"A parent can transfer one site to each child for the purpose of this CGT exemption"

From 1 January 2014 the consideration limited of €750,000 is reduced to £500,000 for individuals aged 66 or over. The limit of €750,000 will continue to apply for individuals aged between 55 and 65.

Disposals within the family of business or farm or shares in family company

Complete exemptions can be claimed by an individual meeting the above conditions if they dispose of their farm/business to their child (or nephew/niece working in the business). However, this exemption is lost if the recipient disposes of the farm/business within six years.

From 1 January 2014 a market value ceiling of €3 million will apply for individuals aged 66 and over.   A charge to CGT will arise to the extent that the market value of the assets disposed of exceeds €3 million.

Budget 2013 - Relief from Farm Restructuring

To enable farm restructuring, relief will be available where the proceeds of a sale of farm land are reinvested for the same purpose.

This relief will apply for the period from 1 January 2013 to 31 December 2015. This will be a once-off relief and will be subject to EU State Aid approval.

Disposal on emigration

Irish non-residents normally pay Irish CGT on disposals relating to Irish property or mineral/exploration rights only, known as "specified assets".

So, if you are emigrating and wish to dispose of "non-specified assets" before you become non-resident any chargeable gain on such disposals e.g. shares in a company will be liable to Irish CGT.

Capital Gains Tax on such disposals may be reduced if the disposal takes place after you become non-resident for Irish tax purposes. It is also important to note that the date of disposal for CGT purposes is the date of contract.

Relief for properties bought between 7 December 2011 and 31 December 2013

Relief from Capital Gains Tax is available for certain properties bought between 7 December 2011 and the end of 2013, where the property is held for more than seven years. The relief means that any gain accruing in the seven year period will not attract CGT. The relief applies to land and buildings situated in all EU member states including Ireland, Norway, Iceland and Lichtenstein.

Computation of gains and losses

Basically, this is done by deducting from the proceeds received, the cost of the disposed asset less any allowable expenses incurred on the acquisition or disposal of the asset.

Indexation relief

When you sell an asset, the original cost and enhancement expenditure may be increased by indexation before any CGT liability is calculated.

Where an asset is acquired prior to 6 April 1974, the "cost" to be indexed is the market value at 6 April 1974, rather than the original cost. Indexation relief does not apply to Development Land.

Indexation relief only applies for the period of ownership up to 31 December 2002.

Windfall tax

For disposals made on or after 30 October 2009, CGT at a rate of 80% applies to the element of a gain which is attributable to the increase in the market value of land from rezoning.

Computation of liability on sale of investment property

In November 2012, a married couple sold a house for €400,000. Sales costs amounted to €25,000. They had bought the house in August 1975 for €32,000. The couple had added an extension costing €20,000 to the house in March 1992.

The house was not their principal residence and they had no other chargeable gains in the tax year 2012.

Capital Gains Tax Computation 2012

		€	€
	Sales Price		€400,000
Less:	Selling Costs		€25,000
			€375,000
Deduct:	Cost in August 1975 adjusted for inflation: i.e. €32,000 x 6.080	€194,560	
	1991/92 Expenditure, adjusted for inflation: i.e. €20,000 x 1.406	€28,120	€222,680
	Capital Gain		€152,320
Less:	Exemption (House in Joint Name)		€2,540
	Taxable @ 30%		€149,780
	Tax Payable	**€44,934**	

Note: The Capital Gains Tax of €44,934 will be payable on 15 December 2012.

Capital gains tax indexation factors

Year of purchase	Year of Disposal					
	98/99	99/00	00/01	2001	2002	2003 et seq
1974/75	6.215	6.313	6.582	6.930	7.180	7.528
1975/76	5.020	5.099	5.316	5.597	5.799	6.080
1976/77	4.325	4.393	4.580	4.822	4.996	5.238
1977/78	3.707	3.766	3.926	4.133	4.283	4.490
1978/79	3.425	3.479	3.627	3.819	3.956	4.148
1979/80	3.090	3.139	3.272	3.445	3.570	3.742
1980/81	2.675	2.718	2.833	2.983	3.091	3.240
1981/82	2.211	2.246	2.342	2.465	2.554	2.678
1982/83	1.860	1.890	1.970	2.074	2.149	2.253
1983/84	1.654	1.680	1.752	1.844	1.911	2.003
1984/85	1.502	1.525	1.590	1.674	1.735	1.819
1985/86	1.414	1.436	1.497	1.577	1.633	1.713
1986/87	1.352	1.373	1.432	1.507	1.562	1.637
1987/88	1.307	1.328	1.384	1.457	1.510	1.583
1988/89	1.282	1.303	1.358	1.430	1.481	1.553
1989/90	1.241	1.261	1.314	1.384	1.434	1.503
1990/91	1.191	1.210	1.261	1.328	1.376	1.442
1991/92	1.161	1.179	1.229	1.294	1.341	1.406
1992/93	1.120	1.138	1.186	1.249	1.294	1.356
1993/94	1.099	1.177	1.164	1.226	1.270	1.331
1994/95	1.081	1.098	1.144	1.205	1.248	1.309
1995/96	1.54	1.071	1.116	1.175	1.218	1.277
1996/97	1.033	1.050	1.094	1.152	1.194	1.251
1997/98	1.017	1.033	1.077	1.134	1.175	1.232
1998/99	-	1.016	1.059	1.115	1.156	1.212
1999/00	-	-	1.043	1.098	1.138	1.193
2000/01	-	-	-	1.053	1.091	1.144
2001	-	-	-	-	1.037	1.087
2002	-	-	-	-	-	1.049
2003 et seq	-	-	-	-	-	-

Note: The indexation rates have remained the same since 2003

Frequently asked questions

1   If I sell my house will I have to pay Capital Gains Tax?

No, if the house (including grounds of up to one acre) has been occupied as your sole or main residence throughout your period of ownership you will be exempt from capital gains tax on the sale.

2   What happens if my property has "development value"?

Where your property has development value i.e. if it is sold for a price higher than its normal current use value then the relief from capital gains tax as outlined above is confined to what it would be if the property did not have development value.

3   What happens when I sell foreign assets?

If you are resident or ordinarily resident, and domiciled in the State you are liable to CGT on worldwide gains.   Therefore, if you dispose of a foreign asset, for example a property in another country or shares in a foreign company, Irish CGT will apply. Where foreign capital gains tax is paid a credit may be available against your Irish CGT for some, or all, of that amount.

4   If I sell part of my garden to a builder, who builds a house on it, am I liable to pay capital gains tax?

Yes. Normally when an individual disposes of their principal private residence and a garden or grounds of up to one acre (excluding the site of the house), then any gain on such a disposal is exempt from capital gains tax. However, where a dwelling house or garden/part of a garden, is sold for greater than its current use value, then this constitutes the sale of development land and principal private residence relief will apply only to the current use value. In general terms the difference between the consideration and the current use value is liable to capital gains tax. Development Land rules do not apply to disposals where the total consideration from such disposals does not exceed €19,050.

5   What happens if I dispose of an investment property?

You will be liable to CGT on any gain you make. In circumstances where the disposal proceeds are less than market value, the market value is used to calculate any gain arising. The gain you make (ignoring indexation and purchase and sale costs) is simply the difference between the purchase price and the sale price.

6   I have an investment property and intend gifting it to my children,
        is this gift liable to CGT?

Disposals also includes a gift and CGT may be payable on a gift.
The market value at the date of the gift is used as the "deemed"
sale proceeds and CGT is then calculated in the normal manner.

7   If I transfer an asset to my spouse do I have to pay CGT?

No, the asset is transferred as if no gain/no loss occurred on the
transfer. The benefiting spouse inherits the base cost and period
of ownership from the spouse making the disposal. In the event
that the benefiting spouse subsequently disposes of the asset the
original base cost and period of ownership is used to calculate any
gain arising. (Transfers between spouses are taxable, if the
benefiting spouse is non-resident in the year the transfer takes
place).

8   Can I offset CGT losses against other income?

CGT losses can only be offset against any other CGT gains which
occur in the same year as the CGT loss, or they can be carried
forward and used against any future capital gain.

9   If I sell an asset that is liable to CGT in July, do I have to pay the
        tax due by 31 October (the pay and file tax deadline)?

If you sell an asset between January and November, you must pay
any CGT liability by 15 December of that year. If you sell an asset
in December the CGT liability must be paid by 31 January of the
following year. i.e. if you sell the item in July 2012 the CGT must
be paid by 15 December 2012.

12 Social welfare benefits

Pay-related social insurance

The main PRSI legislation comprises the Social Welfare (Consolidation) Act, 1993, together with subsequent amendments. The subject is a wide one, and here we outline:

- How much you pay.
- Your benefit entitlements.

Contribution years

The contribution year for PRSI purposes is the same as the tax year. Contribution years are normally referred to as tax years.

Benefit years

The benefit year begins on the first Monday in January each year. Your entitlement to short-term PRSI benefits is normally based on your paid and/or credited contributions in the relevant tax year, which is the second last complete tax year before the benefit year in which you claim.

Example

If you cease to pay PRSI contributions, your entitlement to benefits will normally last for the remainder of that calendar year and the following calendar year.

For a claim made in	The relevant tax year is
2012	2010
2013	2011

PRSI contributions are calculated as a percentage of your gross pay, less any payments to a permanent health benefit scheme which are deducted at source by the employer and approved by the Revenue Commissioners. PRSI contribution costs are normally shared by the employee and employer. For the majority of employees, PRSI contributions are collected through the PAYE tax system.

The following charts show how the Class A1 rate, which is the PRSI Class most employees pay, is calculated in the 2012 and 2013 tax year.

Class A

This class covers employees under the age of 66 in industrial, commercial & service type employment who have reckonable pay of €38 or more per week, for all employments as well as public servants recruited after 5 April 1995.

Class A1	2012	2013
Rate of PRSI	4%	4%

Notes: Employees who earn of €352 or less per week are exempt from PRSI.

Employer

Employee income	2012	2013
Not exceeding €356 per week	4.25%	4.25%
Exceeding €356 per week	10.75%	10.75%

Self Employed

From 1 January 2013, employees who pay PRSI at Classes B, C and D will be liable to PRSI @ 4% in respect of self-employed earned income (from a profession or trade) and any other unearned income e.g. rental income.

	Income	Rate	Minimum contribution	Exemption threshold
2012	All	4%	€253	€5,000 p.a.
2013	All	4%	€500	€5,000 p.a.

Claiming social insurance benefits

Normally, to claim a social insurance benefit it is necessary to have a minimum number of PRSI contributions. PRSI contributions are normally classified as either PRSI paid or PRSI credited.

PRSI contributions are payable each week you are working in insurable employment. There is no charge for PRSI credits, but for many benefits they can be as valuable as PRSI contributions paid.

First PRSI paid

When you become insured for the first time under the Social Welfare Acts you are automatically given PRSI credits for the earlier part of that tax year, in addition to credits for the previous two tax years. For example, if you commenced employment for the first time on the 5 of October you would be entitled to credits from the 1 January to the 4 of October plus the two previous tax years. These credits can help you qualify for Illness and Jobseekers Benefit as soon as you have worked and paid PRSI contributions for 52 weeks.

Credits after you have become insured

If you stop paying PRSI contributions, PRSI credits are normally awarded for the weeks you receive Illness Benefit, Jobseekers Benefit, Maternity Benefit, Adoptive Benefit, Health & Safety Benefit, Carer's Benefit, Invalidity Pension, State Pension Transition or Injury Benefit. Similarly, credits may be awarded for the weeks in which you received Jobseekers Assistance or Carer's Allowance, if you are eligible for credits. If you have never worked, you would not get credits with Jobseekers Assistance.

A break in PRSI

If two consecutive tax years have elapsed without contributions having been paid or credited, no additional PRSI credits can be awarded until a further 26 PRSI contributions have been paid.

Voluntary contributions

A person who ceases to be insured under Pay-Related Social Insurance can, if under 66 years of age, opt to continue insurance on a voluntary basis for limited benefits, provided 260 PRSI contributions have been paid, and you apply within 12 months of the end of the tax year during which you had paid PRSI or had a PRSI credit.

There are three rates of voluntary contributions and the rate you pay is determined by the last rate of PRSI contribution which you paid.

● The high rate of 6%, subject to a minimum payment of €317 applies if you were compulsorily insured at the PRSI class A, E or H. Voluntary contributions at this rate normally provide pension benefits and a Bereavement Grant.

● The reduced rate of 2.6%, subject to a minimum payment of €126, applies to certain Public Servants insured at the lower rates of PRSI. Voluntary contributions at this level normally provide for Widow(er)/surviving civil partner's contributory pension and Orphan's Contributory Allowance and a Bereavement Grant.

● A flat rate voluntary contribution applies to self-employed people insured at Class S who cease self-employment or who are no longer obliged to pay Class S because their income falls below the insurable limit which is currently €5,000. This gives cover for State Contributory Pension, Widow(er)/surviving civil partner's Contributory Pension, Orphan's Contributory Allowance and Bereavement Grant.

Remember, Social Insurance contributions are not a tax but their effect is very similar as you pay contributions out of your gross income. However, it should also be pointed out that benefits are not means-tested and you are entitled to them as a right once you satisfy the necessary contribution conditions.

PRSI benefit entitlements

Summarised on page 210 are:

The main benefit entitlements applicable to the relevant PRSI Classes.

● The page reference to where you will find the necessary back-up information in this guide.

PRSI classes and benefit entitlements	A	B	C	D	E	H	J	M	P	S	See Page
Adoptive benefit	*	-	-	-	*	*	-	-	-	*	227
Bereavement grant	*	*	*	*	*	*	-	-	-	*	239
Carer's benefit	*	*	*	*	*	*	-	-	-	-	235
Family income supplement	*	*	-	*	*	*	-	*	-	-	228
Illness benefit	*	-	-	-	*	*	-	-	*	-	236
Health & safety benefit	*	-	-	-	*	*	-	-	-	-	230
Invalidity benefit	*	-	-	-	*	*	-	*	*	-	224
Jobseekers benefit	*	-	-	-	-	*	-	-	*	-	230
Maternity benefit	*	-	-	-	*	*	-	*	*	*	225
Occupational injuries benefit	*	*	-	*	-	-	*	*	-	-	237
State pension contributory	*	-	-	-	*	*	-	-	-	*	215
Guardian's contributory allowance	*	*	*	*	*	*	-	-	-	*	223
State pension transition	*	-	-	-	*	*	-	-	-	-	212
Treatment benefit -	*	-	-	-	*	*	-	-	*	-	225
Widow(er)/surviving civil partner's contributory benefit	*	*	*	*	*	*	-	-	-	*	220
Working in the EU Jobseekers benefit, health services	*	-	-	-	-	*	-	-	-	-	241

Social welfare pension

Social welfare pensions fall under two main categories;

● Contributory pensions.

● Non-contributory pensions.

Contributory pension

Your entitlement to a contributory pension is based on the amount and contribution class of PRSI you have paid during your working life.

Any other income you have, will not affect your entitlement to a Contributory Pension.

Non-contributory pension

If you don't qualify for a contributory pension you may be entitled to a non-contributory pension. However, the pension age of 66 will increase to 68 (see page 216 for more details). Any income or assets you have, may affect your entitlement to a non-contributory pension.

State pension transition

A State Pension Transition is paid if you are insured for PRSI under classes A, E or H. To qualify for a State Pension Transition you must:

● Be aged 65 or over.

● Be retired from insurable employment.

● Satisfy the PRSI and retirement conditions.

The State Pension (Transition) will no longer be paid from 1 January 2014. This means that from this date there will be a standard pension age of 66 for everyone. However this will change depending on your age (see page 218 for more details). If you have qualified for the State Pension Transition before 1 January 2014 you remain entitled to it for the duration of your claim (1 year).

Contributory conditions

The PRSI contribution conditions which must be met in order to qualify for a State Pension Transition are:

- You must have started paying contributions before you were 55 years of age. **and**

- You must have a certain amount of paid contributions

  - At least 260 if you reach age 65 before 5 April 2012

  - At least 520 if you reach age 65 on or after 6 April 2012, of which at least 260 must be full-rate employment contributions. **and**

- A yearly average of at least 48 full rate contributions paid and/or credited from 1979 to the end of the tax year before you reach age 65 - this will entitle you to a maximum pension. **or**

- For a minimum pension, you must have a yearly average of at least 24 weeks PRSI paid or credited from the year you first become insured. For a maximum pension, a yearly average of 48 weeks PRSI paid or credited from 6 April 1979 to the end of the tax year before you reach pension age.

"At 65 you must 'retire' from work to qualify for State pension transition."

If you were insured in another member state of the EU, as well as in the Republic of Ireland, your full insurance record will be taken into account when deciding whether or not you are eligible for a State Pension Transition. Periods of insurance in countries with which Ireland has a bilateral social security agreement may also be used to help you qualify for a State Pension Transition.

Periods of insurable employment can be combined to ascertain if you would be entitled to a retirement pension from each country.

The age condition for pensions will be changing from 31 December 2013. See page 218 for more details.

Retirement condition

The retirement condition stipulates that at the age of 65 you must not enter into employment which is insurable under the Social Welfare Acts other than class J. This PRSI class applies to people employed under a contract of service whose reckonable earnings are less than €38 per week, or €5,000 per year if self-employed. At the age of 66 you are once more free to take up any employment you choose. Basically, you must actually retire from full-time work at the age of 65 in order to qualify for a State Pension Transition.

State pension transition elements

A State Pension Transition is payable in three distinct elements:

- A personal amount.
- An increase for a qualified adult.
- An increase for each dependent child.

If you qualify for a weekly social welfare payment, you will normally get extra amounts for a qualified adult and child dependents. A qualified adult is usually a spouse but can be the person you are cohabiting with. Your spouse/partner is regarded as your dependent provided they are not getting a social welfare payment in their own right or have income of less than €100 per week and are not on a full-time FÁS non-craft training course. A spouse/partner can have income of up to €310 per week and still be regarded as partially dependent.

If you are entitled to an increase for a dependent spouse/partner and have dependent children you can claim the full rate for a dependent child. If you do not qualify for a payment for a qualified adult you are entitled to half rate for a dependent child.

The following are the maximum rates;

State pension transition / State contributory pension maximum weekly rates	From Jan. 2012 €	From Jan. 2013 €
Maximum rate (under 80)		
Personal Rate	€230.30	€230.30
Person with qualified adult under 66	€383.80	€383.80
Person with qualified adult 66 or over	€436.60	€436.60
Maximum personal rate (over 80)		
Personal Rate	€240.30	€240.30
Person with qualified adult under 66	€393.80	€393.80
Person with qualified adult 66 or over	€446.60	€446.60
Increase per child - Full Rate	€29.80	€29.80
Increase per child - Half Rate	€14.90	€14.90
Living Alone Allowance for people age 66 or over	€7.70	€7.70

From 5 July 2012 you can no longer claim an increase for a qualified child with your state pension (transition) if your spouse/civil partner/ or co-habitant has an income of over €400 per week.

State contributory pension

The State Contributory Pension is payable to insured people from the age of 66. Unlike the State Transition Pension, it is paid to you even if you are still working. It is payable in respect of PRSI class A, E, H and S.

The three main conditions which must be met in order to qualify for the State Contributory Pension are:

- You must have become insured before the age of 56

- You must paid at least 260 full - rate employment contributions (see changes from 6 April 2012, below)

  and

- You must have paid a yearly average of at least 48 paid or credited full-rate contributions from 1979 to the end of the tax year before you reach age 66,

  or

- a yearly average of at least 10 full-rate paid or credited contributions from 1953 (or the time you started insurable employment, if later) to the end of the tax year before you reach age 66.

Note: A yearly average of 10 full-rate contributions will give you the minimum State Contributory Pension. For a maximum pension, you need an average of 48 full rate contributions.

Changes from 6 April 2012

If you reach pension age on or after 6 April 2012

- You must have paid at least 520 full rate employment contributions,

  or

- You can make up the balance of the required 520 with high rate Voluntary contributions provided you have paid at least 260 full rate employment contributions.

"State contributory pension is paid to you even if you are still working."

State non - contributory pension

If you don't qualify for a State Contributory Pension you may qualify for a State non-contributory pension. To claim a State non-contributory pension you must:

● Be aged 66 or over.

● Be living in the State.

● Satisfy a means test.

The following are the maximum rates.

State non-contributory pension/blind pension maximum weekly rates	From Jan. 2012 €	From Jan. 2013 €
Under 80		
Personal rate	€219.00	€219.00
Person with qualified adult under 66	€363.70	€363.70
Aged 80 or over		
Personal Rate	€229.00	€229.00
Person with qualified adult over 66	€373.70	€373.70
Increase per child dependent - Full Rate	€29.80	€29.80
Increase per child dependent - Half Rate	€14.90	€14.90
Living alone allowance	€7.70	€7.70
Blind pension under 66	€188.00	€188.00
Increase for a qualified adult dependent	€124.80	€124.80

Means test

When you make a claim for a non-contributory pension, a Social Welfare Inspector will normally investigate your entitlement to this pension in your own home and attempt to establish your weekly means.

In assessing your means, a Social Welfare Inspector will take account of;

● Cash income.

● The value of any property personally used by you, such as a farm or shop. Your home is excluded unless you are getting an income from it.   Rental income received from a person living with the pensioner is not counted, provided the pensioner is living alone except for that person.

- The value of any investments or capital held.

- The means of your spouse or other person cohabiting with you as husband and wife.

- Income from employment or self employment.   A disregard of earnings from employment (but not self employment) of €200 per week applies to both you and your spouse or partner where applicable.

The formula for assessing the means from capital for all social welfare payments (except Disability Allowance and Supplementary Welfare Allowance) is as follows:

Capital	Weekly means assessed
First €20,000	Nil
Next €10,000	€1 per €1,000
Next €10,000	€2 per €1,000
Balance	€4 per €1,000

From January 2012 for new and existing claimants, income from employment as a home help funded by the HSE will be assessed in means test for social assistance schemes.

State pension (non-contributory), blind pension and carer's allowance

If you are one of a couple and apply for state pension (non-contributory), blind pension or carer's allowance your combined capital is halved and this lower amount is assessed using the relevant formula (see 'rules' above). After you apply the relevant formula the resulting amount is then doubled to get your means from capital.

National Pension Framework proposed changes to pension age

Date	State Pension age	Date of birth of those reaching state pension age	Age in 2010
Present to December 2013	65 (State Pension Transition)		1945 to 1948
January 2014	66		
2014	66	1948 **but** people reaching state pension age during 2014 may have already qualified for State Pension (Transition) at age 65 in 2013	62
January 2015 to December 2020	66		1949 to 1954
January 2021	67		56 to 61
2021	67	No one will reach pension age in 2021 as anyone turning 67 during that year will have already qualified for State Pension at age 66 in 2020	
January 2022 to December 2027	67		1955 to 1960
January 2028	68		50 to 55
2028	68	No one will reach pension age in 2021 as anyone turning 68 during that year will have already qualified for State Pension at age 67 in 2027	
January 2029 onwards	68		49 or younger

Extra benefits - household benefits package

If you are aged 66 or over and you qualify for a full or reduced pension or you satisfy a means test, you may be entitled to free electricity/natural gas allowance, television licence, telephone rental allowance under the household benefits package scheme, subject to the qualifying conditions. All people aged 70 or over qualify regardless of income or who lives with them. Recipients of certain other payments e.g. Invalidity Pension, Carer's Allowance may qualify regardless of their age. You must be residing permanently, on an all year round basis at that address and no other person in the household can be in receipt of the allowances. The accounts must be in your name. The means tested fuel scheme is not part of the household benefits package.

The telephone allowance is available to people aged over 70 who reside in nursing homes, where they have their own telephone accounts.

Free schemes are available to pensioners under the age of 70 who are in receipt of a qualifying payment & whose spouse/partner is getting a Social Welfare payment in their own right and the total income of the spouse/partner satisfies a means test.

"You may be entitled to free electricity/ natural gas, television licence ..."

National pensions framework

The National Pensions Framework was published in March 2010. This framework sets out the Governments intention for radical and wide scale reform of the Irish pension system. A summary of the reforms to social welfare pensions put forward in this framework are as follows;

- Introduction of a 'total contributions' approach for those reaching state pension age from 2020 thereby replacing the current averaging system;

- Apply credits rather than disregards to homemakers and backdate these to 1994 for new pensioners from 2012;

- Introduce a standard age of 66 for the State Pension from 2014 and abolish the State Pension (Transition) thereby removing the retirement condition;

- Gradually increase state pension age to 68 by 2028; **and**

- Arrangements will be put in place to allow people to postpone receiving the state pension beyond pension age and to make up contribution shortfalls.

In relation to legacy issues in pension coverage, pension reform will focus only on future arrangements.

Widow(er)'s/surviving civil partner contributory pension

The Widow(er)'s/surviving civil partner contributory pension is payable on the death of a spouse provided:

- You are widowed/surviving civil partner.

- You are divorced from your late spouse and have not remarried

- You are not cohabiting,   **and**

- You satisfy the PRSI contribution conditions, **or**

- Your late spouse/partner was getting a state transition pension or a state contributory pension which included an increase for you or would have but for the fact that you were getting a carer's Allowance, state non-contributory pension or blind person's pension in your own right.

The PRSI conditions may be based on either your own or your late spouse's PRSI record. However, the two PRSI records cannot be combined. Whichever PRSI record is used must have;

- At least 156 weeks PRSI paid to the date pension age was reached or to the date your spouse died, if earlier,   **and**

- Either an average of 39 weeks PRSI paid or credited over the three or five tax years whichever is more beneficial before reaching pension age (66 years) or before your spouse died, if earlier for a maximum pension, **or**

- For a minimum pension, a yearly average of at least 24 weeks PRSI paid or credited is needed since starting work up to the end of the tax year before reaching pension age (66 years) or the date your spouse dies, if earlier. For a maximum pension, a yearly average of 48 weeks PRSI paid or credited is needed.

With the exception of class J, K, M and P almost all PRSI contributions, including self-employed, civil servants and public sector workers, are included for the contributory widow(er)/surviving civil partner's pension and contributory orphan's allowance. Your entitlement to the contributory widow(er)/surviving civil partner's pension is not affected by any other income you may have.

The total number of paid PRSI contributions needed to qualify for widow(er)/surviving civil partner's pension will increase from 156 to 520 contributions with effect from July 2013.

Island allowance

This is an additional allowance of €12.70 per week for social welfare pensioners aged 66 or over who are living on certain offshore islands. It is also payable to recipients of certain disability payments e.g. Invalidity/Blind pension, Illness Allowance, Injury Benefit, Constant Attendance allowance who are aged under 66.

Widow(er)'s/surviving civil partner contributory pension

The following are the maximum rates of contributory and non-contributory pensions:

Widow(er)'s/surviving civil partner contributory pension maximum weekly rates	From Jan. 2012 €	From Jan. 2013 €
Maximum personal rate - under 66	€193.50	€193.50
Maximum personal rate - aged 66 - 79	€230.30	€230.30
Maximum personal rate - aged 80 or over	€240.30	€240.30
Child dependent	€29.80	€29.80
Living alone allowance	€7.70	€7.70

Widow(er)'s/surviving civil partner non - contributory pension

If you are a widow(er)/surviving civil partner and have no dependent children, you may be entitled to claim a non-contributory widow(er)'s pension on the death of your spouse, provided you are not already entitled to a contributory widow(er)'/civil partner's pension and can satisfy the means test.

Widow(er)'s/surviving civil partner non-contributory pension maximum weekly rates	From Jan. 2012 €	From Jan. 2013 €
Maximum personal rate - under 66	€188	€188

One-parent family payments

The One-Parent Family Payment is a payment for both men and women who, for a variety of reasons, are bringing up a child without the support of a partner.

A person who is unmarried, widowed, a prisoner's spouse, separated, divorced or whose marriage has been annulled and who is no longer living with their spouse, is eligible to apply for this payment.

If you are getting the One Parent Family Payment you can earn up to €130 p.w. and still qualify for full payment.

The upper age limit of the youngest child for new claimants of the one-parent family payment will be reduced to 7 years on a phased basis as shown below.

Date of Application	2012	2013	2014	2015	2016	2017
Pre 27 April 2011	U-18	U-17	U-16	U-7	U-7	U-7
27 April 2011 to 2 May 2012	U-14	U-12	U-10	U-7	U-7	U-7
Post 3 May 2012	U-12	U-10	U-7	U-7	U-7	U-7

Guardian's contributory allowance

Where both parents have died, or one parent has died and the other has abandoned the child, this allowance is payable, provided that the PRSI contribution conditions are met. These require that at least 26 weekly contributions have been paid at any time by the orphan's parent or stepparent, at the appropriate rate.

The PRSI contribution classes which cover the Contributory Guardian's Allowance are the same as those for the Contributory Widow(er)'s Pension. The allowance is payable up to the age of 18, or 22 if the orphan is in full-time education. From January 2013 the rate is €161.00 per week.

Guardian's non - contributory allowance

The Guardian's Non-Contributory Pension is paid for a child or children if:

- Both parents are dead.

- One parent has died and the other is unknown.

- One parent is dead and the surviving parent has abandoned or failed to support the child.

- The child satisfies a means test.

- The child is living in the State.

A claim cannot be made for a child living with stepparents. The allowance may be payable to the guardian of an orphan if the orphan does not already qualify for a Contributory Guardian's Allowance. The maximum rate of allowance payable from 1 January 2012 is €161.00 per week, where the estimated weekly means of the orphan do not exceed €7.60. If the estimated means of the orphan exceed €100.10 no benefit is payable. The allowance is payable up to the age of 18, or 22 if the orphan is in full-time education. However, the means test must be satisfied throughout the entire period.

Invalidity pension

An Invalidity Pension is payable instead of a Illness Benefit if you have been incapable of work for at least 12 months and likely to be incapable of work for a further 12 months or you are permanently incapable of work or you are over age 60 and suffering from a serious illness or incapacity.

You must have paid PRSI at class A, E or H.

In order to claim Invalidity Pension you must have paid the appropriate PRSI contributions for at least 260 weeks and you must have had at least 48 weeks PRSI paid or credited in the last tax year before you apply. The following are the maximum rates.

Invalidity pension maximum weekly rates	From Jan. 2012 €	From Jan. 2013 €
Under 65		
Personal rate	€193.50	€193.50
Person with qualified adult under 66	€331.60	€331.60
Person with qualified adult over 66	€399.80	€399.80
Over 65		
Personal rate	€230.30	€230.30
Person with qualified adult under 66	€368.40	€368.40
Person with qualified adult over 66	€436.60	€436.60
Increases for child dependents - Full rate	€29.80	€29.80
Increases for child dependents - Half rate	€14.90	€14.90
Living alone allowance	€7.70	€7.70

Increases for dependent child payable with the pensions dealt with in this section are paid for children living with you and dependent on you up to the age of 18, or 22 if they are in full time education. The full rate for a dependent child is paid to you if you are entitled to an increase for an adult dependent. If you do not qualify for payment for a qualified adult, the increase for child dependents is paid at half rate.

Qualified adult dependent payment

A qualified adult payment may be payable in addition to the basic benefit in respect of a claimant's spouse/partner, where the claimant's spouse/partner is wholly or mainly maintained by him/her. There are, however, certain exemptions, e.g. if the spouse has income of more than €310 per week or is receiving some other Social Welfare Benefit this supplement may not be paid.

Treatment benefits

Treatment Benefit covers Dental Benefit, Optical Benefit, Contact Lenses and Hearing Aids.

In 2010, the treatment benefit scheme was restricted to the medical and surgical appliances schemes, free dental examinations and free eyesight examinations

Maternity benefits

Maternity benefit is payable to women in current employment or self employed women insured at PRSI Classes, A, E, H and S.

Maternity benefit is not payable on your spouse's insurance. It is payable only where the mother is an insured person and satisfies the PRSI conditions on her own insurance record.

Who can qualify

You will qualify for Maternity Benefit if you;

- Are in employment which is covered by the Maternity Protection Act 1994 immediately before the first day of your maternity leave. The last day of insurable employment may be within 14 weeks of the expected date of birth of the baby;

- Are or have been self-employed,

  and

- Satisfy the PRSI contribution conditions.

Contribution conditions

- You must have at least 39 weeks PRSI paid in the 12 months immediately before the first day of your maternity leave.

  or

- 39 weeks PRSI paid since you first started work and at least 39 weeks PRSI paid or credited in the relevant tax year.

  or

- 26 weeks PRSI paid in the relevant tax year and 26 weeks PRSI paid in the tax year prior to the relevant tax year.

If you are self-employed you must have 52 qualifying PRSI contributions paid:

- In the relevant tax year,

  or

- 52 qualifying PRSI contributions paid in the tax year immediately prior to the relevant tax,

  or

- 52 qualifying PRSI contributions paid in the tax year immediately following the relevant tax

PRSI paid at Class A, E, H, S are deemed as qualifying contributions.

The allowance is payable for a continuous period of 26 weeks. To qualify for the maximum 18 weeks Maternity Benefit you must take a minimum of two weeks and a maximum of 14 weeks before the end of the week in which the baby is due. If your baby is born later than expected and you have less than four weeks maternity leave remaining, you may be entitled to extend your maternity leave to ensure that you have a full four weeks off following the birth.

Where Maternity Benefit has been in payment for a minimum period of 14 weeks, the balance of your payment may be postponed for up to six months if the child is hospitalised. The payment will resume within seven days following written notification of the discharge of the child from hospital.

The weekly rate of maternity benefit is calculated by dividing your gross income, in the relevant tax year by the number of weeks you actually worked in that year. The rate of maternity benefit is 80% of this amount subject to a minimum payment of €217.80 and a maximum payment of €262 per week. For a claim made in 2012 the relevant year is 2010.

Budget 2013

With effect from 1 July 2013 Maternity benefit will be taxed in full, however it will not be liable to the USC.

Adoptive benefit

Adoptive Benefit is payable for 16 weeks to adoptive parents paying PRSI at class A,E, H and S who satisfy the contribution conditions. The rate of payment and the PRSI contribution conditions are the same as those applying to Maternity Benefit (see page 225).

Habitual residence test

The habitual residence test means that in order to get certain payments, you will have to show that you have been habitually resident in Ireland or in the common travel areas of the UK, the Channel Islands or the Isle of Man for a substantial continuous period.

The following payments are now subject to a habitual residence condition:

- Jobseekers assistance.
- State Non-Contributory pension.
- Blind pension.
- Widow(er)'s and Orphan's Non-Contributory pensions.
- One-Parent Family payment.
- Carer's allowance.
- Illness allowance.
- Supplementary welfare allowance (other than once-off exceptional and urgent needs payments).
- Child benefit.

Child benefit

This is a benefit paid every month for each qualified child normally living with you and being supported by you. A qualified child is:

● A child under age 16

and/or

● A child age 16 or 17 who is in full time education or attending a FÁS Youthreach course or is physically or mentally disabled and dependent on you.

Child Benefit ceases when the child reaches age 18.

Child benefit rate

For multiple births higher rates apply.

	From Jan 2012	From Jan 2013
First, second and third child	€140.00	€140.00
Fourth and subsequent child	€160.00	€160.00

Family income supplement

Family income supplement (FIS) is a weekly tax-free payment available to employees (not the self employed) with children. You must have at least one child who normally lives with you or is financially supported by you. Your child must be under 18 years of age or between 18 and 22 years of age and in full-time education.

To qualify for FIS, your net average weekly family income must be below a certain amount for your family size. The FIS you receive is 60% of the difference between your net family income and the income limit which applies to your family.

Conditions

In order to qualify for FIS you must satisfy the following conditions;

- Work 19 hours or more per week (or 38 or more hours per fortnight). You can combine your weekly hours worked with your spouse/civil partner/co-habitant's to meet this condition.

- Be in employment which is likely to last at least 3 months.

- Look after one or more children.

- Earn less than a set amount which varies according to family size.

Generally the payment continues for one year and is not affected by, for example, an increase in earnings or other income in the family.

You cannot get FIS if you are taking part in a Community Employment Scheme, or any FAS schemes except Job Initiative. You cannot get FIS is you are getting one of the following social welfare payments; Jobseekers benefit, Jobseekers allowance; State pension transition or Pre-retirement allowance.

Rates

FIS is calculated on the basis of 60% of the difference between the income limit for the family size and the assessable income of the person(s) raising the child(ren). The combined income of a couple (married, in a civil partnership or cohabiting) is taken into account.

FIS income limits in 2013

If you have	Weekly family income is less than
One child	€506.00
Two children	€602.00
Three children	€703.00
Four children	€824.00
Five children	€950.00
Six children	€1,066.00
Seven children	€1,202.00
Eight children	€1,298.00

It is important to be aware, that no matter how little you may qualify for, you will still get a minimum payment of €20 per week.

Health and safety benefit

This is a weekly payment for women insured at Class A, E or H, who are pregnant or have recently had a baby or are breastfeeding (up to 26 weeks) and who have been awarded Health and Safety Leave under the Maternity Protection Act, 1994.

Health and Safety Leave is granted to an employee by her employer when the employer cannot remove a risk to the employee's health or safety or her pregnancy or breastfeeding, or assign her alternative "risk free" duties.

Jobseekers benefit

Jobseeker's Benefit is a weekly payment to people who are out of work and covered by PRSI.

To qualify for Jobseeker's Benefit you must:

- Be unemployed (you must be fully unemployed or unemployed for at least 3 days in 6).

- Be under 66 years of age.

- Have enough PRSI contributions.

- Be capable of work.

- Be available for and genuinely seeking work.

- Have a substantial loss of employment and as a result be unemployed for at least three days in six.

PRSI contributions

In order to qualify for Jobseeker's Benefit, you must pay Class A, H or P PRSI contributions. Class A is the one paid by most private sector employees and

- Have at least 104 weeks PRSI paid since you first started work **and**

- Have 39 weeks PRSI paid or credited in the relevant tax year (a minimum of 13 weeks must be paid contributions*)

  or

- Have 26 weeks PRSI paid in the relevant tax year and 26 weeks PRSI paid in the tax year immediately before the relevant tax year.

* If you do not have 13 paid contributions in the relevant tax year, you must have the 13 contributions paid in any one of the following years:

- The 2 tax years before the relevant tax year.
- The last complete tax year.
- The current tax year.

The relevant tax year is the second last complete tax year before the year in which your claim is made. So, for claims made in 2012, the relevant tax year is 2010.

There are a number of circumstances in which you will be awarded credited contributions. For example, pre-entry credits are given when you start employment for the first time in your working life. However, you will only qualify for Jobseeker's Benefit when you have 104 contributions actually paid. Credits are also normally awarded while you are getting certain social welfare payments, including Jobseeker's Benefit (provided it is for 6 days), Jobseeker's Allowance or Illness Benefit.

Contributions you have paid in other member states of the EU/EEA will be added to your Irish contributions. If you are applying for Jobseeker's Benefit and need the contributions paid in another EU/EEA country to help you qualify, then your last contribution must have been in Ireland.

You may be disqualified from getting Jobseeker's Benefit for 9 weeks if you:

- Left work voluntarily and without a reasonable cause.
- Lost your job through misconduct.
- Refused an offer of suitable alternative employment or suitable training.
- Are aged under 55 and get a redundancy payment of more than €50,000. The exact length of your disqualification (up to nine weeks) will in practice, depend on the precise amount of redundancy payment you received - see page 233.

How long is jobseeker's benefit paid for

Jobseeker's Benefit is paid for a maximum of 12 months to new claimants who have at least 260 paid contributions.

Jobseeker's Benefit is paid for a maximum of 9 months to new claimants who have less than 260 paid contributions.

If you are under 18 you will only get Jobseekers benefit for a maximum of 156 days (26 weeks).

Budget 2013

- The duration of Jobseeker's Benefit will be reduced from 12 months to 9 months for recipients with 260 or more contributions paid.

- The duration of Jobseeker's Benefit will be reduced from 12 months to 6 moths for recipients with less than 260 contributions paid.

These measures come into effect on 3 April 2013. Claimants getting Jobseeker's Benefit for 6 months or more (or 3 months in case of those with less than 260 contributions paid) on 3 April 2013 will not be affected.

Work and jobseeker's benefit

To get Jobseeker's Benefit you must be unemployed or have lost at least one day's employment and as a result be unemployed for at least 3 days out of 6 days. You may continue to get Jobseeker's Benefit if you can only find part-time or casual work.

Where a jobseeker's benefit recipient is working for part of a week, the payment entitlement will be based on a 5 day week rather than a 6 day week.

Short time working training programme

If you are a systematic short time worker and getting Jobseeker's Benefit, you may qualify for a place on a new Short Time Working Training Programme and continue to get your Jobseeker's Benefit. The Programme will allow you to improve or add to your skills. The training offered will be flexible to allow you to complete your course if you return to full-time work. A limited number of places are available, for more information contact your local FÁS office.

Redundancy

If you are under 55 and get a redundancy payment of more than €50,000 you will be disqualified from claiming Jobseeker's Benefit for the following length of time:

Amount of redundancy payment	Period of disqualification
€50,000 - €55,000	1 Week
€55,001 - €60,000	2 Weeks
€60,001 - €65,000	3 Weeks
€65,001 - €70,000	4 Weeks
€70,001 - €75,000	5 Weeks
€75,001 - €80,000	6 Weeks
€80,001 - €85,000	7 Weeks
€85,001 - €90,000	8 Weeks
€90,001 and over	9 Weeks

On strike

If you are on strike, you are not considered unemployed and not entitled to Jobseeker's Benefit. However, your family may get Supplementary Welfare Allowance.

Rate of jobseekers benefit

Average weekly earnings	Personal rate €	Qualifying adult rate €
Maximum rate	€188.00	€124.80

Jobseeker's Benefit is not paid for the first 3 days you are unemployed (the first 3 days are any 3 days, not necessarily consecutive, in a period of six consecutive days).

If you are unemployed for a second time within 26 weeks of your last Jobseekers benefit payment your application for Jobseeker's Benefit is not treated as a new claim and you do not have another 3 days of non-payment.

Taxation of jobseeker's benefit

Jobseeker's Benefit is taxable. However, if you are getting Jobseeker's Benefit because your normal working week has been reduced (systematic short-time work) your Jobseeker's Benefit is not taxed.

Extra benefits

If you are getting Jobseeker's Benefit, you may be entitled to:

- Mortgage Interest Supplement or Rent Supplement - a payment from the community welfare officer at your local health centre.

- Smokeless fuel allowance - to help low-income households meet the extra cost of using smokeless or low smoke fuels in designated urban areas (payable with Jobseeker's Benefit after 3 months).

- Back to school clothing and footwear allowance - an allowance designed to help towards the cost of uniforms and footwear for children who are attending school. The scheme is payable between June and September each year.

- Medical card - if your income is below a certain level, you may get a medical card. It covers you for free doctor's care, approved prescriptions etc. Contact your local health office for more information.

- School book scheme - each year the Department of Education and Skills provides grants to primary and secondary schools towards the cost of school books for students in financial need. You should contact the school principal for more information. The school principal will also advise you whether the school runs a book loan scheme, whereby your children's books are provided for a nominal rental charge each year.

How to apply

You should apply for Jobseeker's Benefit the first day you become unemployed.

It is important to apply on the first day you become unemployed because you will not get paid for the first three days of your claim.

Jobseeker's Benefit application forms are now available online on www.welfare.ie. You can also get an application form at your local Social Welfare office.

Carer's benefit

Carer's Benefit is payable to PRSI classes A,B,C,D,E and H. It is payable to people who leave work in order to care for a person(s) in need of full-time care and attention.

Who can qualify

You will qualify if you - the Carer:

- Are age 16 or over and under age 65/66.

- Live with the person(s) you are looking after or in close proximity.

- Satisfy the PRSI contribution conditions.

- Give up employment to care for a person(s) on a full-time basis. This employment must have been for a minimum of 16 hours per week or 32 hours per fortnight.

- Are not employed or self-employed outside the home. You may however work up to 15 hours per week. The maximum weekly income which you can earn is €332.50.

- Are living in the State.

- Are not living in a hospital, convalescent home or other similar institution

  and

- The person(s) you are caring for is/are;

  - So disabled as to need full-time care and attention (medical certification is required)

  - Not normally living in a hospital, home or other similar institution.

The rate of carer's benefit from 1st January 2013 is €205.00 per week.

PRSI conditions

For a first claim you must have;

- 156 contributions paid since entry into insurable employment.

  and

- 39 contributions paid in the relevant tax year.

  or

- 39 contributions paid in the 12 month period before the commencement of the Carer's Benefit.

  or

- 26 contributions paid in the relevant tax year and 26 contributions paid in the relevant tax year prior to that.

Respite care grant

An annual Respite Care Grant is paid in June each year and is extended to all carers providing full-time care to an older person or a person with disability, regardless of means, who are not in receipt of an unemployment payment or working outside the home for more than 10 hours per week. This grant is worth €1,700 and is paid in respect of each person being cared for.

Budget 2013

The annual respite care grant is reduced to €1,375.

Illness benefit

Illness Benefit is available to PRSI classes A, E, H and P.

It is payable if:

- You are under 66.

- Are unfit to work due to illness.

- Satisfy the PRSI conditions.

PRSI conditions:

- At least 104 weeks PRSI paid since you started work,

  and

- 39 weeks PRSI paid or credited in the relevant tax year, of which 13 must be paid contributions,

  or

- 26 weeks PRSI paid in the relevant tax year,

  and

- 26 weeks PRSI paid in the tax year immediately before the relevant tax year.

If you do not have 13 paid contributions in the relevant tax year, the following years may be used to satisfy this condition:

- Either of the two most previous tax years.

- The most recent complete tax year,

  or

- The current tax year.

The relevant tax year is the second last complete tax year before the benefit year in which the Illness Benefit claim is made. For claims made in 2012 the relevant year is 2010.

Tax

Illness benefit is taxable, but it will be paid directly to you without income tax deductions. If you are employed, your employer will take your illness benefit into account for PAYE purposes. If you are unemployed, the Revenue will take account the amount paid to you when adjusting your tax credits or reviewing the tax affairs of your spouse.

Occupational injuries benefit

Occupational injury benefit is a weekly payment if you are unfit for work due to;

- An accident at work.

- An accident while travelling on an unbroken journey directly to or from work.

- An occupational disease.

There are a number of benefits available and there are different conditions attached to each benefit which include

- Injury benefit.

- Disablement benefit.

- Incapacity supplement.

- Constant attendance allowance.

- Medical care scheme.

There are also death benefits under this scheme that include

- Widow(er)/surviving civil partner's pension that is paid at a higher rate than ordinary contributory widow(er)/surviving civil partner's pension.

- Orphan's pension.

- Dependent parent's pension.

- Funeral grant.

Occupational Injuries Benefits are available to people covered by PRSI Class A, D, J and M - most workers in Ireland. Injury benefit is not paid for the first three days of your illness or incapacity and payment can be made for up to 26 weeks starting from the date of your injury or the start of your illness.

If you are still unable to work after 26 weeks, you may be entitled to Illness Benefit, Disability Allowance or Supplementary Welfare Allowance. You may be entitled to Disability Benefit if you suffer a loss of physical or mental faculty as a result of the accident or disease. If you don't qualify for Illness Benefit or another social welfare payment and you are getting Disablement Benefit, you may be eligible for Incapacity Supplement.

To check rates and to apply for benefits contact:

> Occupational Injuries Benefit Section,
> Department of Social Protection,
> Aras Mhic Dhiarmada
> Store Street
> Dublin 1
> Tel: (01) 704 3018

Or contact your local Social Welfare office for more information.

Early retirement due to ill health

This scheme applies if you are a Public Servant paying PRSI at Classes B,C and D and have to give up work because of ill health. It basically gives you PRSI credits to keep your insurance record up-to-date and protects your Contributory Widow's/Widower's Pension, Orphan's Contributory Allowance and Bereavement Grant.

To apply for these credited contributions, you should complete the application form CR35.

Bereavement grant

A Bereavement Grant of €850 is available to those paying PRSI at classes A, B, C, D, E, F, G, H, N and S. The grant, based on PRSI contributions, is payable on the death of:

- An insured person.

- The wife or husband of an insured person.

- The widow or widower of a deceased insured person.

- A contributory pensioner (or spouse of a contributory pensioner).

- A child under age 18, or under 22 if in full-time education (where either parent or the person that the child normally lives with satisfies the PRSI contribution conditions).

- The qualified adult of a contributory pensioner, including those who would be a qualified adult but are getting another Social Welfare payments, e.g. Carer's Allowance.

- A qualified child.

- An orphan or a person to whom an orphan's (contributory) allowance is payable.

When an adult dies, a death grant may be paid based on the PRSI record of the deceased or the spouse of the deceased.

When a child dies, a death grant may be paid based on the PRSI record of either parent or on the record of the person the child normally lives with.

PRSI conditions

The PRSI record used must have enough contributions to satisfy the following conditions:

- 156 contribution weeks paid since entry into insurable employment

  or

- At least 26 PRSI contributions paid since entry into insurable employment

  and

- 39 PRSI contributions paid or credited in the relevant tax year

  or

- A yearly average of 39 PRSI contributions paid or credited over the three or five tax years before the death occurred or pension age was reached (age 66 at present)

  or

- A yearly average of 26 weeks PRSI contributions paid or credited since 1979 (or since starting work if later) and the end of the tax year before the death occurred or pension age was reached (age 66 at present)

  or

- A yearly average of 26 weeks PRSI contributions paid or credited since 1 October 1970 (or since starting work if later) and the end of the tax year before the death occurred or pension age was reached (age 66 at present)

The relevant tax year is the second last complete tax year before the year in which the death occurs or pension age was reached.

Claim forms are available from your local Department of Social Protection office.

Widowed parent's grant

A special grant of €6,000 is paid to widows or widowers with dependent children following the death of their spouse. It is payable to widows or widowers who qualify for the Widow/Widower's Contributory Pension or a One-Parent Family Payment or Bereavement Grant. This grant can be paid in addition to the €850 Bereavement Grant.

Funeral grant

If the death was due to an accident at work or occupational disease, a higher Funeral Grant under the Occupational Injuries Scheme may be payable instead of a Bereavement Grant.

Working in the EU

As Ireland is a member of the EU, you are legally entitled to look for work in any Member State without a work permit. Each Member State has a national placement service, similar to FÁS. If you wish to seek work in any of the EU countries, you can apply through a FÁS employment services office for a job in the country of your choice. Details of your application will be circulated abroad through the SEDOC system free of charge and if any suitable vacancies arise, you will be notified.

If you qualify for Jobseekers Benefit here and have been registered and in receipt of benefit for at least four weeks, you may have your Jobseekers Benefit transferred to another EU country for up to 78 days or for a shorter period if you have less than 78 days left on your claim, provided you look for and register for work in that country within seven days. You must register for work within seven days from the date you last claimed Jobseekers Benefit in Ireland for your unemployment payments to be continuous.

"Special Grant of €6,000 is paid to Widow's or Widower's with dependent children following the death of the spouse."

Form E301

This is required to claim Jobseekers Benefit. It gives details of your social insurance and employment record and is available from EU Records Section, Social Welfare Services Office, Floor 2, Oisin House, 212-213 Pearse Street, Dublin 2. Phone (01)7043000. You should also bring your birth certificate as it may be required in certain circumstances.

Health services

EU Regulations also apply to your Health Service entitlements. In the UK you are entitled to UK Health Services, as soon as you have an address in the UK and register with a doctor. If you are on a temporary stay in any other EU country you will be entitled to the same Health Services as the nationals of that country. The European Health Insurance Card is normally required to claim these Health Benefits in all EU countries, excluding the UK.

PRSI/EU documents

Form E104 is required if you are claiming Illness or Maternity Benefit.

Form E301 is required if you are claiming Jobseekers Benefit.

The European Health Insurance Card (EHIC) is required to claim Health Service Benefits in EU countries excluding the UK.

Forms E104 and E301 are available from ;

> E.U. Records Section,
>
> Social Welfare Service Officer
>
> Floor 2, Oisin House,
>
> 212-213 Pearse St.,
>
> Dublin 2.

while the European Health Insurance Card is available from your local Health Board.

Taxation of social welfare payments

Non-taxable

The following payments are not liable to Income Tax:-

- Jobseekers Allowance
- Maternity/Adoptive Benefit (to July 2013)
- Family Income Supplement
- Back to Work Allowance
- Health & Safety Benefits
- Supplementary Welfare Allowance

Taxable

The following payments are taxable:-

- State Pension Transition
- State Contributory Pension
- Illness Benefit
- Widow's/Widower's Contributory Pension
- Jobseekers Benefit
- Maternity/Adoptive Benefit (from July 2013)
- Orphan's Contributory Allowances
- Occupational Injuries Benefit
- Invalidity Pension
- One Parent Family Payment
- Carer's Allowance
- Deserted Wife's Benefit
- Carer's Benefit

Taxation of jobseekers benefit

Jobseekers Benefit, is a taxable source of income. However additional payments for child dependents paid with Jobseekers Benefit, is exempt from tax. Systematic short-term working is exempt from income tax. This is short-term working for a limited time period and is normally 6-8 weeks. Casual short-term working is liable to income tax. Casual short-term working differs from systematic short-term working in that casual working if for an unlimited period.

Taxation of illness benefit

Illness benefit and occupational injuries benefit are taxable sources of income. Prior to 1 January 2012 the first 6 weeks (36 days) of illness benefit and occupational injury benefit payments in a tax year were exempt for tax purposes. Any increases for child dependents are exempt from tax.

State Non-Contributory Pension, Widow's/ Widower's Non-Contributory Pension, Orphan's Non-Contributory Pension, Carer's Allowance, Blind Person's Pension together with social assistance allowance for deserted wives, prisoner's wives and lone parents are also liable to tax. However, as these payments are subject to a means test it would be unlikely that a person in receipt of one of these payments would be liable to tax.

"Fair deal - nursing home support scheme

Also known as the 'Fair Deal' scheme, the Nursing Home Support Scheme has been designed to replace the controversial and often inadequate nursing home subvention scheme from 27 October, 2009.

The subvention scheme is still in effect, and the subvention is paid on a means-tested basis to people who need full time care and go into private nursing homes in Ireland. The means test takes into account the person's income and assets, but not necessarily their family home in every case, say where there is a spouse or partner who remains living there. The subvention was designed to help meet costs, not to replace them and up to now has amounted to a maximum weekly payment of €300. Many families of the elderly found themselves funding the bulk of their relative's care costs or having to sell the elderly person's home to meet the steep costs. Details about the Subvention scheme can be found on the HSE's website: www.hse.ie .

Under the Fair Deal scheme, people who are already getting a subvention can choose whichever scheme is to their advantage.

Fair Deal begins by arranging a Care Needs Assessment by a health care professional from your local Nursing Home Support Group and then a Financial Assessment which determines your contribution to care and the person's corresponding level of financial assistance ("State support").

Under Fair Deal the person is obliged to contribute 80% of their income and 5% of the value of any assets they own per annum. The HSE will then pay the balance of the cost of care. For example, if the cost of care is €1,000 and the person's weekly contribution is €300, the HSE will pay the weekly balance of €700 in State support. Where assets include land and property, the contribution may be deferred during the person's lifetime. Instead, the HSE will collect this deferred payment after death. This is an optional benefit of the scheme called the "Nursing Home Loan" which requires written consent to a Charging Order that is then registered against your house or other asset.

More details of the Fair Deal scheme can be found here:
http://www.dohc.ie/issues/fair_deal/quick_guide.pdf?direct=1

13 Redundancy

When does redundancy arise?

 A redundancy situation arises where an employee's job ceases to exist, and the employee is not replaced because of rationalisation/ reorganisation, not enough work available, the financial state of the firm, company closures etc.

Statutory redundancy payment

As a result of the downturn which we have been experiencing since 2008, redundancy is now a reality for many people in Ireland. The Redundancy Payments Acts, 1967-2007 legally obliges employers to pay redundant employees what is known as a "statutory redundancy entitlement". The amount is related to the employee's length of service and normal weekly earnings (gross weekly wage, average regular overtime and payment-in-kind), all added together, up to a maximum amount of €600 per week or €31,200 per annum.

Which employee's are covered?

Employees, are covered under these Acts if they meet the following requirements.

- Are age 16 or over.

- Have at least 2 years continuous service (104 weeks).

- Are in employment which is insurable for all Social Welfare Benefits. This condition does not apply if you are a part time employee.

- Have been made redundant as a result of a genuine redundancy situation i.e. your job no longer exists and you are not replaced.

Notice of redundancy

An employer who, because of redundancy, intends to dismiss an employee who has at least 104 weeks continuous service with the firm must give notice in writing to the employee of the proposed dismissal. The employer can do so by giving part A (notification of redundancy) of Form RP5O to the employee.

Calculation of statutory redundancy lump sum payments.

The amount of statutory redundancy payments which an employee is entitled to receive from their employer is calculated as follows;

- Two weeks pay for each year of employment continuous and reckonable over the age of 16

- In addition, a bonus week. All excess days are calculated as a portion of 365 days. i.e 4 years 190 days = 4.52 years

- Reckonable service is service excluding ordinary sick leave over and above 26 weeks and an occupational injury over and above 52 weeks.

Reckonable service also excludes absence from work because of lay-offs or strikes. However, short-time work is reckonable.

All calculations are subject to the ceiling of €600 per week.

Statutory redundancy payments are exempt from tax.

"For the purpose of calculating statutory redundancy, a weeks pay is limited to a maximum of €600."

Example

You started working for your current employer on 1 January 2002. As a result of the slowdown in the economy your employer decided to reduce staff numbers and you are made redundant with effect from 31 December 2012. Your current salary is €45,000 per annum.

As you have 11 full years of services you will be entitled to

$$11 \times 2 \text{ weeks} + 1 \text{ bonus week} = 23 \text{ weeks}$$

Your weekly salary is €865.38, however the maximum you can receive by way of statutory redundancy is limited to €600 per week. Therefore your statutory redundancy payment will work out as follows;

$$23 \text{ weeks} \times €600 = €13,800$$

This payment is tax free.

Your employer can receive a refund of 15% of the payment i.e. 15% x €13,800 = €2,070 from the Department of Jobs, Enterprise, & Innovation.

Rebates to employers

Employers who pay the statutory redundancy entitlement and give proper notice of redundancy (at least two weeks) are entitled to a 15% rebate from the social insurance fund, into which they make regular payments themselves through P.R.S.I. contributions.

Due to the high levels of redundancies in recent years there can be a delay in an employer receiving a statutory redundancy rebate.

If a business is waiting on a rebate and is experiencing difficulties in meeting its tax obligations, the amount of the tax refund due to the employer can be paid directly from the Department of Jobs, Enterprise and Innovation to the Revenue Commissioners.

Budget 2013

This rebate is discontinued for redundancies made on or after 1st January 2013.

Employment appeals tribunal

Disputes concerning redundancy payments can be submitted to the Employment Appeals Tribunal, which can provide a speedy, fair, inexpensive and informal means for individuals to seek remedies for alleged infringements of their statutory redundancy rights. The Tribunal also deals with disputes under other labour law areas including the Minimum Notice and Terms of Employment Acts, 1973 to 2001. These cover the right of workers to a minimum period of notice before dismissal, provided they are in continuous service with the same employer for at least 13 weeks and are normally expected to work at least 8 hours per week.

The Tribunal also deals with the Unfair Dismissals Acts, 1977 to 1993 and the Protection of Employees (Employers' Insolvency) Acts, 1984 to 2003 (dealing with such areas, amongst others, as arrears of pay due to an employee, holiday and sick pay etc.) where the employer is insolvent.

Effects of change of ownership of a business on a redundancy lump sum payment

Where there is a change in the ownership of a business and you continue, by arrangement, to work for the new owner with no break in your employment, you are not entitled to any redundancy payments at the time of the change of ownership. Your continuity of employment is also preserved for the purpose of the redundancy payments in the event of your dismissal or redundancy by the new employer at any future date. You are not entitled to a redundancy payment if an offer of employment by the new owner is unreasonably refused by you.

If the new owner merely buys the premises in which you were employed, this will not constitute a change of ownership of the business and your former employer will be liable to pay any redundancy payment which may be due to you.

What happens if an employer fails to pay a redundancy lump sum?

In situations where the employer is unable to pay the employees their entitlements, the Department of Jobs, Enterprise and Innovation pays the full amount direct to the employees from the social insurance fund (S.I.F.). In no circumstances should the employer pay part of the statutory entitlement to the employee.

The employer will then be liable for the payment and will become a preferential creditor to the Department of Jobs, Enterprise and Innovation The employee fills in Form RP50 including the original employer signature and sends it into the Department of Jobs, Enterprise and Innovation Before this claim can be processed an employer must provide a letter from their accountant/solicitor confirming their inability to pay. This confirmation must be based on their own professional view of the companies finances rather than a view based on information provided by the employer and they must be able to support this confirmation should an audit be carried out at any time.

For further information or relevant forms, contact the Department of Jobs, Enterprise and Innovation, Davitt house, Adelaide Road, Dublin 2 or FAS at any of their offices through the country, or www.djei.ie

Ex-gratia payments

Legally your employer is only obliged to pay you statutory redundancy in the event of a redundancy. However many employers also pay an additional, ex-gratia payment to employees. Ex-gratia payments or compensation payments over and above the statutory redundancy payment are taxable.

However, there are a number of exemptions available which reduce the amount charged to tax and "Top Slicing Relief" which reduces the rate of tax paid on ex-gratia lump sums.

Basic exemption

The basic exemption is €10,160 together with an additional €765 for each complete year of service.

Increased exemption

The basic exemption may be increased by €10,000 to a maximum of €20,160 plus €765 for each complete year of service provided:

- You have not made any claims in respect of a lump sum in the previous 10 tax years. **and**

- If you are in an occupational pension scheme, the increased exemption of €10,000 is reduced by the amount of;

  - Any tax-free lump sum from the pension scheme to which you may be immediately entitled **or**

  - The present day value at the date of leaving employment of any tax-free lump sum, which is received or may be receivable from the pension scheme in the future.

If the lump sum from the pension is more than €10,000 you are not due the increased exemption. If it is less than €10,000 you are due the increased exemption of €10,000 less the amount of the pension scheme entitlement.

Revenue approval must be sought for the increased exemption. The application for increased exemption can be found on www.revenue.ie or is available from your local tax office.

Standard capital superannuation benefit (S.C.S.B.)

The third exemption is the Standard Capital Superannuation Benefit. This is arrived at using the following formula:

$$\frac{A \times B}{15} - C$$

A = Average yearly remuneration from the employment for the last 36 months ending on the date of termination.

B = Number of complete years of service.

C = Any tax-free lump sum from an occupational pension scheme to which you may be entitled **or**

The present day value at the date of leaving employment of any tax-free lump sum which is received or may be receivable from an occupational pension scheme.

For the purpose of calculating the increased exemption and the S.C.S.B. amount, the tax-free lump sum receivable from an occupational pension scheme is the present day value of any deferred tax-free lump sum receivable at retirement from the existing occupational pension scheme. A refund of pension contributions which were subject to tax at 20% are excluded.

If you sign a waiver letter i.e. a letter confirming you will not avail of any tax-free lump sum from your current occupational pension scheme now or at retirement, the value of any deferred tax-free lump sum receivable will be Nil. (See C above).

Ex gratia payments made on or after 1 January 2011 will be subject to a maximum exemption limit of €200,000 taking into consideration any prior tax-free payments (including SCSB deduction) which have been received.

Example

You commenced employment with company XYZ Ltd. on 1 December 1990.

You opted for early retirement on 1 November 2012 and you received a lump sum of €60,000 (excluding statutory redundancy).

You received a tax free lump sum of €25,000 from your pension scheme.

The tax-free amount of this €60,000 is the highest of the following:

	€	
01/01/12 - 31/10/12	€41,667	(10 months)
01/01/11 - 31/12/11	€50,000	(12 months)
01/01/10 - 31/12/10	€45,000	(12 months)
01/11/09 - 31/12/09	€7,000	(2 months)
Total salary for 36 months	€143,667	
Average salary for 12 months	€47,889	

Basic exemption

$$€10,160 + (€765 \times 21) = €26,225$$

Only complete years count for the purpose of the additional €765. So even though you had 21 years 11 months service, you only receive €765 x 21.

Increased exemption

As you received a tax-free lump sum from the pension scheme in excess of €10,000, the increased exemption would not apply to you.

Standard capital superannuation benefit (SCSB)

Assuming your salary for the last 36 months was as follows:

Calculation of SCSB

$$\frac{A \times B}{15} \text{ less C} = \frac{€47,889 \times 21}{15} \text{ less } €25,000 = €42,045$$

The highest of the above three exemptions is the SCSB amount of €42,045. This is the amount which you can receive tax-free.

A summary of your position, assuming you pay tax at 41%, is as follows:

		€
	Gross lump sum	€65,000
Less:	SCSB Amount	€42,045
	Taxable	€22,955
	Tax @ 41%	€ 9,411
	USC @ 7%	€1,607
	Total tax and levies	€11,018
	Net Lump Sum	**€53,982**

Subsequent claim

The basic exemption and the SCSB, are generally available against any subsequent lump sum payment. However, they can only be given once against a lump sum from the same employer or an associate employer.

The increased exemption of €10,000 may be claimed if an individual has not made any claims for the increased exemption in respect of a lump sum received in the previous 10 tax years.

How is the lump sum taxed?

Your employer is obliged to deduct PAYE and the universal social charge (USC), on all of the lump sum less the basis exemption or SCSB, as previously outlined. Your employer can give the basic exemption or SCSB without prior approval from your Inspector of Taxes. However, if you are due any increased exemption, either you or your employer should apply to your local tax office well in advance of the payment date for approval to give the increased exemption.

Foreign service and redundancy

Your redundancy lump sum may be completely tax free provided;

- 75% or more of your entire period of employment, ending on the date of termination was foreign service, **or**

- Your period of service exceeded 10 years but the whole of the last 10 years was foreign service, **or**

- One half of your period of service including any ten of the last 20 years was foreign service, provided your period of service exceeded 20 years.

Foreign service is defined as a period of employment the emoluments of which were not chargeable to Irish tax, or if chargeable to Irish tax were chargeable on the remittance basis.

Foreign service not sufficient to exempt

If you have foreign service but do not qualify for full exemption from income tax your redundancy payment, as reduced by the basic/increased or SCSB exemption may be further reduced by the following formula;

$$\frac{P \times FS}{TS}$$

P	=	Gross Lump Sum Payment (as reduced by SCSB or basic / exemption)
FS	=	Number of years of foreign service
TS	=	Number of years of total service

Example

Using the example on page 253 and assuming that you had spent 6 years working in the U.S. foreign service relief would be;

$$\frac{€22,955 \times 6}{21} = €6,559$$

Your taxable lump sum is now reduced by foreign service relief of €6,559

		€
	Gross Lump Sum	€65,000
Less:	SCSB Amount	€42,045
		€22,955
Less:	Relief for foreign service	€6,559
	Taxable	€16,396
	Tax @ 41%	€ 6,722
	USC @ 7%	€1,148
	Total tax & levies	€ 7,870
	Net Lump Sum	**€57,130**

Top slicing relief

This relief is available after the end of the tax year in which you received an ex-gratia lump sum. Top slicing relief works by calculating your average rate of tax for the three years prior to the tax year in which you received an ex-gratia lump sum. If this average rate is lower than the rate of tax which you paid on your ex-gratia lump sum, the tax will be recalculated at the lower rate and you are entitled to a refund of the difference.

The amount of the relief due to you is calculated by the following formula:

Taxable lump sum x (tax rate which you paid on your lump sum less your average rate of tax for the previous three years).

In the case of a couple, taxed under joint assessment, where both spouses have income in any of the three years prior to the tax year in which a termination payment was received, the rate of tax will be based on the income of the spouse who received the termination payment or on the combined income of both spouses, depending on which rate is more beneficial to the couple.

Example

Assuming you received a lump sum in November 2012, the taxable lump sum was €22,800 and you paid tax @ 41% on this, amounting to €9,348. Your average rate of tax over the last three years was 27%.

Your top slicing relief would work out as follows;

Tax paid on lump sum	€9,348
Taxable lump sum	€22,800
Average rate of tax from 2009 - 2011	27%

Top Slicing Relief due to you;

Tax paid - (Taxable lump sum x average rate of tax paid between 2009 - 2011)

€9,348 - (€22,800 x 27%) = €3,192

You would have to wait until the end of the 2012 tax year (i.e. the tax year in which you received the lump sum) in order to claim the top slicing relief.

Budget 2013

Top slicing relief will no longer be available to those receiving an ex-gratia payment, where the payment excluding statutory redundancy exceeds €200,000 or more. This applies to payments made after 1st January 2013.

14 Pensions - financial planning for retirement

Individually, we all need to make financial provision for when we no longer want to work, or are no longer able to work, or indeed when we want to cut back on the amount of time we spend in work – that is, our retirement years.

Financial provision for retirement is made by accumulating a fund of money, or accumulating other assets such as property, stocks and shares, or bonds, that can be used to provide an income when we stop or cut back on work. One important point regarding the provision of an income in retirement is that we need to make sure our retirement provision will be adequate for our needs at that time. Even if we are fortunate enough to have employers that make provision on our behalf, constant monitoring of that provision to ensure it will be adequate is of paramount importance. In other words, we need to take control of our own financial futures.

So, whether you are a self-employed sole trader, a proprietary director, or an employee, **you need to take control of your financial planning for retirement**. Taking this control on your own can be done, but unless you understand financial matters very well, it could be very difficult. This is where taking advice is important, but not just any advice. Your advice should come from a qualified, professional adviser that you can trust to give you the correct advice, and who when it comes to arranging products for you, should be able to give you the choice of a number of different financial institutions.

One important piece of advice that any good financial adviser will give you is that **making provision for retirement should be done as tax-efficiently as possible**.

In this chapter will look at:

- Why we all need to plan for retirement;

- Why, because of their tax-efficiency, contributing to pension plans can make more sense than other forms of savings for most people;

- What sorts of investment funds are available under pension plans;

- The products available for retirement capital accumulation; and

- The products available to provide income following retirement.

Why plan for retirement?

Ask yourself the question **"If I don't make financial provision for my retirement who will?"** Firstly, the State is unlikely to be able to provide you with an adequate income in your retirement. If you are an employee your employer is unlikely to be able to provide you with adequate income in your retirement, either. And, your children will have enough to do to look after themselves and their families.

State pension

At present the maximum weekly pension from the State for an individual is €230.30 per week. This is approximately 1/3rd of the average industrial wage of €36,000 or so per year. Not a very attractive prospect living on 1/3rd or less of your pre-retirement income! Even less attractive if you are earning more than €36,000 per year.

And, things are not going to get any better. Already the retirement age is being moved out to age 66 for all in 2014, 67 in 2021 and 68 in 2028 and qualifying for the maximum benefit is being made more difficult. At present the State Transition Pension is payable for employees that have retired from employment from age 65, with the State Contributory Pension payable from age 66 for all who qualify including self-employed individuals and employees.

Social Welfare Pensions are paid for out of incoming revenue on a "pay as you go basis". This is ok while there are enough people working and making PRSI contributions to pay the pensions to the retired people. But, this situation is changing fast. It's estimated that by 2050 there will be only two people working for every person aged over 65. At present there are almost 6 people working for every person aged over 65. In 2008 the cost to the State of social welfare pensions was 5.5% of GDP and it is estimated that this will have risen to 15% of GDP by 2050. In the boom times the Government set up the National Pension Reserve Fund to help fund pensions for Public Sector workers and Social Welfare Pensions into the future. Unfortunately, this has now been decimated by "investing" in the banks.

So, depending solely on the State to provide an adequate income in retirement is unlikely to be a good idea.

Employer pension schemes

The vast majority of employers are unlikely to be able to provide adequate income in retirement for their employees, and that includes the State and its employees. Already many employers that, in the past, provided Defined Benefit (DB) pension schemes have had to restructure their schemes and, not only in this country but worldwide a huge number of Defined Benefit schemes are closing down. Defined Benefit schemes promise a certain level of benefits at retirement. These benefits are usually related to earnings and service with the employer. Unfortunately, in recent years employers have been finding that Defined Benefit schemes are just too expensive for them to maintain. This is due mainly to the fact that people are living longer and the schemes have to pay out pensions for longer; and, to the fact that the investment returns achieved by the funds have been poor, due to the state of the world economy.

In Ireland Defined Benefit schemes are largely being replaced by Defined Contribution (DC) schemes and by PRSA arrangements. The contribution levels being made to these types of pension schemes are generally totally inadequate to provide worthwhile retirement benefits. While the average contributions to DB schemes are very often likely to be 25% to 30% of salaries in total between employer and employee contributions, the average total contribution rate to DC schemes is only 10% of salaries. Remember, the 25% to 30% of salaries contributions to DB schemes have not been enough to keep many of these schemes going. So, 10% of salaries is unlikely to produce adequate retirement income.

When will I retire?

Another very good question to ask yourself is **"When do I see myself stopping work or cutting back on my workload?"**

Life expectancy rates are increasing. On average people are living now to age 80. That figure is for the total population. Women live 5/6 years longer than men, on average. So, if you see yourself wanting to retire at age 60, for example, what are you going to live off for the following 20 or so years?

As stated earlier the retirement age is being moved out to age 66 for all in 2014, to 67 in 2021 and to 68 in 2028. So if you are going to depend on the State for retirement income you are going to have to work longer before you can start collecting a retirement income. That is assuming the State will be able to afford to pay you a reasonable income.

Women and retirement planning

There is a special need for women to start planning. After all women live 5/6 longer than men on average and assuming that they retire at the same age as men they can be expected to spend 5/6 years longer in retirement. In a recent survey carried out by Mercer more than 20% of Irish women admitted they did not know how they were going to fund their retirement. Also women account for only 47% of those that make private pension provision.

Adequate retirement income

Another very important question to ask yourself is **"What level of income will be adequate for my needs in retirement?"** The word "adequate" is a very important word when talking about retirement planning.

Once you decide on what level of yearly income you will need in retirement – bearing in mind that your mortgage will most likely be paid off, and your children are not likely to be dependant on you are longer – you should multiply this figure by 25 to 30 times to calculate the retirement capital you will need. **So, an income of €30,000 a year is likely to need retirement capital in the region of €750,000 to €900,000**. If you are going to have a dependant spouse/partner to provide for in retirement it is important that you take this into account in your calculations. Of course, if your spouse/partner has independent income currently then they too should be planning for retirement.

The cost of delay

It's very important to start planning for retirement early. Every year can make a big difference as can be seen from the table on page 261. Based upon the assumed investment growth rate and charges shown, an individual who starts contributing to a pension plan 10 years before retirement age will have to contribute more than five times as much as a person starting thirty years before retirement age, in order to accumulate the same amount of money.

Example

€5,000 p.a. (level) pension contribution,6% pa investment growth, 95% allocation & 1% annual management charge.

Term	Illustrative capital	Factor
10 years	€62,732	5.28
15 years	€107,623	3.78
20 years	€164,916	2.62
25 years	€238,039	1.71
30 years	€331,364	1.00

Source: Zurich Life Assurance plc

Why Pension Plans?

When it comes to putting money aside for the future there are many choices available to you. You could use personal investments, such as property, stocks and shares, works of art, etc. Personal savings accounts with banks or credit unions, or through life assurance policies, are another method of accumulating capital for retirement. However, saving through pension plans is for most people the most attractive option. This is due to the tax incentives available from the State.

Although the tax incentives are not as attractive for higher earners as they were in the past, pension plans are still, for the vast majority of individuals, very tax-efficient. Basically a pension plan is a savings plan, with special tax incentives, used to build up a capital sum that will be used to provide an income in retirement for you (and your dependants). The tax incentives are:

- Tax relief on personal contributions.

- Tax-exempt investment growth within the pension investment fund(s).

- Tax-free cash at retirement.

- No tax liability on employer contributions to occupational pensions.

Because of the special tax incentives there are certain rules/criteria that must be observed. Also income draw-down from the different types of pension plans following retirement is liable to taxation. We will look at both these issues in greater depth later in this chapter.

The rules/criteria and the taxation of income from pension plans are the areas that complicate pensions, but it's important to remember the basic concept of pensions is very simple. You, and maybe your employer, pay in money while you are working and at retirement you draw an income out of the fund you have accumulated.

Tax Relief on personal contributions

- Subject to certain limits, for every €100 that you contribute you will pay €41 less in Income Tax if you are a 41% tax-payer and €20 less if you are 20% tax-payer. This is equivalent to a 69.5% subsidy from the State if you are a higher rate tax-payer and a 25% subsidy if you are a standard rate tax-payer.

- The following table shows the limits that apply to the amount of contributions that can be personally made to pension plans in any one year. The maximum earnings to which these limits can be applied are currently €115,000 a year.

Age	Percentage of net relevant earnings/remuneration
Up to 29 Years	15%
30 to 39 Years	20%
40 to 49 Years	25%
50 to 54 Years	30%
55 to 59 Years	35%
60 and over	40%

Notes

- Relevant earnings consist of income from self-employment. A husband and wife have separate relevant earnings, which cannot be aggregated for retirement saving purposes. Income from a claim under a Permanent Health Insurance (PHI) policy is considered to be relevant earnings for retirement saving purposes. Investment earnings are not treated as relevant earnings and cannot be taken into consideration in calculating your maximum allowable pension contributions. Net relevant earnings consist of relevant earning less capital allowances, trading losses and certain other charges e.g. covenants and mortgage interest, for which you can claim tax relief.

- Remuneration applies to the earnings of employees and directors who pay tax under the PAYE system. It can include basic pay, bonus payments, over-time payments and any other payments that are subject to Schedule E tax (PAYE) including the value of any benefit-in-kind.

- For some specific occupations the 30% limit applies irrespective of age (e.g. certain professional sports people)

- With the exception of Additional Voluntary Contributions made through a Personal Retirement Savings Account (AVC PRSAs), regardless of age and net relevant earnings an annual contribution of €1,525 to a Personal Retirement Savings Account (PRSA) will attract tax relief, even if this exceeds the figures shown on page 262

- For the self-employed and individuals in non-pensionable employment, the limits on page 262, relate to the total of personal contributions, and any employer contributions, made to Personal Pension plans or PRSA contracts.

- For employees who are members of occupational pension schemes the limits shown on page 262 apply to the total of personal contributions, Additional Voluntary Contributions (AVCs), and/or PRSA AVCs made. Employer contributions to Occupational pension schemes are not taken into account in calculating the maximum contributions for personal tax relief.

- Where an individual has more than one source of income the total figure of €115,000 applies to the aggregated income. Where one of the incomes is pensionable through an occupational pension scheme, they must use up all the relief available in respect of that pensionable income if they wish to maximise their full tax relief entitlement, and claim relief on contributions relating to their non-pensionable income after that, if there is scope to do so.

Individuals who make personal contributions to pension plans by October 31st in any given tax year can back-date the tax relief to the previous tax year, provided they advise the Revenue of their intention to back-date the relief by October 31st. This does not apply where contributions are made by salary deduction as the tax relief is given at source.

For those who are registered to file their tax returns and pay their tax bills on-line through the Revenue Online System (ROS) the Revenue allow an extension on the October 31st deadline to mid-November. These individuals have until this date to make their pension contributions and notify the Revenue of their intention to back-date the relief.

Budget 2013

In his Budget 2013 speech the Minister for Finance announced that the Government's aim was that there would be no tax relief for contributions to a pension fund that would give an annual income on retirement in excess of €60,000 per annum. Details of how this will be achieved are not likely to be published until 2014 following a consultation process with interested parties.

Tax-Exempt Investment Growth

- The fact that pension funds can grow without any liability to Income Tax on investment income and without any Capital Gains Tax on investment growth means that there is the potential to accumulate larger amounts of capital than under personal savings and investments where investment returns are taxable (e.g. DIRT on Deposit Accounts).

- Although the Government has introduced a temporary levy of 0.6% p.a. on pension for four years from 2011 to 2014 this levy will have a minimal effect on the returns from pension funds over the long term, particularly where contributions to pension plans are made on a regular basis.

Budget 2013

In his Budget 2013 speech the Minister for Finance stated that this levy will not be extended beyond 2014.

Tax-Free Cash at Retirement

- Every individual who funds for retirement through a pension plan or plans is entitled to take a lump sum benefit at retirement. The maximum lump sum will depend on the type of pension plan that the individual has.

- For Personal Pensions and PRSAs the maximum lump sum is 25% of the accumulated fund. For Defined Benefit occupational pension schemes up to 150% of "final remuneration" can be taken, depending on their length of service with their employer. Members of Defined Contribution occupational schemes have a choice between the 25% of fund and the earnings and service related bases.

- The maximum lump sum that can be taken is currently €575,000 and the first €200,000 of this can be taken tax-free, with the next €375,000 taxed at only 20%. This figure of €200,000 is a lifetime figure and all retirement lump sums taken since Dec 5th 2005 are taken into account.

No Tax Liability on Employer Contributions

- For employees there is no liability to Income Tax, PRSI or USC on the contributions their employers make to occupational pension schemes on their behalf. (Due to an anomaly, there is a USC liability on employers' contributions to PRSAs and Personal Pensions. Also, if employers' contributions to PRSAs or Personal Pensions cause the total contributions to exceed the maximum allowable personal contribution limits as detailed on page 262, there is a liability to Income Tax and PRSI on the amount by which the limits are exceeded.)

- Being a member of an occupational pension scheme makes a great deal of sense for an employee even if they are obliged to make contributions to the scheme. For example, if the employer is contributing 5% of salary and the employee is obliged to contribute a further 5%, the employee is getting the value of 10% of salary being contributed, all for a net outlay of 2.95% of salary if they are a 41% tax-payer, and 4% of salary if they are a 20% tax-payer.

- For individuals who own their own companies (i.e. Proprietary Directors) having their companies contribute to occupational pension schemes is an excellent way for them to take profits from their companies and put these profits away for their futures without any immediate liability to tax. Their spouses can also be employees/directors of these companies and their retirement capital can be funded separately through occupational pension plans.

- Self-employed individuals can also employ their spouses and other family members, and accumulate retirement capital for them through occupational pension schemes. The employer contributions are invested for the spouses / family members without any liability to benefit-in-kind taxation on the employer contributions. The self-employed individual can also receive tax relief on their contributions to the schemes.

ENGAGE WITH YOUR
PENSION

www.pensionsboard.ie

Pension calculators   **Information booklets**   **Pension checklists**

Standard Fund Threshold

- In order to deter the abuse of the rules regarding the tax incentives offered to those contributing to pension plans the Government has introduced a maximum limit on the value of the accumulated pension fund (or, the capital equivalent of the benefits accrued under a Defined Benefit occupational pension scheme) in recent years. This limit is known as the Standard Fund Threshold, and this has been €2.3 million since 7 December 2010.

- Those whose accrued value exceeded €2.3 million at 7 December 2010 were allowed to apply to Revenue to have their value recognised as a Personal Fund Threshold. For Defined Benefit schemes the capitalisation factor to be used in converting the value of the total accrued pension benefit to a capital value is 20, before the deduction of any lump sum benefit. In other words, the current SFT of €2.30 million is equivalent to a pension benefit of €115,000 per annum.

- At retirement those whose fund value exceeds the Standard Fund Threshold / Personal Fund Threshold must pay a once-off additional tax of 41% on the excess over their respective threshold amount. This is in addition to the normal taxation of income from pension plans which will be covered later in this chapter.

Pension investment funds

An important area where you need to take control is with regard to the funds into which your pension contributions are invested. Again, using the services of a qualified financial adviser who can explain how investment funds work and who can offer you lots of choice, may be a good idea.

You need to understand what caveats such as "Past performance is not a reliable guide to future performance" or "The value of your pension fund may go down as well as up" actually mean. You need to think about how you would feel if your retirement investments dropped in value by 10%, 20% or even more overnight. Would you be very upset or would you understand that in all likelihood they would eventually gain back that loss again over time. This is what is known as your level of "risk tolerance".

A good financial adviser should be able to help you decide what your level of risk tolerance is and should be able to help you decide what sort of funds suit you best.

It is important that you are comfortable with the funds you choose. After all it is your money that is being invested and your retirement that is being funded for. However, investment theory tells us that the greater the level of risk taken the greater the chances of making more profits in the long term.

This does not mean that a pension fund investment manager is likely to offer you funds that are so risky that you could lose all your investment. Usually a pension fund will hold a wide range of assets, and even a fund that is invested in one asset class, such as equities, will usually hold a large number of different equities. Investment theory also tells us that the lesser the number equities held within such a fund the higher the risk, but also the greater the potential for higher returns. Most providers will give you full details of the spread of assets held within a fund.

Unit-Linked Funds

There are the four main asset classes into which pension fund managers will invest:

- Equities – i.e. stocks and shares in companies.

- Property.

- Fixed Income Securities (Bonds) – i.e. loans issued by governments and larger companies.

- Cash.

There are other asset classes, such as commodities, but these are not used as much as these four main classes.

Investment returns are achieved by investment income from these assets and by growth in the value of the assets.

Examples of investment income are dividends being paid to the shareholders who own shares in the companies; rental income from property; dividends paid by governments and companies on bonds; and, by interest earned by cash on deposit. This income is usually re-invested back into the fund by purchasing further assets.

Investment growth is achieved by the assets increasing in value, although the opposite can also happen from time to time, as a result of less favourable economic conditions. However, over the years it would be expected that most assets and the funds invested in them would grow in value particularly over the longer term.

- Most pension funds in Ireland are operated on a unit-linked basis. That is, the contributions into the pension plan buy "units" in the fund. These units reflect the value of the assets held by the fund. If the value of the assets increases either by their sale value increasing or as a result of investment income being used to purchase more assets, the value ("price") of the units owned by the fund will increase. Depending on investment conditions unit prices can also fall in value from time to time.

- The unit-linked funds in the Irish market would mainly invest in established markets in one or more of the asset classes mentioned above, although alternative markets or assets may also be used. Where assets are owned outside the Eurozone there can be an exposure to currency fluctuations, but the effect of this may be offset through "hedging".

- A long term historical view of the returns achieved on the different asset classes shows that, equities produce the highest average returns in real terms (i.e. when compared to inflation). When it comes to pensions or any other savings or investments inflation beating returns are what count. Maintaining the purchasing power of the money you invest is very important.

- However, investing in equities can be risky as again historically statistics show that equities can be more volatile than other assets. That is, they are likely to rise and fall in value more often and the ups and downs are likely to be of a greater magnitude.

- The most popular funds in terms of moneys invested are Managed or mixed funds that would use a mix of the different asset classes, but with more of an emphasis on equities than on the other asset classes – with 70% or more invested in equities normally.

- "With-profit" funds, which are more traditional type funds also invest in a mix of asset classes, but try to give a more systematic distribution of investment profits than managed funds, through yearly bonus declarations, and maturity bonuses. In good investment years they hold profits in reserve in order to be able to pay yearly bonuses to be added to policyholders' investments in poor years for investment returns. The maturity bonuses which may be paid when the policy is being matured or surrendered will reflect the underlying assets in the fund at the time the policy is being matured or surrendered. With-profit funds may also have certain levels of guarantee built into the contract. In recent times a number of the with-profit funds available on the Irish market have been closed to new business. And, many of the funds have had "Market Level Adjustments (MLAs)" imposed. This means that on surrender of the fund the value payable to the contract owner has been reduced due to the fact that the total underlying value of the assets in the fund is less than the total value as shown in the clients' investment accounts.

- Absolute Return Funds are a recent development. They seek to make positive returns in either a rising or falling stock-market cycle by employing investment management techniques that differ from traditional unit-linked funds. They will hold a diverse range of asset classes and use a range of investment techniques that will try to make a profit from both ups and downs in the markets and in individual stocks. Investment techniques include using short selling, futures, options, derivatives, arbitrage, leverage and unconventional assets. There are no guarantees that these techniques will work and only time will tell how well they will do in the future.

- It is important to note that the returns on the different funds will depend on the skills of those managing the funds. This is why investment return figures can vary from investment manager to investment manager even where the investments are broadly within the same sectors. The managers may be investing in similar assets but the specific assets, such as specific company shares, that they buy and the time at which they buy and/or sell these assets will make a difference to the returns achieved.

- Passive investment strategies where the investment managers attempt to achieve the returns on a specific sector (e.g. Eurozone Equities) through buying assets that track the assets held within an index of that sector (Euro Stoxx 50) have also grown in popularity in recent years. Consensus Funds are a similar idea in that the managers try to mirror the average of the assets held by other fund managers operating within a sector in order to achieve the average returns earned in that sector.

- With certain pension products a self-directed option is available, whereby the individual can decide on the individual stocks and shares, or bonds etc that they wish to invest in. Currencies other than the Euro can also be accessed through this option. In the past self-investment in property has been popular, but those who went this route now have lots of problems as a result of the massive fall in property values.

So, as retirement planning is a long term exercise pension investors may be better off to take the risk of the higher volatility to achieve better long term returns. But, not all of us will want to take that risk. It is important, therefore, to ensure that you understand fully the risks involved.

Another important point is that as retirement age approaches if you have a large exposure to equity based investment, a move away from this position to less volatile investments may suit, depending on how the funds are to be used to provide an income in retirement.

Retirement capital accumulation products

This brings us to the types of specific pension products that can be used for the accumulation of retirement capital. There are a number of different types of pension contracts available.

Firstly though, it is important to understand the difference between Defined Contribution plans and Defined Benefit plans.

Defined Contribution Plans

- Defined Contribution plans also known as "Money Purchase" plans are the more common type of pension plan being arranged in current times.

- Under individual Defined Contribution pension plans the individual has their own retirement account into which contributions are invested. Group occupational pension schemes can also be Defined Contribution arrangements arranged under a group trust. Under these schemes the individual scheme member also has an individual investment account.

- The investment will purchase units in the fund or funds that are chosen for investment. These units may produce investment growth which, when added to by further contributions and growth should mean that the individual's investment account grows over the years.

- The size of the retirement account will depend on the total contributions made, the investment growth achieved and the charges deducted.

- Obviously, the earlier the contributions start being made the more contributions are likely to be made by retirement age, and the more time the money has to accumulate.

Defined Benefit Schemes

Defined Benefit plans are usually confined to large occupational pension schemes where the employer promises a certain level of pension income to employees at retirement. This promise to pay benefits is funded through contributions made by the employer and the employee members of the scheme. The promised pension is normally based on a proportion of salary at retirement multiplied by the number of years service with the employer at retirement age – for example, 1/60th of final earnings for each year of service. Part of the pension income can normally be given up ("commuted") in lieu of a lump sum benefit at retirement.

The Superannuation scheme for Public Sector employees is a Defined Benefit pension scheme. However, there is no pre-funding of benefits and the benefits are paid from the exchequer on a pay as you go basis. The pension benefit is normally based on 1/80th of pensionable salary at retirement for each year of service, with a gratuity (i.e. lump sum) payment based on 3/80ths of pensionable salary for each year of service, payable when the individual reaches normal retirement age. New employees joining the public sector from Jan 1st 2012 will have their retirement benefits based on the average of their earnings over their careers rather than on earnings at retirement age.

Personal Retirement Savings Accounts (PRSAs)

First introduced in 2003 PRSAs are intended to be low-cost, simple to understand, accessible, portable retirement savings plans. They are Defined Contribution arrangements.

- Any resident of Ireland can contribute to a PRSA but only those with income from self-employment or from non-pensionable employment (i.e. are not members an occupational pension scheme) will get tax relief on their contributions. However, where an individual intends returning to the workforce at sometime in the future they can make contributions to a PRSA and carry the tax relief entitlement forward to future years. An individual can have more than one PRSA but the contribution limits apply to the total contributions being made.

- Members of occupational pension schemes may make Additional Voluntary Contributions (AVCs) to enhance the benefits provided by their occupational schemes through PRSAs. See page 281 for more details.

- PRSAs may also be used to accept in transfers of occupational pension scheme members' pension fund values when a member leaves the scheme or the scheme is being wound-up. Conditions and criteria apply, the main one being that a transfer to a PRSA may only take place if the individual has been a member of the scheme or of any other scheme related to that individual's employment with, or any person connected with, the employer for less than 15 years.

- PRSAs are personally owned contracts. An employer may make contributions to an employee's PRSA, but once contributions are made by the employer they become the property of the individual employee through their PRSA.

- Employers that do not provide membership of an occupational pension scheme for employees within six months of joining employment must provide a facility whereby the employees involved can have their PRSA contributions deducted from salary at source. This applies to temporary or permanent, full-time or part-time employees.

- Tax relief on contributions to PRSAs is subject to age-related limits as outlined on page 262. Employer contributions are counted in calculating the maximum contributions and if limits are exceeded the excess amount is subject to benefit-in-kind taxation.

- Due to an anomaly in the legislation all employer contributions to PRSA's are treated as a Benefit-in-Kind for USC purposes.

- Employers receive tax relief on their contributions to employees' PRSAs, and are not liable for Employers' PRSI on their contributions. If the employer is a company, tax relief is against Corporation Tax, if the employer is a self-employed individual or a partnership the tax relief will be against Income Tax. Employers do not receive any relief against Employers' PRSI on the employees' contributions deducted from salaries at source.

- Back-dating of tax relief on contributions made by an individual plan-holder to the previous tax year is allowed, subject to the age-related limits and earnings cap as detailed on page 262

- The legislation governing PRSAs allows for two different types of PRSAs – Standard and Non-Standard. For Standard PRSAs, charges are restricted to a maximum of 5% of contributions and 1% p.a. of the accumulated fund, and "pooled investment" funds must be used. There are no maximum charge restrictions on Non-Standard PRSAs, but they can have a wider fund choice than Standard PRSAs.

- All PRSA contracts must have a default investment strategy, which must be designed to fulfil the reasonable expectations of a typical PRSA investor who does not possess an in-depth knowledge of investment matters.

- The cost of risk benefits (i.e. life assurance cover, serious illness cover, or Permanent Health Insurance cover) cannot be deducted from PRSA contributions or investment accounts.

- No costs can be charged on transfers to PRSAs from other retirement contracts or on transfers from PRSAs to other retirement contracts.

- Normally, you can mature a PRSA contract any time after you reach age 60. Benefits must be taken before age 75 and it is not necessary to stop working to draw benefits after age 60. Employees who are retiring from employment can draw benefits after age 50.

- On maturing your PRSA you will entitled to take 25% of your fund as a lump sum benefit, subject to a maximum of €575,000. Under current legislation the first €200,000 of the lump sum will be tax-free with the excess over €200,000 being taxed at 20%. For PRSA AVCs the accumulated fund will be aggregated with the main scheme benefits and the maximum lump sum that can be taken will be subject to the rules governing Occupational Pension Schemes.

Personal Pensions / Retirement Annuity Contracts (RACs)

Personal Pensions have been available in Ireland since 1968. Personal Pensions are very similar to PRSAs, but there are some differences.

- As with PRSAs, Personal Pension plans are personally owned by the individual. An employer may make contributions to an employee's Personal Pension plan, but once contributions are made by the employer they become the property of the individual employee through their Personal Pension plan.

- One area of difference between Personal Pensions and PRSAs is that only those with income from self-employment or from non-pensionable employment (i.e. are not members an occupational pension scheme) can contribute to Personal Pension plans.

- Tax relief on contributions to Personal Pension plans is subject to the same age-related limits that apply to PRSAs or any personal contributions to pension arrangements. These limits are outlined on page 262. As with PRSAs, employer contributions are counted in calculating the maximum contributions and if limits are exceeded the excess amount is subject to Benefit-in-Kind. An individual can have more than one Personal Pension but the contribution limits apply to the total contributions being made.

- Due to the same anomaly as applies to PRSAs all employer contributions to Personal Pension plans are treated as a Benefit-in-Kind for USC purposes.

- As with PRSAs, employers receive tax relief on their contributions to employees' plans, and are not liable for Employers' PRSI on their contributions. If the employer is a company, tax relief is against Corporation Tax, if the employer is a self-employed individual or a partnership the tax relief will be against Income Tax. Employers do not receive any relief against Employers' PRSI on the employees' contributions deducted from salaries at source.

- Back-dating of tax relief on contributions made by an individual plan-holder to the previous tax year is allowed (see page 262), subject to the age-related limits and earnings cap as detailed on page 262.

- The cost of life assurance cover can be deducted from Personal Pension contributions or investment accounts. Also, Personal Pension plan legislation allows plans to be put in place that solely provide a benefit on death before retirement. This can be a very tax-efficient method of providing life assurance protection.

- Normally, you can mature a Personal Pension plan contract any time after you reach age 60. Benefits must be taken before age 75 and it is not necessary to stop working to draw benefits after age 60.

- On maturing your Personal Pension plan you will entitled to take 25% of your fund as a lump sum benefit, subject to a maximum of €575,000. Under current legislation the first €200,000 of the lump sum will be tax-free with the excess between €200,000 and €575,000 being taxed at 20%.

- A wider fund choice can be available under Personal Pension plans than under PRSAs, particularly Standard PRSAs.

Occupational Pension Schemes

Otherwise known as employer-sponsored pension schemes, company-paid pensions, or employee pensions, occupational pension schemes are the most attractive retirement funding product from a tax-efficiency perspective. This is because the individual employee or director is not liable for tax on the employer contributions to the scheme.

Employers will often establish an occupational scheme for their employees out of a sense of duty to those employees; to reward their employees for their hard work and loyalty; to attract better quality employees to their employment; and, to retain better quality employees.

- Employers receive tax relief on their contributions to occupational pension schemes and are not liable for Employers' PRSI on their contributions. If the employer is a company tax relief is against Corporation Tax, if the employer is a self-employed individual or a partnership the tax relief will be against Income Tax. Employers do not receive any relief against Employers' PRSI on the employees' contributions deducted from salaries at source.

- Employees receive relief against Income Tax on their contributions subject to the age-related limits (see page 262).

- In order to qualify for the pension tax incentives Occupational Pension schemes must be established under trust for the benefit of the sponsoring employer's employees and their dependants, and they must be approved by the Revenue Commissioners.

MyFolio

Investments made easy

Choose one of our five MyFolio funds expertly managed to suit your attitude to risk.

Talk to your financial adviser about accessing these funds through our pensions, savings and investment products or visit **standardlife.ie**

Warning:	If you invest in these funds you may lose some or all of the money you invest
Warning:	The value of your investment may go down as well as up
Warning:	This investment may be affected by changes in currency exchange rates

The Way Forward

Pensions and Investments since 1834
standardlife.ie

- Only employees and directors who are taxed under the PAYE system may become members of occupational pension schemes.

- An administrator must be appointed to the scheme. This can be a Life Assurance Company or a specialist pension administration firm.

Occupational Pension Schemes can be arranged on Defined Contribution basis or a Defined Benefit basis.

- Defined Contribution schemes can be arranged on an individual basis ("Executive Pensions") using individual trusts or on a group basis ("Group Defined Contribution Pension Schemes") using a group trust. The members of the scheme will each have their own individual investment account into which contributions are placed, and the account is then invested in pension funds. Benefits at retirement are provided for the individual members from their accounts.

- Defined Benefit schemes are normally arranged on a group basis using a group trust. The scheme will normally have one pooled fund, into which contributions are placed, and the pooled fund is then invested. The retirement benefits will very often be paid to the individual scheme members out of this fund. However, as an alternative, the trustees of Defined Benefit schemes may purchase annuities to provide the retirement income for the scheme members.

- Occupational Pension Schemes are subject to a set of rules laid out by Revenue Commissioners under the Revenue Practice Notes. These rules lay down a set of maximum benefits that can be paid to scheme beneficiaries on retirement at the scheme's normal retirement age, on the early retirement of the scheme member, and on the death of the scheme member. These limits are detailed later in this chapter.

- The maximum contributions that can be paid on behalf of an employee by the employer and employee to a Defined Contribution scheme are much greater than those allowed to PRSAs or Personal Pension plans. Samples of the maximum allowable rates are shown on the table on page 280, and the earnings ceiling of €115,000 does not apply to the employer contributions. However, the Standard Fund Threshold (€2.3 million) – or, Personal Fund Threshold – does apply to each individual member.

Maximum Allowable Contributions to Defined Contribution
Schemes

Years to NRA	NRA 60	NRA 65
5	432%	379%
10	216%	189%
15	144%	126%
20	108%	95%
25	86%	76%
30	72%	63%

NRA = Normal Retirement Age

- As all contributions are pooled there are no limits on the total contributions that can be made to a Defined Benefit pension scheme but the eventual retirement benefits are limited by the Revenue rules. For Defined Benefit scheme members the Standard Fund Threshold is calculated by applying the benefit formula applying to the scheme, and currently using a multiplier of 20.

- In recent years many self-employed individuals have established companies in order to avail of the more attractive tax regime that applies to occupational schemes. They become proprietary directors of the companies and draw income from the companies. They then put Executive Pension plans in place in respect of their company incomes.

- The spouses and family of proprietary directors can also be made employees or directors of the companies and paid an income by the company provided they are genuine employees. This income can also be pensioned under Occupational Pension plans. This means that the spouse then has their own separate Standard Fund Threshold and can draw a separate lump sum benefit at retirement, the first €200,000 of which will be tax free under current legislation.

Employees of the State are usually provided with pensions on a Defined Benefit basis. However, these pensions are not funded in advance. Instead benefits are paid from revenue collected by the State through taxes.

Small Self-Administered Pension Schemes (SSAPS) are occupational pension schemes established by an employer where the company directors wish to have more choice and more control over the investments made by the scheme. There are Revenue rules regarding the types of investment that a SSAPS can make and the pensioner trustee, that must be appointed to SSAPs, must ensure that these are adhered to.

Additional Voluntary Contributions (AVCs)

Employees and directors who are members of Occupational Pension Schemes may enhance the benefits (i.e. lump sum and/or pension) provided by their schemes by making traditional AVCs to the scheme itself, or by making traditional AVCs to a separate group AVC arrangement established under trust, or by making AVCs through PRSA contracts (i.e. PRSA AVCs). Scheme benefits cannot be enhanced to a degree whereby they exceed the maximum benefits as allowed by the Revenue.

Although put in place to enhance Occupational Scheme benefits at normal retirement age, AVCs are very often used to help employees retire early from employment, where it is possible to retire early.

- Traditional AVCs must be arranged under trust on a group basis – either the main scheme trust or a separate trust.

- PRSA AVCs need not be arranged under trust. They are owned by the individual scheme member. They give more control over the investment of the contributions to the scheme member. As they can be arranged with a different provider to the provider of the main scheme, they can give the scheme member more choice.

- Traditional AVCs can be arranged on a Defined Contribution basis or a Defined Benefit basis. PRSA AVCs are arranged on a Defined contribution basis only.

- The majority of traditional AVCs are now arranged on a Defined Contribution basis.

- Defined Benefit AVCs are often referred to as "added years" AVCs. At this point in time the added years option applies mainly to the schemes for Public Sector employees. They will provide additional lump sum and additional pension benefits. It is not possible to fund solely for additional lump sum benefits through the added years option.

- Defined Contribution AVCs and PRSA AVCs can be used to fund solely for additional lump sum benefit, subject to the overall maximum lump sum benefit allowed by Revenue.

- AVCs / PRSA AVCs are subject to the rules of the main occupational scheme in that benefits must be taken at the same time, either on retirement at the schemes normal retirement age or on early retirement.

- The overall total benefits provided by the main scheme and the AVCs / PRSA AVCs are subject to the Revenue rules regarding maximum benefits.

Budget 2013

In his Budget 2013 speech the Minister for Finance announced that for a period of three years from the passing of the Finance Act 2013 individuals will be able to access up to 30% of the fund they have accumulated in AVC contracts. The withdrawals they make will be subject to Income Tax at their marginal rate. It is not clear whether PRSI and USC will also be payable at the time of going to print. The Finance Act 2013 will clarify this.

- The normal rules regarding tax relief apply, and the scheme member's total contributions, including AVCs / PRSA AVCs, are subject to the age-related limits. (Page 262).

- When putting an AVC / PRSA AVC in place the scheme member needs to consider carefully how tax-efficient the exercise will be. In simple terms, unless some of the accumulated AVC fund can be taken back on a tax-free or reduced tax lump sum basis making AVCs may not be tax efficient.

- AVCs and PRSA AVCs can be made either by salary deduction at source, where the employer transfers them on to the AVC provider, or by direct debit from the individual's bank account.

- Back-dating of tax relief on lump sum contributions not made by salary deduction to the previous tax year is allowed.

Long Term Savings Plans

For certain individuals for whom further retirement funding through pension plans is not tax-efficient, using long-term savings plans to fund for their retirement may be an option. Examples of where contributing to pension plans may not be tax-efficient for certain individuals are as follows:

- They are higher earning self-employed individuals who are already maximising the tax relief limits on pension contributions to PRSAs or Personal Pensions, and forming companies is not practical for them.

- They are higher paid employees in non-pensionable employment who are already maximising the tax relief limits on pension contributions to PRSAs or Personal Pensions.

- Their accumulated retirement fund is likely to exceed the Standard Fund Threshold of €2.3 million.

- None of their AVC fund will be available to them on a tax-free or reduced tax basis.

- If they have more than one source of income, and one of these sources is a pensionable employment for which they are paid more than €115,000 per annum, they must use up their contribution tax relief allowances by way of AVCs in respect of that employment. If they wish to make retirement provision in respect of their non-pensioned income they cannot do this tax-efficiently through pension plans as they are not entitled to tax relief on the contributions.

While there is no tax relief available on contributions to savings plans and while the investment growth or interest accumulated is subject to tax (at 36% on life assurance policies and at 33% on deposit account with effect from 1 Jan 2013) the proceeds of the savings plan can be taken on a tax-free basis as a lump sum. For life assurance policies investment fund options similar to those available under pension plans are available.

Income in retirement products

Over the coming pages we will look at the products that are used to provide an income from the retirement capital, individuals have accumulated through pension plans and long term savings plans. We will also look at the tax treatment of the income drawn from these products.

However, we will first look at the options available to pension plan holders when they get to retirement.

As already noted those with Personal Pension plans and PRSAs can take up to 25% of their accumulated retirement capital as a lump sum benefit up to a maximum of €575,000, with the first €200,000 of this being payable tax-free, and the balance taxed at 20%. The balance of their capital can then be used to provide an income in line with the Flexible Retirement Options outlined below.

Members of Defined Contribution Occupational Pension schemes, individual or group, have a choice of options. One is to take up to 25% of their accumulated retirement capital as a lump sum benefit up to a maximum of €575,000, with the first €200,000 of this being payable tax-free, and the balance taxed at 20%, provided the rules of their scheme allows this. If they choose this option the balance of their capital can then be used to provide an income in line with the Flexible Retirement Options outlined below.

The other option available to them is to base their lump sum benefit on a formula based on their service with the employer and their "Final Remuneration", as outlined in the Revenue Practice Notes. If they choose this option then they must opt for an annuity to provide the retirement income.

Members of Defined Benefit Occupational Pension schemes must base their lump sum benefit on the formula based on their service with the employer and their "Final Remuneration", as outlined in the Revenue Practice Notes. The retirement income must be taken from the scheme's overall fund, unless the trustees buy an annuity using capital from the scheme's overall fund. This applies also to Defined Benefit AVCs.

Capital accumulated within a traditional AVC Defined Contribution arrangement or a PRSA AVC contract can be used to provide an income in line with the Flexible Retirement Options outlined on next page.

Flexible Retirement Options

If your retirement fund is in a Defined Contribution (DC) arrangement (i.e. a DC pension scheme, a PRSA, a Personal Pension etc.) you have a choice of using the balance of accumulated retirement capital, after taking your tax-free cash, to provide you with an income through any combination of the following:

1. Buying an annuity.

2. Investing in an Approved Retirement Fund (ARF) and gradually drawing down an income.

3. Taking your money in cash form, subject to an immediate tax liability.

Those with PRSAs, but not PRSA AVCs (see page 273), have an option also to leave the retirement capital in the PRSA up to age 75, but not after age 75, rather than investing it in an ARF or buying an annuity. Once the retirement lump sum is taken from a PRSA the PRSA becomes known as a "Vested PRSA".

To avail of options 2 and 3 above there are requirements one of which you are obliged to fulfil at retirement:

● Have reached age 75.

● Have a guaranteed pension income of €18,000 per year (i.e. 1.5 times the maximum rate of Contributory State Pension for a single person, read to the nearest €100) which is payable for your lifetime ("Specified Income").

● Have €119,800 (i.e. 10 times the maximum rate of Contributory State Pension for a single person read to the nearest €100) invested in an Approved Minimum Retirement Fund (AMRF), or have used €119,800 to purchase an annuity.

The pension income of €18,000 can include any ordinary pension annuity or Social Welfare Pensions (single rate) and foreign pensions.

For employees and directors, who make AVCs / PRSA AVCs, when it comes to the tax-free cash element of their pensions at retirement they are subject to the Revenue rules relating to the overall maximum benefits that can be provided by their occupational schemes (see page 277), and cannot take 25% of the AVC / PRSA AVC fund in addition to the maximum allowable benefit under those rules.

Annuities

An annuity operates on the basis of you paying all or part of your retirement fund (i.e. the annuity purchase amount) to the life assurance company and, in return, the life assurance company guaranteeing to pay you a pension income (annuity) for the rest of your lifetime. Depending on the type of annuity you purchase, income may also be payable for the lifetime of your financial dependants after your death.

● The amount of your income will be expressed in terms of a percentage of the capital used to buy the pension - the annuity rate. For example, if your pension plan had a value of €500,000 and the annuity rate quoted was 5% then your pension income would be €25,000 p.a.

● The factors that usually decide the annuity rate are age, the on the government bonds purchased by the life assurance company prevailing at the time the annuity is purchased, the type of annuity (i.e. single life or joint life annuity) and additional benefits purchased such as annual increases on the annuity income and a guaranteed minimum payment period, should you die early in retirement.

● Annuity income is made up of both the bond yield on the investment of your money and a return of part of the original capital invested. With annuities, those who live well into old age benefit to a greater degree than those who die earlier in retirement, and the total of all the years' income they receive back from the annuity before they die is likely to be much larger than their original investment.

● Annuity income is subject to Income Tax and the Universal Social Charge (USC) but is not subject to PRSI. The normal credits and exemption limits apply. Pension income paid directly from the fund of a Defined Benefit Occupational Pension Scheme is subject to tax in a similar manner.

Approved Retirement Funds (ARFs) & Approved Minimum Retirement Funds (AMRFs)

An Approved Retirement Fund (ARF) is an investment contract, owned by the individual retiree, from which the individual can draw down income as required.

● The investment is in tax-exempt pension funds, including a self-directed fund option from some ARF providers.

- An Approved Minimum Retirement Fund (AMRF) is similar to an ARF, except that only investment growth can be drawn down, before age 75, unless the AMRF becomes an ARF at an earlier date. An AMRF becomes an ARF once the Specified Income requirement is fulfilled, or on the death of the AMRF owner.

- The ARF option was designed to give the individual involved more control over the use of their accumulated retirement fund; to address the problem of lower annuity rates; and to address the needs of those who wish to pass on the value of their pension funds to their dependants on death. The purpose of AMRFs is to address the criticism that a spendthrift could dissipate their retirement benefits too quickly.

- Any withdrawal from an Approved Retirement Fund or Approved Minimum Retirement Fund taken out after 6th April 2000 is liable to Income Tax under the PAYE system. Withdrawals from ARFs and AMRFs are also subject to PRSI up to age 66 and to USC.

- From the year when an individual turns age 61 Income Tax, PRSI and USC are payable on "imputed distributions" from ARFs, but not AMRFs. An imputed distribution is an assumed withdrawal from the ARF of 5% of its value as at 30th Nov each year. If an ARF-holder withdraws this amount or more from the ARF during the year ending on 30th Nov then there is no imputed distribution and the tax is payable only on the amount withdrawn. Where withdrawals are less than 5% in the year the actual withdrawals made from both ARFs and AMRFs during the year can be deducted from the 5% value. The annual imputed distribution rate on ARFs is 6% in respect of ARFs with asset values in excess of €2 million (or, where an individual owns more than one ARF or Vested PRSA, where the combined value of the assets in those ARFs and/or Vested PRSAs exceeds €2 million). Where the combined value exceeds €2 million the 6% rate applies to the total value and not just the excess over €2 million.

- You are not restricted to one ARF, you can spread your retirement amongst a number of the Qualifying Fund Managers that provide ARFs and AMRFs, but you can have only one AMRF.

- A disadvantage of ARF investment is that if the investment funds do not provide sufficient investment returns to cover withdrawals or imputed distributions the ARF may potentially dissipate before the individual ARF holder dies.

- On death the tax treatment of an ARF will depend on who benefits from the proceeds. The following chart shows the tax treatment on death of ARFs taken out after 6 April 2000.

Tax treatment of ARFs on death

ARF funds left to	Tax due
ARF in surviving spouse's / civil partner's name	No tax on transfer to surviving spouse's / civil partner's ARF. All subsequent withdrawals by spouse / civil partner, including imputed distributions, will be liable to Income Tax, USC & PRSI under PAYE system. Exempt from Capital Acquisitions Tax.
Directly to surviving spouse / civil partner	The full amount is treated as income of the deceased in year of death and taxed accordingly under PAYE. Exempt from Capital Acquisitions Tax.
Children aged 21 or over at date of parent's death	Income Tax charge of 30% on amount inherited, deducted at source. Exempt from Capital Acquisitions Tax.
Children under age 21 at date of parent's death	No Income Tax liability. Capital Acquisitions Tax due at 33% - normal thresholds apply.
Others	The full amount is treated as income of the deceased in year of death and taxed accordingly under PAYE. Capital Acquisitions Tax due at 33% - normal thresholds apply.

Note: If you intend leaving the money in your ARF to an ARF in your spouse's name on your death you are probably best advised to make provision for this in your Will. This will have the effect of ensuring that the proceeds will not be treated as a transfer of capital directly to your spouse.

Vested PRSAs

As stated earlier, those with PRSAs, but not PRSA AVCs, have an option to leave the retirement capital in the PRSA up to age 75, but not after age 75, rather than investing it in an ARF or buying an annuity. Once the retirement lump sum or any income is taken from a PRSA the PRSA becomes known as a "Vested PRSA".

- If the individual does not have a guaranteed pension income of €18,000 per year which is payable for their lifetime, or does not have €119,800 invested in an Approved Minimum Retirement Fund (AMRF), or has not used €119,800 to purchase an annuity they must leave €119,800 invested in the PRSA until age 75.

- As with ARFs Income Tax, PRSI and USC are payable on "imputed distributions" from ARFs and in effect the Vested PRSA is treated as if it were an ARF, with the 6% rate applying where the combined asset value of an individual's ARFs and Vested PRSAs exceeds €2 million. Where an individual is required to keep €119,800 in the PRSA until age 75, based on the paragraph immediately preceding this one, the imputed distribution tax does not apply to the €119,800.

- If an individual wishes to avail of the Vested PRSA option, and if they have a fund accumulated in another pension product, they must firstly transfer the fund to the PRSA before taking the lump sum benefit. Not all pension product funds can be transferred to Vested PRSAs. The funds from Personal Pensions plans can be transferred. However, the funds from occupational pension schemes can only be transferred if the individual has been in the scheme, or any other scheme connected to the same employment, for less than 15 years. And, unless the scheme has been wound-up a "Certificate of Benefit Comparison" from a qualified actuary is required – and, there will be an expense involved in producing this comparison.

- Income drawn from a vested PRSA is liable to Income Tax, USC and PRSI in the same way as income from an ARF.

- Because it is not allowed to take income from PRSAs after age 75 a Vested PRSA fund should be taken as income, or transferred to a PRSA, or used to purchase an annuity, by age 75.

- It is possible to make further contributions to a Vested PRSA, but as future withdrawals are liable to taxation it is unlikely to be tax-efficient to make such contributions. It is possible to put another PRSA contract in place to receive in further contributions, however, and this PRSA can be matured at a later date and a lump sum benefit of up to 25% of the fund value to be taken as a lump sum, with €200,000 tax-free rule applying.

- A disadvantage of investment in a Vested PRSA is that if the investment funds do not provide sufficient investment returns to cover withdrawals the Vested PRSA fund may potentially dissipate before the individual dies.

- In the event of the death of a Vested PRSA holder the fund within the Vested PRSA is treated similar to the way the fund within an ARF is treated on the death of the ARF holder.

Long term savings plans

As mentioned earlier the proceeds of long term savings plans are available as a lump sum payment and are not subject to taxes as income.

- The proceeds of the plan can be used to provide an income in retirement in a number of different ways, such as investing it in a life assurance bond or putting it on deposit, and drawing an income from the bond without liability to tax.

- •The proceeds can also be used to purchase an annuity (known as a "Purchased Life Annuity"). These are similar to pension annuities except with regard to how they are taxed. The part of the income drawn from the purchased life annuity that is seen to be a return of the capital is tax-free, and the part that is seen to be interest is taxed as income.

Maximum allowable benefits under occupational pension schemes

As mentioned earlier the benefits payable by an Occupational Pension Scheme at retirement or on earlier death may not exceed the maximum limits set down by the Revenue Commissioners. The calculation of some of the maximum benefits can be very complicated indeed for the ordinary individual to understand, particularly with regard to early retirement. Normally your pension provider or financial advisor will be able to explain the calculations to you, if the need arises.

Maximum Pension at Normal Retirement Age

- In general, a maximum pension of at least 1/60th of final remuneration for each year of service with the employer up to a maximum of 40 years may be provided for an employee at normal retirement age. This is referred to as the n/60ths scale where "n" is the number of years service the employee will have had with the employer at retirement.

- If the employee has more than five years service with the employer an "uplifted 60ths" scale may be used, as follows:

Years of service at normal retirement age	Maximum pension as a fraction of your final remuneration
1	4/60ths
2	8/60ths
3	12/60ths
4	16/60ths
5	20/60ths
6	24/60ths
7	28/60ths
8	32/60ths
9	36/60ths
10 or more years	40/60ths (i.e. 2/3rds)

- The overall maximum pension that can be provided for an individual retiring at Normal Retirement Age from his employer's pension scheme is the lower of:

- A pension based on the up-lifted scale shown on the previous page, **and**

- 2/3rds of final remuneration less any retained pension benefits, if the resultant amount is greater than that calculated under the n/60ths scale.

Retained pension benefits are pension benefits arising from a previous occupational pension scheme, including buy-out bonds, or from any paid-up benefits under a Personal Pension Plan or PRSA. Benefits accumulated through AVCs and PRSA AVCs in respect of the same employment are treated as benefits arising from the main scheme and not as retained benefits.

- The maximum pension figure must include the pension equivalent, based on current annuity rates, of the value of any retirement lump sum taken at retirement.

- Where an individual is retiring from a Defined Contribution scheme and opts for 25% of the accumulated fund as a retirement lump sum and the flexible retirement options for the balance, the accumulated fund must first be tested to ensure that the maximum allowable pension, based on then current rates, is not exceeded.

Final remuneration

Final remuneration may be defined as any one of the following:

A   Remuneration for any one of the five years before the retirement date. "Remuneration" means basic pay for the year in question plus the average of any fluctuating emoluments (e.g. bonuses, over-time payments etc.) over a suitable period, usually three years or more **or**

B   The average of the total emoluments (i.e. salary plus bonuses etc) of any three or more consecutive years ending not earlier than 10 years before your normal retirement age **or**

C   The rate of basic pay at the date of retirement, or on any date within the year ending on that date, plus the average of fluctuating emoluments over three or more consecutive years, ending with the date of retirement.

Notes:

- "Remuneration" includes all income and benefits that are assessable to income tax under PAYE in the relevant employment e.g. BIK on a company car can be included as part of your final remuneration.

- In the case of the first two definitions each year's remuneration may be increased in line with the Consumer Price Index from the end of the relevant year up to your retirement date. This is referred to as 'dynamising' final remuneration.

- If you own or control more than 20% of the voting rights in your company (i.e. "a proprietary director") you can only use definition B on page 292 when calculating your final remuneration. This is to stop controlling directors substantially inflating their earnings in the last years before retirement in order to increase the tax-free lump sum they can take from their pension.

Maximum tax free cash lump sum at Normal Retirement Age

- Where a member of a Defined Contribution pension scheme is retiring from employment they have the option of taking 25% of the value of their pension fund as a lump sum benefit and availing of the flexible retirement options as outlined earlier, provided the scheme rules allow them to do this. Defined Contribution scheme members who do avail of these options, and Defined Benefit scheme members are generally entitled to a maximum lump sum amount of at least 3/80ths of final remuneration for each year of service up to a maximum 40 years, or 1.5 times final remuneration on retirement at Normal Retirement Age.

- For those using the remuneration and service basis of calculating the maximum lump sum benefit if the individual has more than eight years service with the employer, an "uplifted 80ths" scale may be used as follows:

- The overall maximum tax-free lump sum that can be provided for an individual with more than 8 years service in the employment from which they are retiring is the lower of:

  - A lump sum based on the up-lifted scale shown above, **and**

  - 1.5 times final remuneration less any retained lump sum benefits, if the resultant amount is greater than that calculated under the 3n/80ths scale.

Retained lump sum benefits are benefits arising from a previous occupational pension scheme, including buy-out bonds, or from any paid-up benefits under a Personal Pension plan or PRSA. Benefits accumulated through AVCs and PRSA AVCs in respect of the same employment are treated as benefits arising from the main scheme and not as retained benefits.

Maximum pension on ill health early retirement

- Whereas there is no specific definition of ill health in the Revenue pension guidelines, incapacity is defined as follows

Years of Service at Normal Retirement Age	Maximum tax free lump sum as a fraction of your final remuneration
1 -8	3/80ths for each year
9	30/80ths
10	36/80ths
11	42/80ths
12	48/80ths
13	54/80ths
14	63/80ths
15	72/80ths
16	81/80ths
17	90/80ths
18	99/80ths
19	108/80ths
20 or more year	120/80ths

"Physical or mental deterioration which is bad enough to prevent the individual from following their normal employment, or which very seriously impairs their earning capacity. It does not mean simply a decline in energy or ability."

- If an individual retires early due to ill health, the maximum pension they can receive is the equivalent of the one they could have expected to receive had they worked until normal retirement age.

Example

John commenced employment with his current employer at age 35. The normal retirement age under the scheme rules is 65 years.

Five years later, John aged 40 retired on grounds of ill health, after suffering a serious illness. He has no retained pension benefits. His final remuneration prior to ill health was €50,000 per annum.

John would have had 30 years of service to normal retirement age, entitling him to a maximum pension on the "up-lifted 60ths" scale of 40/60ths of final remuneration.

His maximum ill health retirement pension is:

40/60ths x €50,000   =   €33,333 per annum

- In the case of early retirement due to ill health, "final remuneration" is calculated by a reference to the period preceding actual retirement.

- If John were a member of a Defined Contribution scheme he is very unlikely to have accumulated enough capital to be able to provide that level of benefit. This is where his PHI cover is likely to be called on to provide him with an income until normal retirement age, when the pension benefits would become payable. It would be important to have contribution protection cover in place to ensure the continuation of John's pension contributions up to retirement age.

- In the case of a Defined Benefit scheme, only the very large schemes may be able to afford to pay him this level of benefit at such an early age. PHI cover is often provided with these schemes also, and the pension would become payable at retirement age.

- If an individual is retiring in 'exceptional circumstances of serious ill health' (i.e. the expectation of life is less than 12 months) the Revenue will allow them to take the pension entitlement in cash form. The non tax-free part of the full lump sum taken in these circumstances is liable to income tax at 10%.

Maximum pension on voluntary early retirement

- Where early retirement is taking place after age 50 other than due to ill health, then the maximum immediate pension allowed is the greater of:

- 1/60th of final salary remuneration for each year of actual service completed, or

- The pension worked out by the following formula - N/NS x P

N   =   The actual number of years service to early retirement,

NS =   The number of years of potential service to normal retirement age.

P   =   The maximum pension allowable if the scheme member had remained in service to your normal retirement age.

Example

John joined his employer at age 35. The normal retirement age under the scheme rules is 65. John is now aged 50 with a final remuneration figure of €40,000 and he elects to take voluntary early retirement with his employer's consent. He has no retained pension or lump sum entitlements from previous employments or self-employment.

N is 15, actual years service completed to age 50.

NS is 30, Potential Service to Normal Retirement Age.

P is 2/3rds of final remuneration – Revenue maximum pension.

So, John's maximum early retirement pension is to be the greater of:

15/60ths x €40,000 = €10,000 per annum. **and**

15/30 x 2/3rds x €40,000 = €13,333 per annum.

- If the individual has less than 10 years service completed by the date of early retirement the maximum immediate pension is the lowest of:

  - N/NS x P, as calculated above,

  - The maximum pension as calculated on the uplifted scale shown earlier, taking account of actual service to date, **and**

  - 2/3rds of final remuneration less retained pension benefits.

- While the above outlines the maximum pension benefits that may be allowed by Revenue on early retirement, it would be rare for most employers to provide this level of benefits on early retirement. Typically, the rules of a Defined Benefit scheme would provide for the calculation of benefits based on the n/60ths scale, related to service to the date of retirement, with penalties for early retirement. For example, these penalties could mean a reduction of 0.5% per month for each month between the date of early retirement and the normal retirement age (i.e. a 60% reduction if you are retiring 10 years early).

- For Defined Contribution schemes the early retirement benefits would be dependent on the fund accumulated at that stage and, in reality it is very unlikely that this would be sufficiently large to exceed the Revenue maximum allowable figures.

- Also, Defined Contribution scheme members have the right to take 25% of their accumulated fund as a lump sum benefit and avail of the flexible retirement options for the balance.

Maximum tax free lump sum on early retirement

- In the case of ill health early retirement, the maximum tax-free lump sum is similar to that available had the individual remained in the employer's service up to normal retirement age. This would give up to a maximum of 1.5 times final remuneration at the date of retirement, if the individual were to have had 20 years service at normal retirement age.

- In the case of voluntary early retirement the maximum tax-free lump sum is normally calculated by taking the greater of:

  - 3/80ths of remuneration for each year of actual service, **or**

  - the sum calculated in accordance with the following formula
    - N/NS x LS

N = number of years service completed up to early retirement.

NS = the potential number of years that could have been completed by normal retirement.

LS = the maximum allowable tax-free lump sum which could have be provided at normal retirement age, after the restriction for any retained lump sum benefits where relevant.

Example:

Mary has 25 years service with her employer when she retires voluntarily at age 50 with the approval of her employer. She has no retained lump sum benefits from previous employment or self-employment. Her final remuneration figure is €50,000 and her scheme's NRA is 60.

N =	25	Mary's actual service
NS =	35	Potential service
LS =		150% of final remuneration

So, Mary's maximum retirement lump sum is the greater of:

75/80ths of €50,000 = €46,875 **and**

25/35 x €75,000 = €53,571

Also, if Mary is a member of a Defined Contribution Scheme she also has the option of taking 25% of her accumulated retirement fund.

● If the individual has less than 20 years service completed by the date of early retirement the maximum immediate lump sum benefit is the lowest of:

  ● N/NS x LS, as calculated above;

  ● The maximum lump sum on the uplifted scale as shown earlier, taking account of actual service completed to the date of early retirement; **and**

  ● 150% of final remuneration less retained lump sum benefits.

Example

Robert has 17 years actual service, 25 years potential service, final remuneration of €40,000 and no retained lump sum benefits. He is restricted to the lowest of:

● N/NS x LS, i.e. 17/25 x €60,000 = €40,800;

● 90/80ths (i.e. figure applicable to 15 years service from the uplifted scale above) x €40,000 = €45,000; **and**

● 150% x €40,000 = €60,000

So, overall in this example Robert is limited to a lump sum benefit of €40,800.

- If a retirement lump sum is taken on voluntary early retirement the early retirement pension benefit has to be reduced by the pension equivalent of the lump sum.

- In the case of Defined Benefit schemes, the lump sum on voluntary early retirement may be restricted by the scheme rules; in the case of Defined Contribution schemes taking the maximum lump sum benefit, based on the remuneration and service formula, could potentially deplete the retirement fund completely, leaving no capital to provide an income.

- If Robert is a member of a Defined Contribution scheme he has the option of taking 25% of the accumulated fund as a retirement lump sum and using the balance of the fund in accordance with the flexible retirement options .

Maximum death-in-service benefits

- A pension scheme may provide two benefits if a member dies in service before normal retirement age.

- The maximum allowable lump sum benefit is four times remuneration at the date of death, together with a refund of any personal contributions to the scheme with "reasonable interest". This benefit would be payable to the trustees who, under the rules of the scheme, would have some discretion as to which of your dependants should receive the proceeds.

- The maximum allowable death-in-service pension, which could be paid to your spouse or to any one or all of your dependants, is 100% of the maximum pension that you could have received if you had retired on grounds of ill health at the date of your death.

Maximum Death-in-Retirement Benefit

- Many pension schemes provide a guaranteed period of pension payments after retirement in the event of early death. This guaranteed period may be up to 10 years. If the guaranteed period is five years or less the remaining instalments may be paid at the trustees' discretion in a lump sum to your dependants. If the guarantee is more than five years, the outstanding instalments will be paid in pension form to the beneficiaries.

- Spouses' and dependants' pensions may be provided in addition to this guarantee. The maximum pension that may be provided for the spouse, or for any one or all of the dependants, is 100% of the maximum pension that could have been provided for you at retirement.

- The term "maximum pension" is defined as the maximum pension at normal retirement age, increased in line with the Consumer Price Index from the date of retirement up to the date of death.

Maximum pension increases

- Generally speaking, a pension may be increased in line with the rise in the Consumer Price Index each year. Alternatively, increases at a rate of 3% per annum compound may be promised and paid, regardless of the Consumer Price Index. However, if the pension at retirement was less than the maximum Revenue allowable pension at retirement age, this pension may be increased at a faster rate than the increase in the Consumer Price Index until it reaches the level of the maximum allowable pension.

15 Marriage

Tax and financial issues arising from marriage are spread throughout our tax and financial system. To make everything as simple and as straight forward as possible, we shall look at marriage under a number of different headings:

- Legal Impact.
- Income Tax.
- Capital Gains Tax.
- Capital Acquisition Tax.
- Social Welfare.

Legal impact

Marriage or a civil partnership changes the legal status of two people from a couple to spouses, with many consequential and financial implications. For example, a surviving spouse/civil partner's legal entitlements under the 1965 Succession Act are as follows:

If there is a Will

Irrespective of what is indicated in the Will, the minimum legal requirements of a surviving spouse/civil partner are:

Spouse/civil partner and No Issue	One-half of estate to the surviving spouse/civil partner.
Spouse/civil partner and Issue	One-third of estate to the surviving spouse/civil partner.

No Will in existence

Spouse/civil partner and No Issue	Whole estate to the surviving spouse/civil partner.
Spouse/civil partner and Issue	Two-thirds to the surviving spouse/civil partner, one-third to issue in equal shares.

Succession Act rights may be voluntarily renounced by a prenuptial agreement.

Income tax

A marriage/civil partnership ceremony in itself does not give rise to any income tax advantage.   To obtain these benefits, a couple must be married and "living together".

Under the income tax rules, a couple who are married or in a civil partnership are deemed to be "living together" unless

- They are separated under an order of a Court of competent jurisdiction or by Deed of Separation,

   or

- They are in fact separated in such circumstances that the separation is likely to be permanent.

A couple who are married or in a civil partnership may choose to be taxed jointly, separately or as single people.

A couple who are married or in a civil partnership and claiming joint assessment under Income Tax rules are entitled to the following:

- A married/civil partners tax credit which is double the single person tax credit.

- Home carer's tax credit.

- Double a single person's mortgage interest relief on their principal private residence.

- Trading losses incurred by one spouse/civil partner can be set against income of the other spouse/civil partner.

- Double the age tax credit even though only one spouse/civil partner may be over the age of 65 years.

- Increased blind person's tax credit where both spouses/civil partners are blind.

- Tax relief can be obtained by one spouse/partner in respect of a person employed to take care of the incapacitated other spouse/civil partner.

Individualisation

For the tax year 2012 and 2013 the standard rate tax band for a couple who are married or in a civil partnership is €41,800. Where both spouses/civil partners have income this can be increased by the lower of ;

- €23,800

  or

- The income of the lower earning spouse.

To gain the maximum benefit from the 'individual' band increases for a two income couple, the lower earning spouse/civil partner must have a minimum 'individual' income of €23,800 in the year 2012 and 2013.

For example, a two income couple where one spouse/partner earns €50,000 in the tax year 2012 and 2013 and the other earns €8,000, the maximum standard rate band for couples who are married or in a civil partnership of €41,800 can be utilised by the higher earning spouse/civil partner but only €8,000 of the 20% band can be utilised by the lower earning spouse/civil partner. The balance of €15,800 is left unused.

Once you get married or enter into a civil partnership you should inform the tax office of the date of your marriage or civil partnership, quoting your PPS Number and that of your spouse.

Year of marriage/civil partnership

In the year of marriage/civil partnership, you and your spouse/civil partner are treated as two single people for income tax purposes for the entire tax year. However, if you pay more tax than that which would have been payable as a couple who are married or in a civil partnership, you can claim a refund. This refund will be the excess of the tax paid as two single people over the tax payable as a jointly assessed couple who are married or in a civil partnership, reduced in proportion to the part of the tax year in which you were not married or in a civil partnership.

"In the year of marriage or civil partnership, you and your spouse or civil partner are treated as two single people for income tax purposes for the entire year."

Example

A married couple have income of €60,000 and €30,000 respectively. Their date of marriage was 1 June 2012. Their tax liability for 2012 will be as follows:

	2012 €		2012 €
Salary	€60,000		€30,000
Tax payable			
€32,800 @ 20%	€6,560	€30,000 @ 20%	€6,000
€27,200 @ 41%	€11,152		€ 0
	€17,712		€6,000
Less: Tax credits			
Personal	(€1,650)		(€1,650)
PAYE	(€1,650)		(€1,650)
Net tax	**€14,412**		**€2,700**
Total tax as single people			**€17,112**

At the end of the year, they may apply for a reduction in their tax liability on the basis of joint assessment as illustrated:

		2012 €
	Total salaries	€90,000
	Tax payable	
	€65,600 @ 20%	€13,120
	€24,400 @ 41%	€10,004
		€23,124
Less:	**Tax credits**	
	Personal	(€3,300)
	PAYE	(€3,300)
	Net tax	**€16,524**
Less:	Tax paid (See above)	(€17,112)
	Excess of single over joint basis of assessment	€588
	Restriction for pre married period €588 x 5/12	€245
	Tax refund due	**€343**

The tax refund due to each spouse/civil partner will be in proportion to the amount of tax each has paid.

Couples who are married or in a civil partnership / income tax options

After the year of marriage/civil partnership, you have three options as to how you are taxed.

Joint assessment

Joint assessment is automatic, unless either spouse/partner gives notice of election for separate or single assessment to the Revenue Commissioners.

The assessable spouse is the spouse/civil partner with the higher income and will continue to be so unless you jointly elect to change it.

Repayments made are allocated between each spouse/civil partner according to the amount of tax they paid in the year.

Separate assessment

A claim may be made for separate assessment of income tax liability where the joint assessment basis applies. The claim must be made in the period beginning three months before and ending three months after the start of the tax year i.e. between 1 October and 31 March. A claim for separate assessment cannot be backdated and lasts until it is withdrawn. An application for a withdrawal of separate assessment must be made in writing by whichever spouse/civil partner made the initial claim. Where separate assessment is claimed the tax credits are divided between the spouses/civil partners. If at the end of the tax year, the total tax payable under separate assessments is greater than the amount payable if an application for separate assessment had not been made, you can apply for a tax refund.

Single assessment/(separate treatment)

As a couple who are married or in civil partnership, you may each elect for single assessment. Each spouse/civil partner is treated as a single person with no right of transfer of allowances or relief's between spouses/civil partners. Single assessment is normally only beneficial where one spouse/civil partner has foreign employment income.

Assessable spouse/nominated civil partner

If you are jointly assessed one spouse/civil partner is nominated to be the assessable spouse/civil partner. They are taxable on the total income of both spouses/civil partners and are responsible for making a return of income for both parties.

Both spouses/civil partners nominate the assessable spouse/civil partner jointly by completing the Assessable spouse/civil partnership form available from www.revenue.ie or your local tax office. This should be submitted to the tax office before 31 March in the relevant tax year. If you do not nominate an assessable spouse/civil partner, the tax office will treat the spouse/civil partner with the highest income in the last tax year as the assessable spouse/civil partner.

Capital gains tax (CGT)

A couple must be married/ in a civil partnership and "living together" in order to maximise their benefits under Capital Gains Tax which include:

- Entitlement to dispose of assets to each other without being subject to CGT.

- Capital losses available to one spouse/civil partner can be used by the other spouse/civil partner.

Capital acquisitions tax (CAT)

The "living together" rules do not apply to CAT and all gifts and inheritance given by one legally married spouse / couple in a registered civil partnership to the other are exempt from CAT regardless of their "living together" status.

Pension benefits

Any pension benefit taken by a person, other than the pension member, is treated as a gift or inheritance for tax purposes.

However, the spouse/civil partner exemption from CAT means any lump sum death benefit or dependent's pension benefit received by your spouse/civil partner from a pension scheme of which you were a member is exempt from tax.

Life assurance policies

An interest in possession in life assurance policies is only deemed to occur when a benefit becomes payable under the policy. So if you effect a Life

Assurance policy on your own life for the benefit of someone else, no gift or inheritance tax will arise until the benefit becomes payable under that policy. Any sums received by you or your spouse/civil partner from a life assurance policy, of which you or your spouse/civil partner were the original beneficial owners, are exempt from tax.

Stamp duty

Transfer of all assets between spouses/civil partners is exempt from stamp duty. This exemption includes a direct transfer of assets from one spouse/civil partner to another or a transfer from one spouse/civil partner into joint names.

Social welfare

Social welfare widow(er)/surviving civil partner's contributory pension is payable to the widow(er)/surviving civil partner following the death of their spouse/civil partner, for as long as the widow(er)/surviving civil partner does not remarry or cohabit with someone else. A spouse/civil partner may qualify for this pension either on their own PRSI contribution record, or on that of the other spouse/civil partner.

If the widow(er)/surviving civil partner does not have the required PRSI contributions either on their own PRSI record or on their spouses/civil partners, then non-contributory social welfare widow(er)/surviving civil partner's pension maybe payable as long as they do not remarry or cohabit with someone else.

Example: 2012 Income Tax options

A couple are married with two children, with salaries of €50,000 and €30,000 respectively. The higher earning spouse pays pension contributions of €5,400 in the 2012 tax year. Their tax options are illustrated on page 308.

Method of assessment	Joint Assessment		Assessment - Separate				Assessment - Single			
	€	€	€		€		€		€	
Salary	€80,000		€50,000		€30,000		€50,000		€30,000	
Less: Pension	(€5,400)		(€5,400)		(€0)		(€5,400)		(€0)	
Taxable Income	€74,600		€44,600		€30,000		€44,600		€30,000	
Tax Payable	Amount	Tax	Amount	Tax	Amount	Tax	Amount	Tax	Amount	Tax
20%	€65,600	€13,120	€32,800	€6,560	€30,000	€6,000	€32,800	€6,560	€30,000	€6,000
41%	€9,000	€3,690	€11,800	€4,838			€11,800	€4,838		
Total		€16,810		€11,398		€6,000		€11,398		€6,000
Less: Tax Credits										
Personal	(€3,300)		(€1,650)		(€1,650)		(€1,650)		(€1,650)	
PAYE	(€3,300)		(€1,650)		(€1,650)		(€1,650)		(€1,650)	
Total		€10,210		€8,098		€2,700		€8,098		€2,700
Total Payable	**€10,210**		**€10,798**				**€10,798**			

Note: Separate assessment results in an additional tax bill of €588 which can be reclaimed at the end of the tax year. Single assessments result in the same additional bill. However under single assessment this amount could not be reclaimed back at the end of the year.

16 Separation and divorce

To make everything in this section as simple as possible, we will look at each of the issues relating to "Separation and Divorce" under the same headings as those used in the previous chapter entitled "Marriage Matters". To get a better understanding of the tax implications of "Separation and Divorce", we advise you to first read the previous chapter outlining the tax issues arising on marriage.

Marriage breakdown is a major and traumatic event for couples and it is best approached in a logical and non-confrontational manner. A brief checklist of points to consider in relation to separation and divorce is included at the end of this section.

When a married couple decide to separate, they will normally go about it in one of the following ways:

- They decide to live apart.

- They seek a Legal Separation.

- They seek a Judicial Separation.

Living apart

Legal impact
Living apart does not change the legal status of your marriage.

Succession rights
There is no automatic loss of your Succession Act entitlements if you live apart from your spouse. However:

- A spouse who is guilty of desertion, which continues for two years or more up to the death of the other spouse, is precluded under the Succession Act from taking any share in the estate of the deceased, either as a legal right or on intestacy.

- If a surviving spouse is deemed to be "guilty of conduct which justified the deceased separating and living apart", then the surviving spouse could be deemed to be guilty of desertion and hence precluded under the Succession Act from taking a share in the deceased spouse's estate. For example where a wife leaves home because of violent behaviour on the part of her husband, he could be found guilty of desertion and lose his Succession Act rights to her estate while, conversely, she could in fact, retain her rights to his estate.

- Any spouse who has been found guilty of a serious offence against the deceased spouse or against a child of the deceased spouse, is also precluded, under the Succession Act, from taking any legal right under the estate of the deceased.

Income tax

A couple's Income Tax position following separation is determined by three main factors:

- Whether the separation is likely to be permanent.

- Whether maintenance payments are being made by one spouse to the other.

- If maintenance payments are being made, whether these payments are *legally enforceable*.

If the separation is not likely to be permanent, there is no change in the Income Tax position and you can elect for Joint, Separate or Single Assessment.

If the separation is likely to be permanent and if there are no legally enforceable maintenance payments, the spouses are assessed for Income Tax under Single Assessment. Any voluntary maintenance payments are ignored for income tax purposes.

If the separation is likely to be permanent and if there are legally enforceable maintenance payments being made, then the couple may generally opt for either Single Assessment or if both spouses remain resident in Ireland, Separate Assessment. If Single Assessment applies, maintenance payments are tax-deductible for the payer and are taxable in the hands of the recipient. Under Separate Assessment, maintenance payments are ignored for income tax purposes.

Capital Gains Tax (CGT)

If the separation is not likely to be permanent, there is no change in the spouse's status for CGT purposes.

If the separation is likely to be permanent, the spouses are treated as two unconnected persons for CGT purposes:

- Transfers between spouses are no longer exempt from CGT. However, any transfer by virtue of, or in consequence of, the separation will not trigger a CGT liability.
- No transfer of unused CGT losses is permitted between spouses.

Capital Acquisition Tax (CAT)

Spouse's exemption from Capital Acquisitions Tax will continue to apply.

Pensions/death-in-service benefit

If a member of a pension scheme dies while still working for an employer, Death in Service Benefits may be paid to the member's dependants. Many pension schemes give discretion to the pension trustees as to how these death-in-service benefits may be paid e.g. the pension rules may require a spouse to be living with, or ordinarily residing with, their spouse at the date of death.

Life assurance

The proceeds are normally exempt from tax, provided you or your spouse were the original beneficial owners of the relevant policy.

Stamp duty

Exemption from Stamp Duty will continue to apply on relevant property transactions.

Social welfare

The contributory widow(er)/surviving civil partner's pension is payable to the widow(er)/surviving civil partner, following the death of their spouse/civil partner, for as long as the widow(er)/surviving civil partner does not remarry and does not cohabit with someone else. A widow(er)/surviving civil partner may qualify for this pension either on their own PRSI contribution record or that of their late spouse/civil partner.

Qualifying adult dependent payment

A qualifying adult dependent payment is generally payable to a claimant who is separated, provided their spouse/civil partner is wholly or mainly maintained by the claimant.

Legal separation

Under a Legal Separation, both spouses voluntarily enter into a legal agreement. This legal agreement is often referred to as a "Deed of Separation".

A Deed of Separation will usually include:

- An agreement to permanently live apart.

- Arrangements for custody of, and access to, children.

- Provision for maintenance to be paid by one spouse for the benefit of the other spouse and/or children.

- Succession Act rights: one spouse may voluntarily renounce rights to the other's estate, etc.

Legal impact

A Deed of Separation will not change the legal status of your marriage.

Succession rights

- There is no automatic loss of your entitlements under the Succession Act.

- Your entitlements under the Succession Act may be voluntarily renounced under a Deed of Separation

- Any specific bequest in your Will to your spouse will stand until you make a new Will or change your existing Will.

Income tax

A couple's Income Tax position following separation is determined by three main factors:

- Whether the separation is likely to be permanent.

- Whether maintenance payments are being made by one spouse/civil partner to the other.

- If maintenance payments are being made, whether these payments are *legally enforceable*.

If the separation is not likely to be permanent, there is no change in the income tax position and you can elect for joint, separate or single assessment.

If the separation is likely to be permanent and if there are no legally enforceable maintenance payments, the spouses are assessed for Income tax under single assessment. Any voluntary maintenance payments are ignored for income tax purposes.

If the separation is likely to be permanent and if there are legally enforceable maintenance payments being made, then the couple may generally opt for either single assessment or if both spouses remain resident in Ireland, separate assessment. If single assessment applies, maintenance payments are tax deductible for the payer and taxable in the hands of the recipient. Under separate assessment, maintenance payments are ignored for income tax purposes.

Assessable spouse

The spouse with the greater income in the year of marriage will generally be deemed to be the assessable spouse from year to year.

The assessable spouse may be changed provided both spouses elect jointly for an alternative option. The assessable spouse is generally responsible for submitting the annual return and paying any tax due.

Year of separation

The married tax credit and double rate tax band can be claimed for the year of separation by the assessable spouse providing:

- Separation does not occur on the first day of that tax year.

  or

- The non-assessable spouse has not submitted a claim for single assessment prior to separation.

The assessable spouse is liable to income tax for the tax year of separation on their own income under joint assessment if they were previously taxed jointly for the full year, and on the other spouse's income up to the date of separation. A tax deduction will be available for legally enforceable maintenance payments.

Year of separation/Single assessment

If a couple were paying tax under single assessment before the separation, each spouse would have been responsible for submitting their own tax returns and paying their own tax. No change in their status for income tax purposes would have occurred on separation.

Subsequent tax years

How you will be taxed in subsequent tax years will depend on a number of factors e.g.

- Voluntary maintenance payments.

- Legally enforceable maintenance payments.

- Single parent credits.

- Mortgage repayments etc.

Maintenance payments

Tax is not deducted at source from legally enforceable maintenance payments from one spouse to the other. Such payments may be allowed for tax purposes as a deduction against the income of the payer and may be chargeable to income tax, in the hands of the recipient. A spouse will not be entitled to the marriage credit where he/she claims a deduction for maintenance payments made.

Where maintenance is received for the benefit of a child:

- The payment is to be made without deduction of income tax,

- The amount is to continue to be treated as the income of the payer,

   and

- The payer's income tax liability is calculated without any allowance for the payments made.

PRSI

If you are legally separated and you receive maintenance payments from your spouse, PRSI will be payable on the maintenance received if you are taxed as a single person. If you have opted for separate assessment, maintenance payments are ignored for income tax purposes and PRSI is not payable on the maintenance.

The PRSI payable would be the Class S1 rate, which in 2012 is 4% of the gross income.

Universal social charge (USC)

From 1 January 2011 the income levy and health levy were abolished and replaced with the universal social charge (USC). This USC may apply to maintenance depending on whether they are voluntary payments or legally inforceable payments.

Voluntary maintenance payments (if the payment is paid under an informal arrangement)

The spouse making the payments does not receive exemption from the universal social charge (USC) on the portion of their income which they pay as maintenance.

The spouse who receives the payments is not subject to the USC on the maintenance payments they receive.

Legally enforceable maintenance payments (payable under legal obligation)

The spouse making the payments is entitled to receive an exemption from the USC on the portion of their income which they pay as maintenance either directly or indirectly to their spouse. There is no USC exemption due in respect of any portion of the maintenance payments paid towards the maintenance of children.

The spouse who receives the payments is subject to the USC on the portion of the maintenance payments they receive in respect of themselves. Any portion of the maintenance payments paid towards the maintenance of children is not subject to the USC.

Note: In the case of a legally enforceable maintenance arrangement, where a separated couple has jointly elected to be treated as a married couple for income tax purposes, the spouse making the payments does not receive exemption from the USC on the portion of their income which they pay as maintenance. The spouse who receives the payments is not subject to the USC on the maintenance payments they receive.

Example

You and your spouse agree to separate.

- Your income is €50,000 p.a. for the tax year 2012. Your spouse has no income.

- You agree to pay your spouse €200 per week.

The arrangement is informal and nothing is legally enforceable.

Your tax position

	2012	
	Joint assessment married €	Single assessment separated €
Salary	€50,000	€50,000
Tax payable		
€41,800 @ 20%	€8,360	
€32,800 @ 20%		€6,560
€8,200 @ 41%	€3,362	
€17,200 @ 41%		€7,052
	€11,722	€13,612
Less: Tax credits		
Personal	(€3,300)	(€3,300)
PAYE	(€1,650)	(€1,650)
	€6,772	**€8,662**

The €200 p.w. maintenance which you pay is not tax deductible. Your additional tax payable as a separated person under single assessment is €1,890

Notes:

- The marriage tax credit will be granted to you under single assessment because your spouse is wholly or mainly maintained by you. You are not entitled to deduct the maintenance payments as these are voluntary and not legally enforceable.

- Your spouse is not living with you and you are not entitled to the benefit of the double tax bands because the maintenance payments are not enforceable.

Example

You and your spouse agree to separate. Your spouse works in the home.

- Your salary is €56,000 p.a. in the 2012 tax year.

- You agrees to pay your spouse €200 per week and the arrangement is legally enforceable.

Your tax position

As legally enforceable maintenance payments are tax-deductible, reduction in tax payable under single assessment is €2,374.

	2012	
	Joint assessment married €	Single assessment separated €
Salary	€56,000	€56,000
Maintenance paid	€0	€10,400
Taxable	€56,000	€45,600
Tax payable		
€41,800/€32,800 @ 20%	€8,360	€6,560
€14,200/€12,800 @ 41%	€5,822	€5,248
	€14,182	€11,808
Less: Tax credits		
Personal	(€3,300)	(€3,300)
PAYE	(€1,650)	(€1,650)
	€9,232	**€6,858**

Capital gains tax (CGT)

Normally, under a legal separation the spouses are treated as two unconnected persons for CGT purposes:

- Transfers between spouses are no longer exempt from CGT. However, any transfer by virtue of, or in consequence of, the Deed of Separation will not trigger a CGT liability.

- No transfer is permitted between spouses of unused CGT losses.

Capital acquisition tax (CAT)

Spouse's exemption from Capital Acquisitions Tax will continue to apply.

Pension benefits

Pension rights negotiated under a Deed of Separation may not be enforceable, unless the agreement is backed up by a formal court order.

Life assurance

Specific rights obtained under a Deed of Separation in relation to life assurance policies may not be legally enforceable - to avoid problems make sure that your interest in a life assurance policy is backed up by a relevant court order e.g. Financial Compensation Order, under the Family Law Act 1995.

Stamp duty

Exemption from Stamp Duty will continue to apply on relevant property transactions.

Social welfare

The contributory widow(er)/surviving civil partner's pension is payable to the widow(er)/surviving civil partner following the death of their spouse/civil partner, as long as the widow(er)/surviving civil partner does not remarry or cohabit with someone else . The surviving spouse/civil partner may qualify for a widow(er)/surviving civil partner's pension either on their own PRSI contribution record, or that of their late spouse/civil partner.

- A qualified adult dependent supplement may not be payable to a claimant if that claimant's spouse/civil partner is no longer wholly or mainly maintained by the claimant.

Judicial separation

A decree of judicial separation can be obtained by a spouse applying to the courts under the Judicial Separation and Family Law Reform Act 1989. The application may be made on one or more of the following grounds:

- The other spouse has committed adultery.

- That the other spouse has behaved in such a way that the applicant spouse cannot reasonably be expected to live with the other spouse.

- That the other spouse has deserted the applicant spouse for a continuous period of at least one year immediately preceding the application and that the spouses have lived apart from one another for a continuous period of at least one year immediately preceding the application and that the other spouse consents to a decree being granted.

- That the spouses have lived apart from one another for a continuous period of at least three years immediately preceding the application and that the marriage has broken down to the extent that the court is satisfied in all circumstances that a normal marital relationship has not existed between the spouses for at least one year immediately preceding the application.

Ancillary orders

On the granting of, or following, a decree of Judicial Separation, the Circuit or High Court can make a number of orders relating to maintenance or specific assets. These orders are known as Ancillary Orders.

Under a Judicial Separation either spouse, or, in some cases, a person acting on behalf of a dependent child, can apply to the courts to have one or more Ancillary Orders made in relation to:

- Maintenance.

- The family home.

- Property.

- Pension benefits.

- Life assurance policies.

- Succession rights etc.

While the Courts retain the discretion to grant an Ancillary Order sought by a spouse, or a person acting on behalf of a dependent child, the Family Law Act 1995 does provide specific factors which the Court is obliged to take into account before making a decision.

- The income, earning capacity, property and other financial resources which each of the spouses has, or is likely to have in the foreseeable future. The financial needs, obligations and responsibilities which each of the spouses has or is likely to have in the foreseeable future (whether in the case of remarriage of the spouse or otherwise).

- The standard of living enjoyed by the family concerned before the proceedings were instituted or before the spouses separated, as the case may be.

- The age of each of the spouses and the length of time during which the spouses lived together.

- Any physical or mental disability of either of the spouses.

- The contributions which each of the spouses has made or is likely in the foreseeable future to make to the welfare of the family, including any contribution made by each of them to the income, earning capacity, property and financial resources of the other spouse and any contribution made by either of them by looking after the home or caring for the family.

- The effect on the earning capacity of each of the spouses of the marital responsibilities assumed by each during the period when they lived together and, in particular, the degree to which the future earning capacity of a spouse is impaired by reason of that spouse having relinquished or foregone the opportunity of remunerative activity in order to look after the home or care for the family.

- Any income or benefits to which either of the spouses is entitled by or under statute.

- The conduct of each of the spouses, if that conduct is such that in the opinion of the court it would in all the circumstances of the case be unjust to disregard it.

- The accommodation needs of either of the spouses

- The value to each of the spouses of any benefit (for example, a benefit under a pension scheme) which by reason of the decree of judicial separation that spouse will forfeit the opportunity or possibility of acquiring.

- The rights of any other person, other than the spouses but including a person to whom either spouse is remarried.

Enforcing maintenance orders

Experience has shown a relatively high rate of defaulting on regular maintenance payments; a court can enforce these payments in one of two ways:

- *Secured Payments*. Here the periodic payments are secured on some capital asset or investment. For example, the court could order the sale of an investment property to generate the necessary funds.

- *Attachment of earnings order* where the court may order an employer to deduct the periodic payments from the earnings of one spouse and pay it to the other spouse.

Payments orders will normally specify the period, or periods, during which the payments are to be made, which can be a fixed number of years, or for the lifetime of either spouse. However, payment orders will generally cease on:

- The death of either spouse.

- The date of remarriage of the applicant spouse.

Legal impact

A Judicial Separation does not change the legal status of your marriage.

Succession rights

- There is no automatic loss of entitlements under the Succession Act.

- Your entitlements under the Succession Act may be voluntarily renounced under a Judicial Separation.

- Any specific bequest in your Will to your spouse will stand until you make a new Will or change your existing Will.

Income tax

If there are no legally enforceable maintenance payments being made, the spouses are assessed for Income Tax under Single Assessment. Any voluntary maintenance payments are not tax-deductible for the paying spouse and are not taxable in the hands of the receiving spouse.

If there are legally enforceable maintenance payments being made, then the couple can generally either opt for single assessment or if both spouses remain resident in Ireland, separate assessment. If single assessment applies, maintenance payments made for the benefit of the spouse are tax deductible for the payer and taxable in the hands of the recipient. Under separate assessment, maintenance payments are ignored for tax purposes.

"A judicial separation does not change the legal status of your marriage."

If you have a Judicial separation, your income tax position is the same as under a legal separation.

Capital gains tax (CGT)

Normally, under a judicial separation the spouses are treated as two unconnected persons for CGT purpose:

- Transfers between spouses are no longer exempt from CGT. However, any transfer by virtue of, or in consequence of, a decree of Judicial separation will not trigger a CGT liability.

- No transfer of unused losses is permitted between spouses.

Capital acquisitions tax (CAT)

Spouse's exemption from Capital Acquisitions Tax will continue to apply.

Pension benefits

The Family Law Act 1995 envisages a number of ways in which a spouse's pension benefits might be taken into account in the event of a judicial separation:

Earmarking	A charge is set against a spouse's pension benefits, so that when they become payable a designated part of these benefits are payable to the other spouse.
Pension Splitting	The relevant pension benefits are split on an agreed basis between both spouses.

| Offsetting | If proper financial provision can be made by other orders (e.g. a financial compensation order), or a property adjustment order the court may decide to offset these benefits against any relevant pension rights rather than "splitting everything down the middle". |

Life assurance

Once a decree of Judicial Separation is granted, a spouse or a person acting on behalf of a dependent child may seek a Financial Compensation Order which can compel either or both spouses to:

- Effect a policy of life insurance for the benefit of the applicant or the dependent child.

- Assign the whole or a specified part of the interest in a life insurance policy effected by either, or both, spouses to the applicant or for the benefit of a dependent child.

- Make or continue to make the payments which either, or both, of the spouses is, or are, required to make under the terms of the policy.

A Financial Compensation Order will generally cease on the death or remarriage of an applicant spouse.

Stamp duty

Exemption from Stamp Duty will continue to apply on relevant property transactions.

Social welfare

The contributory widow(er)/surviving civil partner's pension is payable to the widow(er)/surviving civil partner following the death of their spouse/civil partner as long as the widow(er)/surviving civil partner does not remarry or cohabit with someone else. The surviving spouse/civil partner may qualify for a widow(er)/surviving civil partner's pension either on their own PRSI contribution record, or that of their late spouse/civil partner.

An adult dependent supplement may not be payable to a claimant if that claimant's spouse/civil partner is no longer wholly or mainly maintained by the claimant.

Divorce

The grounds on which a court may grant an application for a decree of divorce are those set out in Article 41.3.2 of the Constitution:

At the date of the institution of the proceeding, the spouses must have lived apart from one another for a period of, or periods amounting to, at least four years during the previous five years.

- There is no reasonable prospect of a reconciliation between the spouses, **and**

- Such provisions as the court considers proper, having regard to the circumstances that exist, will be made for the spouses, any children of either or both of them and any person prescribed by law **and**

- Any further conditions prescribed by law are complied with.

Ancillary orders

The courts, on application by either spouse or by someone acting on behalf of a dependent child, can issue one or more of a number of Ancillary Orders including the following:

- Periodical payments and secured periodical payments order.

- Lump sum payments order.

- Property adjustment order.

- Order regarding occupation or sale of family home.

- Order regarding title of property.

- Variation of benefit of either spouse, or any dependent family member, of any pre or post nuptial agreement.

- Order regarding partition of property.

- Financial compensation orders.

- Pension adjustment orders.

- Order extinguishing succession rights.

- Order for sale of property, except the family home where a remarried spouse ordinarily resides with their spouse.

- Maintenance pending relief order.

- Order for provision for one spouse out of the estate of the other spouse.

Legal impact

Divorce legally dissolves the marriage and each spouse may legally remarry after the decree.

Succession rights

Each spouse's succession rights are automatically extinguished by the decree of divorce. Any specific bequest in a Will to a former spouse will stand until a new Will is made or an existing Will is changed.

Income tax

If there are legally enforceable maintenance payments being made then the couple can generally either opt for single assessment or if both spouses remain resident in Ireland, separate assessment. If single assessment applies, maintenance payments for the benefit of the spouse are tax-deductible for the payer and are taxable in the hands of the recipient. Under separate assessment, maintenance payments are ignored for income tax purposes.

If you are divorced, your income tax position is the same as that under legal separation.

Capital gains tax

Divorced spouses are treated as two unconnected persons for CGT purposes:

- Transfers between spouses are no longer exempt from CGT. However, transfers by virtues of, or in consequence of, the divorce will not trigger a CGT liability.

- No transfer of unused losses between spouses.

Capital Acquisitions Tax

After divorce, you are no longer legal spouses and the spouse exemption ceases to apply in respect of any future gifts or inheritances for CAT purposes. The "stranger threshold" will apply for CAT purposes after the divorce. However, property transfers between former spouses on foot of a court order governing a decree of divorce will be exempt from Capital Acquisitions Tax.

Pensions

The Family Law (divorce) Act 1996 envisages a number of ways in which a spouse's pension scheme benefits might be taken into account in the event of a decree of divorce:

Earmarking	A charge is set against a spouse's pension benefits, so that when they become payable a designated part of these benefits is payable to the other spouse.
Pension Splitting	The relevant pension benefits are split on an agreed basis between both spouses.
Offsetting	If proper financial provision can be made by other orders, e.g. financial compensation order or property adjustment order, the court may decide to offset these benefits against the relevant pension rights rather than "splitting everything down the middle".

"Divorce legally dissolves the marriage and each spouse may legally remarry after the decree."

Life assurance

After the granting of the decree of divorce, a spouse, or a person acting on behalf of a dependent child, may seek a financial compensation order which can compel either or both spouses to:

- Effect a policy of life insurance for the benefit of the applicant or the dependant child.

- Assign the whole or a specified part of the interest in a life insurance policy, effected by either or both spouses, to the applicant or for the benefit of a dependent child.

- Make or continue to make the payments which either, or both, of the spouses is, or are, required to make under the terms of the policy.

Such an order will cease on the death or remarriage of an applicant's spouse.

Social welfare

There is no change in either spouse's entitlement to a Social Welfare widow(er)/surviving civil partner's pension following a decree of divorce provided that the other spouse/civil partner has not remarried or is not cohabiting with someone else.

If the deceased spouse/civil partner had remarried both their current spouse/civil partner and their ex-spouse/civil partner are entitled to claim a widow(er)/surviving civil partner's pension if they meet the normal qualifying conditions.

17 Death - and taxes

While tax and financial matters are not the foremost consideration when somebody dies, they are nevertheless areas that must be sorted out before a deceased person's estate can be finalised.

Before looking at the tax consequences arising on a death it might be helpful to look briefly at some key terms, at the ways in which property passes on a death to the beneficiaries and at certain procedures that must be gone through before assets are handed over to the beneficiaries.

What is an "estate"?

A deceased's estate consists of whatever assets (e.g. bank accounts, stocks and shares, house, land, livestock, jewellery, car, etc.) which can be passed on to beneficiaries following the deceased's death.

How does the estate pass on to the beneficiaries?

The assets, which make up the deceased's estate, can be passed on in a number of ways. Assets left by Will pass to the beneficiaries in accordance with the terms of the Will. If there is no Will (a situation known as intestacy), assets that would otherwise have passed by Will pass instead under special rules laid down by law. In addition, assets can also pass outside of the Will or intestacy.

Examples of assets which pass under the Will or intestacy

- Assets owned in the deceased's sole name.
- Assets owned by the deceased but placed in the name of another person for convenience or some similar reason.
- Assets placed by the deceased in the joint names of the deceased and another person without the intention of benefiting that other person.

Examples of assets which pass outside of the Will or intestacy

- Assets passing by nomination, e.g. the deceased may have instructed An Post to pay Saving Certificates on their death to a particular person, called the nominee.

- Death benefits passing under a life insurance policy or pension scheme where the beneficiaries are particular family members named in the policy or scheme.

- Assets passing in which the deceased had an interest for their life only.

- Assets placed by the deceased in the joint names of the deceased and another person with the intention of benefiting that other person on the deceased's death.

"A beneficiary is a person who inherits either the whole or part of the deceased's estate ..."

The personal representative

The personal representative is the person who is responsible for finalising the deceased's affairs. He or she must, within a reasonable time, collect the assets passing under the Will or intestacy, pay any debts and distribute the surplus assets to the beneficiaries entitled to them.

If there is a Will, it is likely that the Personal Representative has been appointed by being named in the Will as its executor and has taken on the responsibility, because he or she is the deceased's spouse or one of the next-of-kin. A Personal Representative who has not been appointed by Will is known as an administrator.

Beneficiary

A beneficiary is a person who inherits either the whole or part of the deceased's estate whether passing under the Will or intestacy or outside of the Will or intestacy.

Trustee

Instead of providing for property to be given directly to the beneficiary, the deceased's Will may provide that, for a specified period, the property is to be held in trust on behalf of the beneficiary by trustees named in the Will. Such trusts may arise because the beneficiary concerned is very young, or because the deceased wishes the property to be held for the benefit of one person for life and, on the death of that person, to be transferred to another beneficiary. The trustees will take over the management of the trust property only after the estate has been administered by the personal representative. The trust will then continue until the time specified in the Will for the ultimate handing over of the property.

The same person can have more than one role; for example, a personal representative can also be a beneficiary.

Before assets are handed over to the beneficiaries certain procedures must be gone through. Broadly, these are as follows:

Assets passing outside of the Will or intestacy

In the case of an asset passing outside of the Will or intestacy, production of a death certificate by the beneficiary is often all that is required to establish the beneficiary's entitlement to receive the asset in question.

Assets passing under the Will or intestacy

In order to get legal confirmation of their appointment, the personal representative must apply to the Probate Office of the High Court for a document known as a Grant of Representation. The Grant of Representation acts as an assurance to financial institutions (e.g. banks, building societies, credit union, etc.) and to others that they can safely place the deceased's assets in the hands of the person named as personal representative in the grant. The Grant of Representation is also known as a Grant of Probate (where there is a Will) or Letters of Administration (where there is no Will).

The application for the Grant of Representation will normally be made by a solicitor acting on behalf of the Personal Representative. In straightforward cases, it may be possible to make a personal application for the grant through the Personal Application Section of the Probate Office.

Special additional procedure relating to money in joint names

In the absence of a letter of clearance from the Revenue Commissioners, banks, building societies and other financial institutions are prohibited by law from releasing monies (other than current accounts) lodged or deposited in the joint names of the deceased and another person or persons. This applies if, at the date of death, the total of all the amounts standing with the institution in the joint names of the deceased and that other person or persons exceeds €6,350. It does not apply, however, to monies which have only been held in the joint names of the deceased and their surviving spouse.

Applications for letters of clearance for production to financial institutions should be made to the Capital Taxes Office of the Revenue Commissioners.

If you are a personal representative

In summary this is what you should do about tax and when you should do it.

Sort out the deceased's pre-death tax affairs

As Personal Representative, you are responsible for settling any outstanding tax matters for the period up to the date of death. Depending on the circumstances, you may need to pay additional taxes or claim a repayment of tax.

Notifying the tax office

The deceased's tax office should be advised as soon as possible of the date of death and the name and address of the Personal Representative. This will ensure that correspondence will be addressed to the Personal Representative until such time as the administration of the estate is finalised.

The address of the deceased's tax office can be found on any correspondence from that office to the deceased. If you are in any doubt as to which tax office to contact, get in touch with your local tax office.

Remember that:

- If you distribute the estate without paying any outstanding tax liabilities, you may have to pay the tax out of your own pocket.

- If you fail to claim a tax rebate due to the estate, you may have to make good the loss to the estate.

If the deceased was *self-employed*, you will most likely get the deceased's accountant to file any outstanding Income Tax returns and business accounts with the deceased's tax office. As well as Income Tax, you will also need to ensure that any outstanding VAT, employer's PAYE/PRSI, or other taxes in respect of the period up to the date of death are fully paid.

If the deceased was an employee, there may be a PAYE tax rebate due, as the deceased's tax credits for the year of death may not have been fully used up. The deceased's employer will send Form P45 to the tax office which dealt with the deceased's tax affairs. Any tax rebate will form part of the deceased's estate.   As Personal Representative, it is your responsibility to file any outstanding tax returns on behalf of the deceased.

Income and capital gains during the administration period

It may take the Personal Representative some time to administer the estate during which time income may be earned or capital gains may be made. Broadly the position is as follows.

Income tax

- The Personal Representative is liable to pay income tax at the standard rate on income earned during the administration period. There is no entitlement to personal tax credits or to any of the reliefs otherwise available to individual taxpayers.

- In certain circumstances, the tax office may concessionally agree to treat the beneficiary as succeeding to the inheritance from the date of death.   In such circumstances, the beneficiary will take full responsibility for paying income tax on the post-death income as if they had been entitled to the asset - and the income - from the date of death.

Capital gains tax (CGT)

- Death does not give rise to a Capital Gains Tax liability. For example, if the deceased bought shares for €10,000 and they were worth €15,000 at the date of death, the €5,000 capital gain is not taxable.

If the Personal Representative sells any property during the administration period, there may be a liability to Capital Gains Tax - but only to the extent that the value of the property in question has increased between the date of death and the date of sale. Following on from the example above, if the Personal Representative sells the shares during the administration period for €16,000, the relevant capital gain is €1,000 and is taxable. The distribution of property by the personal representative to the beneficiaries does not give rise to a Capital Gains Tax liability.

If you are a surviving spouse / civil partner

This section gives an outline of the main tax exemption and reliefs specifically for surviving spouses / civil partners.

Main tax exemptions reliefs for surviving spouses / civil partners.

In summary these are covered under the following headings:

- Inheritance tax;

- Income tax;

"Death does not give rise to a Capital Gains Tax liability."

Inheritance tax

If you take an inheritance from your late spouse /civil partners you do not have to pay Inheritance tax. The exemption is unlimited - it doesn't matter how much you inherit, it is entirely exempt. There is no necessity to claim this exemption and you don't have to fill in any Inheritance tax forms.

Income tax - for the year in which your spouse / civil partners has died

Your Income Tax treatment for the tax year (i.e. the year to 31 December) in which your spouse / civil partner has died will depend on how you and your spouse / civil partners were treated before bereavement.

Your tax office will help you do the calculations and make sure you have the right tax credits. Broadly, the position is as follows:

- If your late spouse was the "assessable spouse/civil partner", i.e. the person responsible for making a joint tax return on behalf of both of you, then you will be entitled to a special increased widowed person/surviving civil partner's credit from the date of your spouse /civil partner's death up to the following 31 December. The single person's rate bands will apply for this period.

- If you yourself were the "assessable spouse/civil partner", you will continue to get the married person/civil partner's credit and rate bands for the remainder of the tax year. You will be taxable on your own income for the full tax year and your spouse/civil partner's income from 1 January to date of death.

- If you were both taxed as single persons, you will get the special increased widowed person/civil partner's credit and single rate bands for the year.

Special credit for surviving spouse/civil partner with a dependent child

If you have any dependent children you may be entitled to a special Income tax credit (called "widowed parent's credit") for the five tax years after the year of your spouse/civil partner's death. You may also be entitled to the "one-parent family credit" for as long as you have any dependent children.

Widowed person's tax credit

A widowed person/surviving civil partner whose spouse/civil partner has died in a given tax year is entitled to the widowed person's bereaved credit, for that year only. This credit is the same as the married person/civil partner's credit but is not available to a surviving spouse/civil partner who is the subject of a joint assessment for the same year. A widowed person/surviving civil partner with dependent children is also entitled to;

- The one parent family credit

   and

- Widowed/surviving civil partner parent credit

Widowed/surviving civil partner parent tax credit

This credit is available for the five years following the year of death. For the 2012 and 2013 tax year the amount of the credit are as follows;

€3,600	in first tax year after death.
€3,150	in second tax year after death.
€2,700	in third tax year after death.
€2,250	in fourth tax year after death
€1,800	in fifth tax year after death.

Widow(er)/surviving civil partner in year of bereavement

The tax treatment for individuals in the year of death depends on whether they were taxed under joint or separate assessment and whether it was the assessable spouse/civil partner who died.

- If your late spouse/civil partner was the assessable spouse/civil partner, i.e. the person responsible for making the joint tax return on behalf of both of you, then you will be entitled to a special increased widowed person/surviving civil partner's credit from the date of your spouse/civil partner's death up to the following 31 December. The single person's rate bands will apply for this period.

- If your late spouse/civil partner was not the "assessable spouse/civil partner", you will continue to get the married person/civil partner's credit and rate bands for the remainder of the tax year. You will be taxable on your own income for the full tax year in which your spouse/civil partner died plus your late spouse/civil partner's income from 1 January to the date of death.

- If you were both taxed as single persons, you will get the special increased widowed person/surviving civil partner's credit and single rate bands for the year.

Note: The surviving spouse/civil partner can elect for joint assessment for the year of death before the end of that tax year.

Widow(er)/surviving civil partner in subsequent tax years

The tax position of a widow(er)/surviving civil partner in subsequent tax years is as follows;

- A reduced personal tax credit.

- A single person's tax band.

- A single person's PAYE tax credit.

- Reduced mortgage interest relief, if applicable.

- Single parent tax credit.

- Widowed parent tax credit (for five years following bereavement).

Example

A married couple/widow(er) with one dependent child and a salary of €55,000 p.a. (only one spouse working).

Widow(er) in subsequent year

	2012			
	Married €		**Widow(er)** €	
Gross salary	€55,000		€55,000	
		Tax		Tax
Taxable @ 20%	€41,800	€8,360	€36,800	€7,360
@ 41%	€13,200	€5,412	€18,200	€7,462
Total tax payable	€13,772		€14,822	
Less: Tax credits				
Married person	(€3,300)		(€1,650)	
PAYE	(€1,650)		(€1,650)	
Widowed person	(n/a)		(€1,650)	
Single parent	(n/a)			
Net tax payable	**€8,822**		**€9,872**	

Where there's a Will there's a relative!

This old proverb is never out of date. It has also been said that nothing is more inevitable than death and taxes. While, good financial planning cannot lessen your sense of loss on the death of a loved one, it can reduce your tax bill.

Issues that need to be considered when you have assets to pass on, include:

- Making a Will.

- Testate and Intestacy.

- The Succession Acts.

- Capital Acquisition Tax.

- Probate.

Anyone who owns property or other assets such as a life assurance policy, savings plan or even a simple deposit account, should make a Will. A Will not only ensures that you can distribute your wealth as you wish, but it also means that your family and beneficiaries are spared the expense and distress of a complicated and drawn-out administration of your estate, as set out by the Succession Act 1965.

Wills should be drawn up with the assistance of a solicitor. The simpler the terms of the Will, the less work involved and the lower the fee. However, it will be money well spent.

Many people do not realise that a Will is revoked on marriage unless it is clearly made with the marriage in mind. An important time to make a Will, if you haven't done so already, or to review an existing one, is when you have children. This is in order that you name a legal guardian for the child(ren) in the unlikely event that both you and your spouse should die together, or soon after each other.

When you make a Will you have to name an executor, someone who has the responsibility of seeing that your wishes are carried out and your assets distributed. Married couples often name each other, or an adult child or a family advisor - a solicitor or accountant - to act as executor. Others choose a business partner, bank manager or friend. Even if you, as a spouse, are named as Executor, your family advisor can assist with the various procedures involved.

Planning ahead

Before you meet your solicitor, gather up a list of your assets and the names and addresses of the people whom you wish to be beneficiaries and make sure your Executor consents to being named in your Will.

- A Will must be in writing - verbal ones are not valid.

- A Will must be witnessed by two people, neither of whom can be beneficiaries.

- You cannot disinherit your spouse.

- Your Will will remain in force until death or marriage unless it is clearly made with the marriage in mind. If a new Will is made, it automatically revokes any previous Wills you may have made.

- You should always keep a copy of your Will in a safe place - a strongbox or bank safety deposit facility. Let your Executor and family know where it is and where your other valuable papers are kept.

Dying "intestate"

If you die without making a Will, this is known as dying "intestate" and all your property will be distributed according to the 1965 Succession Act. (See page 340).

Since there is no official Executor, the Personal Representative of the deceased - who can be a spouse, relative or even friend, will need to obtain what is known as a grant of Letters of Administration, in order to distribute the proceeds of your estate to your beneficiaries.

Legal rights of spouse under a Will

Irrespective of what the deceased leaves to his spouse, the spouse has a legal entitlement as follows:

Relatives surviving	Spouse's share by legal right
Spouse/civil partner and issue	One-third of estate
Spouse/civil partner and no issue	One-half of estate

SUCCESSION ACT 1965	
Relatives surviving	**Distribution of estate where the deceased dies intestate**
Spouse / civil partner and issue	2/3rds to spouse/civil partner, 1/3rd to issue in equal shares. Children of a deceased son or daughter take their parent's share.
Spouse / civil partner and no issue	Whole estate to spouse / civil partner.
Issue and no spouse/civil partner	Whole estate to issue in equal shares Children of a deceased son or daughter take their parent's share.
Father, mother, brothers and sisters	1/2 to each parent.
Parent, brothers and sisters	Whole estate to parent.
Brothers and sisters	All take equal shares. Children of a deceased brother or sister take their parent's share.
Nephews and nieces	All take equal shares.
Remoter next-of-kin	All take equal shares.

Death and taxes

Inheritance tax

If after your death the beneficiaries of your estate receive sums in excess of the Thresholds for Capital Acquisitions Tax (CAT) purposes Inheritance Tax will be payable.

Gift tax

A liability to gift tax arises when a person receives a benefit liable to capital acquisitions tax other than on a death.

Tax-free threshold for Capital Aquisitions Tax (CAT)

There are three tax free thresholds which apply for CAT purposes. From 7 December 2011 these threshold amounts were as follows:

Group A   €250,000 where the recipient is a child, or minor grandchild of the benefactor, if the parent is dead. In some cases this threshold can also apply to a parent, niece or nephew who have worked in a family business for a period of time.

Group B   €33,500 where the recipient is a brother, sister, niece, nephew or linear ancestor/descendent of the benefactor or where a gift is made by the child to the parent.

Group C   €16,750 in all other cases.

The Group A Threshold applies to gifts/inheritance taken from a foster parent to a foster child provided the foster child was cared for and maintained from a young age up to the age of eighteen for a period of five years. The foster child must also have lived with the foster parent for the period.

Budget 2013

For gifts and inheritances taken after 5 December 2012 the CAT tax free thresholds have been reduced as follows;

Group A   Reduced from €250,000 to €225,000

Group B   Reduced from €33,500 to €30,150

Group C   Reduced from €16,750 to €15,075

"You cannot disinherit your spouse."

CAT rates

For benefits taken on / after 6 December 2011	
Amount	Rate
Below Threshold	Nil
Balance	30%

Budget 2013

For gifts or inheritances taken after 5 December 2012 the CAT rate is increased to 33%.

Some benefits are not subject to CAT:

- Any inheritance or gifts made between spouses,

- The first €3,000 of all gifts received from a benefactor in any calendar year,

- Any inheritance received from a deceased child which had been given to that child as a gift by the parent,

- Irish Government stock given to a non-Irish domiciled beneficiary, so long as it had been held by the beneficiary for at least six years previously.

- A family home, provided the following conditions are met;

    - It is the principal private residence of the disponer and/or the recipient.

    - The recipient had been living in the home for the three years immediately preceeding the transfer.

    - The recipient does not have an interest in any other residential property.

The relief will be withdrawn if the recipient disposes of the home within six years of the transfer. This does not apply where the recipient is over 55 years of age.

For gifts (not inheritances) taken on or after 1 February 2007, any period during which a child of a disponer occupied a house that was during that period the disponer's only or main residence, will not be treated as a period of occupation in the three year period prior to the date of the gift. Accordingly, a parent cannot gift free of CAT the family home they share with their child unless the parent has moved out of the home at least three years prior to the gift, while the child remained in the occupation of it as their principal residence.

This does not apply in cases where a disponer is compelled by old age or infirmity to depend on the services of the donee.

Inheritance/gift from a child to a parent

If a "child" gives a gift to a parent the Group 2 threshold applies. However, the Group 1 threshold applies if a parent receives an inheritance from "a child".

Business relief

Relief from CAT is available where business property is acquired under a gift or inheritance. This relief works by reducing the value of the qualifying asset which pass under a gift or inheritance by 90%.

The following condition apply to this relief;

- The qualifying business assets must have been owned by the disponer for at least five years in the case of a gift or at least two years in the case of an inheritance.

- Qualifying business assets are;

  - Unquoted shares or securities of an Irish company.

  - Land, buildings, machinery or plant owned by the disponer but used by a company controlled by the disponer.

  - Quoted shares or securities of an Irish company which were owned by the disponer prior to them being quoted.

The relief will be clawed back if the assets are disposed of within six years of the gift/inheritance.

Agricultural land

Agricultural lands which are passed on as part of an inheritance enjoy some additional CAT relief's. Instead of the land being assessed for CAT purposes at its full market value, it is assessed at 10% of its value. The relief will be disallowed, however, if the property is disposed of within six years of the inheritance (or gift) and partly disallowed if disposed of within six to ten years.

CAT payments

You must pay and file your CAT liability on the 31 October. All gifts and inheritances with a valuation date in the 12 month period ending on the previous 31 August will be included in the return to be filed by 31 October. That means that where the valuation date arises between the 1 January and the 31 August, the pay and file deadline would be the 31 October in that year. Where the valuation date arises between the 1 September and the 31 December, the pay and file deadline would be the 31 October in the following year.

Example

Valuation date

21 February 2012   File IT38 and pay taxes by 31 October 2012

6 November 2012   File IT38 and pay taxes by 31 October 2013

Section 60 policy

CAT can be avoided by a beneficiary if a Section 60 life assurance policy was taken out for the purpose of paying CAT. Policies like these appeal to people who are leaving large estates to their families or other beneficiaries.

Since Capital Acquisitions Tax in the form of an inheritance or gift are subject to aggregation - a rolling up of benefits from various sources - the relevant thresholds can be affected. The calculations can be very complicated and you should always consult your financial or tax advisor.

Foreign Inheritance

If you receive an inheritance or gift from another jurisdiction there may be a tax liability to be met in that country and here. However, you may be entitled to a tax credit on the tax paid abroad to ensure you don't pay double tax. The credit will not exceed the Irish rate of tax payable.

Death - capital gains tax

A liability to capital gains tax does not arise on death. When you inherit an asset you are treated for capital gains tax purposes as receiving the asset at the market value at the date of death.

Index

A

Absolute return funds ...57

Adoptive benefit ...227

Age credit ...119

Alternative investments ...60

Annuity mortgage ...85

Approved retirement fund
(ARF's) ...286

Assessable spouse ...305

AVC's ...281

B

Benefit in kind (BIK) ...144

Accommodation ...157

Car pools ...154

Company cars ...145

Company vans ...154

Medical insurance ...155

Preferential loans ...156

Share schemes ...158

Bereavement grant ...239

Blind person's credit ...116

Bonds ...34

Borrowing ...63

Bridging loan interest ...81

Budgeting ...69

Buying a home ...77

C

Capital acquisition tax (CAT) ..341

Capital allowances ...172

Capital gains tax ...199

Annual allowances ...200

Chargeable assets ...199

Disposals ..199

Exemptions and reliefs ...200

Indexation factors ...204

Married couples ...199

Principal private residence
...200

Rates ...199

Retirement relief ...201

Site from parent to child
...201

Windfall tax ...203

Carers benefit ...235

Car pools ... 154

Charge cards ..67

Child benefit ...228

Childcare service relief ...130

Civil service mileage rates
... 141

Code of conduct on mortgage
arrears ... 91

Coming to live in Ireland ...193

Company cars ...145

Company van ...154

Company car or mileage allowance
...149

Compensation and guarantees
schemes ...17

Consolidation loans ...67

Contributory pension ...212

Contributory widows pension ...220

Convertible term cover ...94

Corporation tax ...169

Credit unions ...23

D

Death and taxes

   CAT business relief ...343

   CAT payments ...344

   CAT rates ...342

   CGT ...333

   Beneficiary ...330

   Foreign inheritance ...344

   Income tax ...333

   Inheritance tax ...334

   Inheritance tax thresholds ...341

   Intestate ...339

   Personal representative ...330

   Succession Act ...340

   Surviving spouse/civil partner ...334

   Trustee ...330

   Widow(er)/surviving civil partner in year of bereavement ...336

   Widowed parent's tax ...335

   Widowed person/surviving civil partner's tax credit ...335

   Wills ...331

Decreasing term cover ...94

Deed of covenant ...120

Defined benefit pension scheme 273

Defined contribution pension scheme ...271

Dental expenses ...125

Dependent relative credit ...115

Deposit accounts ...20

Deposit guarantee & compensation schemes ...17

D.I.R.T. free accounts for over 65's ...27

Disability insurance ...99

Dividend income ...40

Divorce ...324

Domicile ...183

Double taxation ...185

E

Eligible liabilities guarantee scheme ...19

Emergency tax ...138

Employee benefits ...144

Employee share purchase plans (ESPP's) ...163

Employee share ownership trust (ESOT) ...159

Employee tax efficient benefits ...142

Endownment mortgage ...85

Exchange traded funds (ETF's) ...42

Exemption limits   111

Ex gratia payments ...250

Exit tax ...97

F

Fair deal nursing home support scheme ...244

Family income supplement ...228

Film investment ...130

Fixed term accounts...20

Fixed interest accounts ...21

Foreign earnings deduction ...192

Foreign income ...181

Foreign inheritance ...344

Foreign service and
        redundancy ...254

Funeral grant ...241

G

Gilts ...35

Guardian's contributory allowance
                ...223

Guardian's non-contributory
                allowance ...223

Guaranteed "whole of life" cover
                ...95

Gold - investing in ...60

H

Health & safety benefit ...230

Health & medical insurance ...103

Home carers credit ...113

Home equity release loans ...83

Home insurance ...105

Hospital cash benefit plan ...104

Household benefits package ...219

I

Illness benefit ...236

Incapacitated child credit ...114

Incapacitated person (employing a
                carer) ...115

Income exemption limits ...111

Income protection insurance..99

Income tax ...107

Income tax bands & rates ...110

Income tax credits ...109

Income tax credits

    Age credit ...115

    Blind person's credit ...116

    Bridging loan interest ...118

    Chargeable person ...107

    Childcare service relief ...130

    College fees ...128

    Deeds of covenant ...120

    Dental expenses ...125

    Dependent relative credit
                ...115

    Donations/gifts ...128

    Employment investment
                incentive ...129

    Film investment ...130

    Home carers credit ...113

    Incapacitated child credit
                ...114

    Incapacitated person
        (employing a carer) ...115

    Income exemption limits 111

    Job assist ...127

    Marginal relief ...111

    Married credits ...112

    Medical expenses ...123

    Medical insurance ...123

    Mortgage interest relief ...116

    One parent family credit
                ...113

    PAYE credit 119

    Permanent health

insurance (PHI) ...126

Proprietary director ...107

Rent relief ...127

Retirement annuity pension contributions ...121

Single credit ...112

Tax credit ...109

Tax bands & rates ...110

Universal social charge (USC) ...130

Widowed parent credit ...113

Indexation - CGT ...204

Individualisation ...111

Inheritance tax ...341

Insurance ...93

Insuring your home ...88

Invalidity pension ...224

Investing ...33

Investing in gold ...60

Investment bonds ... 56

J

Job assist ...127

Jobseekers benefit ...230

Joint assessment ...305

L

Leaving Ireland ...194

Level term insurance ...94

Life assurance ...93

Loan protection insurance ...101

Local property tax ...53, 88

M

Managed funds ...55

Marginal relief ...111

Married credit ...112

Marriage

Assessable spouse ...305

Income tax ...302

Individualisation ...303

Income tax options ...305

Legal impact ...301

Year of marriage/civil partnership ...303

Maternity benefit ...225

Medical expenses ...123

Medical insurance ...103, 123

Mileage rates ...141

Mortgages

Annuity ...85

Bridging loan interest ...79

Code of conduct on arrears ...91

Debt ...90

Endowment ...85

Home choice loans...81

Interest relief (TRS)...77, 116

Pension mortgage ...87

Stamp duty ...48, 78

Trackers ...87

Variable & fixed ...87

Mortgage protection ...102

Mortgage interest relief ...79

N

National instalment savings ...22

National Pensions Framework ...219

National solidarity bond ...22

Non-contributory guardian's
            allowance ... 223
Non-contributory state pension
            ...212
Non-principal private residence
            (NPPR) charge ...52

O

Occupational injuries benefit ...237
Occupation/employees pension
            scheme ..277
One parent family credit ...113
One parent family payment ...222
Ordinarily resident ...182
Overdrafts ...65

P

P21 ...140
PAYE credit ...119
PAYE ...133
Partnership ...175
Pensions ...257
        Defined contribution plans
                ...271
    Annuities ...286
        Approved retirement funds
                (ARF's) ...286
        Approved minimum retirement
                fund (AMRF) ...286
        AVC's ...281
        Death in retirement benefits
                ...299
        Death in service benefits ...299
        Defined benefit schemes
                ...273
        Employer pension schemes
                ...259

Final remuneration ...292
Maximum allowable
            benefits ...291
Maximum pension ...291
Maximum tax free cash ...293
Occupational pension scheme
            ...277
Pension investment funds
            ...267
Pension mortgages ...87
PRSA's ...273
Personal   pension   plans/
retirement Annuity contracts
            (RAC) ...276
Retirement capital
accumulation products ...271
Standard fund threshold
            ...267
Tax relief ...262
Tax relief limits ...262
Tax free cash at retirement
            ...264
Unit linked funds ...268
Vested PRSA's ...289
Pension mortgage ...87
Permanent health insurance (PHI)
            ...126
Personal credit (tax) ...112
Personal pension plans ...276
Preferential loan ...156
Preliminary tax ...167
Private residential tenancy board
            (PRTB) ...51
Property...43
        Commercial property ...46

Stamp duty ...48, 76

PRSA's ...273

PRSI - self employed ...178

Price earning ratio ...40

Prize bonds ...22

R

Redundancy ...247

    Basic exemption ...251

    Employment appeal tribunal (EAT) ...249

    Ex gratia ...250

    Foreign services ...254

    Increased exemption ...251

    Notice of redundancy ...247

    SCSB ...251

    Statutory redundancy ...247

    Top slicing relief ...255

Regular income accounts ...21

Regular savings accounts ...20

Relocation expenses ...157

Relief for investment in film industry ...130

Remittance basis of taxation ...184

Relocation costs ...157

Rental income

    Income tax ...48

    Renting while abroad ...189

    Tax on disposal ...203

Rent a room scheme ...55

Renting while abroad ...189

Rent paid to non resident landlord ...190

Rent relief ...127

Residence ...181

Restrictive stock units ...164

Retirement annuity pension contributions ...121

Revenue audit ...177

ROS ...176

S

Savings ...15

Saving for your children ...27

SAYE schemes ...162

SCSB ...251

Self-employed ...167

    Basis of assessment ...174

    Calculation of profit ...172

    Capital allowances ...172

    Corporation tax ...169

    Limited company ...169

    Partnerships ...175

    Preliminary tax ...167

    PRSI ...178

    Registering for income tax ...171

    Revenue audit ...177

    ROS ...176

    Sole trader ...170

    Surcharge ...168

    USC ...180

    VAT ...171

    Withholding tax ...174

Separate assessment ...305

Separation and divorce ...309

    Capital acquisition tax ...311

    Capital gains tax ...311

Divorce ...324

Income tax ...310

Life assurance ...311

Judicial separation ...319

Legal separation ...312

Living apart ...309

Maintenance ...314

Pension benefit ...311

PRSI ...314

Social welfare ...311

Stamp duty ...311

Succession rights ...309

Universal social charge ...315

Year of separation ...313

Serious illness insurance ...102

Share schemes ...158

Shares incentive scheme ...163

Single assessment ...305

Single credit ...112

Single parent credit ...113

Split year treatment ...188

Social welfare benefits ...207

Social welfare pensions ...212

Stamp duty rates ...48, 78

Standard rate cut off point ...134

State contributory pension ...215

State non contributory pension ...216

State pension transition ...212

Statutory redundancy ...247

State savings ...21

Stock options ...161

Stocks & shares ...37

Succession Act ...340

Surcharge ...168

T

Tax bands & rates ...110

Tax credits & relief's ...109

Tax efficient benefits ...142

Taxation of social welfare benefits ...243

Term loans ...64

Top slicing relief ...255

Tracker mortgages ...87

Treatment benefits ...225

TRS (Mortgage interest) ...116

U

UCITS ...59

UK dividends ...41

UK double taxation agreement ...195

UK gilts ...37

UK income ...195

UK interest ...26

UK tax rates & allowances ...198

Universal social charge (USC) ...130, 180

V

VAT ...171

Variable or fixed mortgages ...87

Voluntary contributions (social welfare) ...210

W

Widow(er)/ surviving civil partners pension

contributory ...220

non-contributory ...221

Widowed parents grant ...241

Widowed parent credit ...113

Wills ...338

Working abroad ...181

Working in the EU ...241

Y

Year of arrival ...187

Year of death ...334

Year of departure ...188

Year of marriage/civil partnership
...303

Year of separation ...313